W9-COD-993

Illinois Hiking and Backpacking Trails

Walter and George Zyznieuski

Southern Illinois University Press
Carbondale and Edwardsville

Library of Congress Cataloging in Publication Data

Zyznieuski, Walter.
  Illinois hiking and backpacking trails.

  Bibliography: p.
    1. Hiking—Illinois—Guide-books. 2. Backpacking—
Illinois—Guide-books. 3. Trails—Illinois—Guide-books.
4. Illinois—Description and travel—1981–   —Guide-
books. I. Zyznieuski, George, 1961–   . II. Title.
GV199.42.I3Z98 1985   796.5'1   84-23470
ISBN 0-8093-1230-1
ISBN 0-8093-1203-4 (pbk.)

To our parents, Anna and Nick

Contents

Illustrations

Foreword

As Director of Campus Recreation's Outdoor Program at Illinois State University, I have been responsible over the last ten years for assisting college students, faculty, staff, and community members in planning a wide variety of outdoor trips throughout Illinois, Wisconsin, Indiana, Missouri, and many other states. Inevitably, the most difficult activity to obtain specific information about has been hiking and backpacking. In many states, including Illinois, it is often necessary to write several different agencies or individuals to obtain the exact information needed to plan a hiking or backpacking trip. There are always questions to be answered when planning a trip: Where are the hiking and backpacking trails located in Illinois? Where do I write to obtain the information I need and who do I write to? Who owns the land the trail crosses? May I camp along the trail and is there a cost? Is water available and may I build a campfire in this area? The difficulty in obtaining this information in Illinois demonstrates the need for a guide that specifically addresses itself to this type of information. This guide, *Illinois Hiking and Backpacking Trails*, has filled that need. The authors, Walter and George Zyznieuski, both competent outdoorsmen, have visited and remapped each trail site in the guide and have gathered the information needed to help plan our hikes.

In the last ten years I have seen a steady increase in the popularity of backpacking and hiking. This popularity, I believe, has paralleled our awareness of both the environment as well as the importance of individual physical fitness. Day hiking and backpacking are inexpensive, provide physical exercise which can easily be varied to meet the needs of the individual, can be done alone or with the entire family, and, probably most important, put us in direct contact with our natural environment where we can enjoy some solitude and beauty. A short hike can put us in areas rarely seen by those who visit our state and national lands.

There is one danger associated with the publication of this type of guide: the possible destruction of these areas due to overuse and abuse. This guide will make it much easier for individuals and groups to visit these trail sites, thus increasing the wear on them. If we do not concern ourselves with the preservation of our natural areas, we could easily destroy them. I ask that we all show respect for our environment and these trail sites so that future generations may enjoy our natural areas as we have enjoyed them.

James E. Rogers

Acknowledgments

We wish to thank the many individuals who in one way or another have contributed and helped us with the completion of the book.

Thanks to Bev Sherer for her editorial assistance and valuable suggestions which, from the beginning, have helped us refine our ideas and manuscript from the rough draft to the final product.

Deb Nixon helped us tremendously by inputting data and by reviewing the manuscript.

Laura Lee Hoffman provided us with valuable ideas and comments, many of which stem from completing several trails with us.

Special thanks also to Kay Etling, Dan Irwin, Peter Ives, Beth Kidd, John Romuk, and Max Schnorf for their assistance and comments.

Additional thanks to all of the site superintendents and staff at the state parks, conservation areas, agencies, park districts, Shawnee National Forest, and all other areas where hiking trails are located, for providing us with valuable trail information.

We would especially like to thank our family and all of our friends everywhere, who have persevered during the course of writing this book and have given us their full support.

Introduction

Hiking is one of the fastest growing, most popular, and healthiest recreational activities in America today. Increasingly, various federal, state, and local departments, organizations, and groups have been promoting hiking outings or developing new trails for the public to enjoy.

There are many reasons why the general public has gained a new interest in hiking. First, hiking offers a person the chance to get away from worries, other people, noise, and pollution, as well as a chance to relax and enjoy the solitude that may be found along the trail. Many times we've hiked all day and not seen another person on the trail. (This may also be explained partly by the public not knowing that the trail exists in the first place!)

Second, people today want to keep in shape and stay healthy. Hiking—especially long distance hikes or extended backpacking trips—is an excellent way to stay fit and to exercise the cardiovascular system. Third, many people want a chance to travel and explore the lands, historical areas, and unique geological formations. Illinois has many fine archaeological, historical, and forested and wild areas that are not frequently visited. By getting out in the woods on a trail, the hiker has the chance to explore, discover, and enjoy these beautiful sites that never will be seen from inside cars. Fourth, hiking is usually free; therefore, it is a cheap form of recreation. And finally, hiking is a sport that may be enjoyed by all age groups. Several times we've seen both scout troops and retired couples out hiking for exercise.

Some of our experiences, including many bad ones, led us to write a guidebook for hiking trails in Illinois. There were many reasons why we saw a need for this book. These include the need for the public to know where the hiking trails are located in the state, how to get there, how long the trails are, if trail maps are available, what trail rules and regulations are in effect, and where they may write or call to request additional trail information.

Since there are numerous groups and federal, state, and local organizations which manage or own hiking trails in the state, the information on these trails is located in a variety of sources; the material was not organized into one single guide. *Illinois Hiking and Backpacking Trails* was written specifically to fill this gap, and to provide appropriate and up-to-date trail information to interested parties.

This book includes information about fifty-nine trails. For our purposes these trails had to be at least 4 miles in length or connected with another trail to total 4 miles. The trails also had to be marked either with paint blazes or posts along the trail, or with a trail marker, or with a trailboard at the trailhead. All of the trails described in this book were hiked between March 1983 and May 1984; therefore, some trail changes may have occurred since then.

The trails are located at state parks, conservation areas and nature preserves, Shawnee National Forest, county and municipal parks, forest preserves, conservation districts, not-for-profit organizations, and along utility and railroad rights-of-way. The authors did not hike any Boy Scout trails (unless they were part of an existing trail), because they were usually located at their scout camps where restrictions are put on public access or the trails were actually roads for their entire length. In addition, many times the scout trails are part of a trail that has another name (e.g., the Red Caboose Trail is really the Illinois Prairie Path). Horse trails, bike trails, or fire lanes were not hiked either unless the organization or park noted that the trail was for hiking also. This does not prohibit the outdoor enthusiasts from hiking there.

The state was divided into three regions to categorize the trails—northern, central, and southern Illinois—and the book is arranged according to those divisions. Each of the trails described has the trail length, location, county, highway map coordinates, appropriate topographical map, history, trail description, facilities, permits needed, trail rules and regulations, mailing address for additional information, and a trail map which we have drawn for each trail (see Map Information). We have also included some general directions by which you can locate the parks and trails; in some instances there may be additional access routes to the park or trail.

In addition, a bibliography lists additional books related to the subject.

The Illinois Highway Map Coordinates listed under each trail description are those that are seen on the State of Illinois Highway Map issued by the Illinois Department of Transportation. Should the hiker have another map of Illinois that was not issued by the state, the map coordinates may not necessarily match. All of the trail histories were taken directly from the appropriate park booklet or pamphlet that was issued for that particular trail.

Additionally, we have listed the various park permits required under "Permits Required" in the trail description. Most state parks and some other areas require a camping permit; however, you do not need to reserve or purchase these permits in advance. In most instances, after you have chosen a campsite, a park employee will come to your site to collect the appropriate fees and issue you your camping permit.

In order for the hiker to enjoy the hike comfortably, Part 1 recommends what the hiker needs to bring along on the trail and where the hiker can obtain additional information. Part 2 lists trails in northern Illinois; Part 3 lists trails in central Illinois; and Park 4 lists trails in southern Illinois.

By following the information presented in this book and by taking our advice, you should be able to arrive at the trail properly. We hope that you enjoy some of the beautiful hiking trails in Illinois as much as we did. Get out and enjoy Illinois' hiking trails!

PART I

General Information

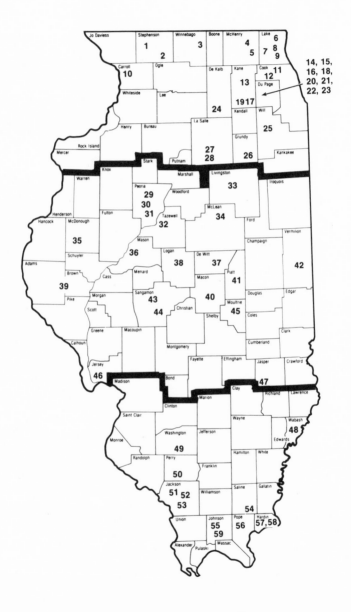

Figure 1. Hiking trails in Illinois

Trail Locations

Illinois is a large state encompassing 55,947 square miles. The state is 385 miles long from north to south and about 218 miles wide. Although Illinois is not noted for its large tracts of forested lands, there are some unique and beautiful areas that would astonish many people. The Illinois Department of Conservation (IDOC) and the U.S. Forest Service both own and administer large acreages of land that offer many trails for recreation. The IDOC owns and administers 101 recreation sites in the state totaling over 155,000 acres in size. These include both state parks and conservation areas. The U.S. Forest Service owns and administers recreation sites in the Shawnee National Forest in southern Illinois. The Shawnee National Forest covers over 260,000 acres. In addition to offering hiking trails, these recreation areas offer facilities, such as campgrounds, picnic areas, and playground equipment; many areas also allow swimming, fishing and boating, and hunting.

The hiking trails in Illinois are scattered throughout the state and vary in length from short nature trails to unmarked trails that measure 80 miles. These trails vary in difficulty from very easy to extremely difficult. Figure 1 shows the location by counties trails described in this book, and how the state is divided into three regions. The numbers on the map in Figure 1 correspond to the total number of trails described in this book (59) and are arranged in descending order of location, from 1 in the northwest tip of Illinois to 59 in the southeast part of southern Illinois.

Three other figures, located at the beginning of each section, show the locations of the trails in that division. (Please note that in cases where a trail covers two or more counties, the map indicates only the county in which the trail begins.)

For convenience, the state was divided into three regions: northern, central, and southern. The boundaries for these regions do not correspond to any specific regional boundary, but were arbitrarily determined by the authors. There are twenty-eight trails located in northern Illinois; nineteen trails in central Illinois; and twelve trails in southern Illinois.

The majority of the trails throughout the state are located at state parks and recreation areas administered by IDOC. While this may be said for the state as a whole, it is not true for the specific regions in the state.

In northern Illinois most of the hiking trails described in this book are located at forest preserves. There are twenty-eight hiking trails located in northern Illinois, ten of which are located within the forest preserve districts for McHenry, Lake, Cook, Du Page and Will counties.

In central Illinois, the majority of the hiking trails are located at state parks, forests or conservation areas scattered throughout the region. Nine of the nineteen trails are located at state parks, conservation areas or rights-of-way.

In southern Illinois, most of the hiking trails are located within the Shawnee National Forest boundaries. In fact, the longest and perhaps the most challenging and difficult trail described in this book, the River-to-River Trail, is located in the Shawnee National Forest.

In addition, numerous hiking trails in the state are located at municipal parks, parks owned by not-for-profit organizations, nature preserves, boy and girl scout camps, other park district lands and county parks. Appendix H lists other trails that may be found in northern, central and southern Illinois, their lengths, and who owns/administers these trails. The list in Appendix H includes trails that are less than 4 miles, unmarked trails, horse trails, bike trails and scout trails.

Since most of the trails are located in state parks or recreation areas or in the Shawnee National Forest, it would be appropriate to list the rules and regulations that are in effect for these areas. Appendix A lists the rules and regulations that must be followed while at state parks or conservation areas. Appendix B lists the rules and regulations for recreation sites in the Shawnee National Forest. Some of the trails lie within state nature preserves. These areas are protected by law; therefore, the hiker needs to know the appropriate rules and regulations which are in effect for these areas. Appendix C lists the regulations that must be followed at nature preserves.

In addition, the appropriate rules and regulations for the other hiking trails included in the book are listed under the trails section titled "Park Rules and Regulations."

Trail Signs and Markers

The hiking trails listed in this book were included because they were all identified with a trail sign or some other sort of trail marking. Numerous other hiking trails also exist in Illinois but may be unmarked, or the markings may change periodically and may confuse the hiker. Generally, these types of trails are not maintained and are undeveloped.

The trails described here are marked either with trailboards, which may be found at the trailhead, along the trail, or at a trail intersection, or with trail markers, such as paint blazes on trees and rocks, or wooden or metal markers displaying some appropriate symbol.

Our reasons for describing only marked, established hiking trails were that: (1) additional information is usually available for the marked hiking trails; (2) many times the unmarked trail may be obscure, overgrown with vegetation, or joined with other unmarked trails; and (3) most important, the public needs information about the location of existing, developed trails. Trail signs and markers are the hiker's "road signs" in the woods.

While each trail may have a trail sign or marker, not all of them are marked the same. Even the state park and conservation areas differ on the type of trail markers used. Some parks or areas administered by the same agency may have the same marking system. For instance, the trails in the Shawnee National Forest are usually all marked with white paint blazes along the trail and usually have a hiker sign identifying the hiking trail location.

Some trailboards provide very detailed trail descriptions; others may show just a layout of the trail and the trail name. Trailboards typically include some of the

High Point trailboard, Mississippi Palisades State Park

Trailhead sign, Greene Valley Forest Preserve

Trail marker, Mississippi Palisades State Park

following information: (1) trail name; (2) trail length; (3) park boundaries or layout; (4) facilities available on the trail; (5) rules in effect on the trail; (6) the organizational name; and (7) trail difficulty.

Most trail markers are wooden or metal posts, usually three feet high; they are found at various locations on the trail, and will usually have a symbol of a hiker, biker, horseback rider, or cross-country skier on them. This symbol may be made out of wood, metal or plastic.

One problem with these markers is that many times they may be missing or may have been vandalized. On several occasions the authors noted missing posts or symbols. If this situation occurs along the trail, you should report it to the organization in charge of the trail. Each trail description has the address for the agency in charge of the trail. The agency should be informed if there are any problems on or along the trail.

As an alternative to symbols, paint blazes are used along some trails. These blazes may be either painted on the trees or on other objects, such as large rocks or bluffs. The paint blaze will usually be in the shape of a diamond. Paint blazes stand out better on the trail, especially if they are properly marked. Typical paint blaze colors marking the trail include white, orange, and blue.

It should be pointed out that not every trail has a trailboard. Many times there might be just a metal hiker sign or a wooden post marking the trail's beginning. In addition, the trail blazes along the trails may not be uniform along the entire length of the trail. Many times the authors discovered missing trail blazes or blazes that were marked on the wrong trail. Any trails which were marked incorrectly or sparingly are identified as such in the trail description.

In order to keep from getting lost while hiking, either due to improper trail marking or other reasons, the hiker should always carry a trail map and compass. (More on maps in the next section). A compass is critical, and the hiker should carry one at all times. In some situations the hiker may have strayed off the trail or started hiking down the wrong trail spur. By using a compass, the hiker should be able to realize that he is straying off course. Some of the longer trails, such as the ones found in the Shawnee National Forest, may be easy to get lost on because some areas of the trail may not be marked correctly or the trail signs may not exist.

The bibliography lists some books that discuss the correct ways to mark trails and how to use a map and compass. In addition, local or university orienteering clubs often sponsor classes for basic map reading or sponsor orienteering meets; both are excellent ways to learn how to use a compass and a topographic map.

Map Information

Every trail described in this book has a trail map. The maps were redrawn from the United States Geological Survey's (U.S.G.S.) topographic quadrangle maps and the U.S. Forest Service Shawnee Sportsman's Maps. Some trail maps were modified from park maps that were provided, and this will be indicated on the bottom of those maps accordingly. Additional information was added to each of these maps to identify pertinent areas for the hiker.

While trail maps were available for most of the trails and parks hiked by the authors, these maps usually were not marked or drawn correctly. For instance, many times the trail layouts seen on the Department of Conservation park brochures are outdated, contain errors, or simply do not list the trail or new trails.

One of the reasons this book was written was to provide the hiker with an accurate and detailed map which would show the trail layout and length correctly. In order to check map accuracy, the authors hiked each trail. We then used a topographic map measurer to measure the trail mileage for each map. The trail mileage we have listed under the trail description is what we measured. All of the trail maps were then drawn in a similar style. This makes reading the maps a little easier and more convenient for the hiker.

Each trail description lists the name of the topographical (or "topo") map on which the trail is located. These maps are issued by the U.S.G.S. and have the contour lines, streams, lakes, roads, and buildings that may be found in that area. Appendix E lists agencies from which one may order topographic maps. The U.S.G.S. is in the process of printing a new index for topographic and other maps for Illinois, as well as a catalog of topographic maps. The U.S.G.S. also has a pamphlet which explains the symbols for topographic maps. The index shows the location of the topographic map and name. The index (when available) and the pamphlet are both free and may be ordered from the U.S.G.S. at the address listed in Appendix E.

Appendix E also lists agencies from which one may order other maps for Illinois, including county maps, township maps, and general statewide maps. Some maps, such as the county road maps, may prove to be useful for locating a particular road which may lead to the park or trail junction.

If the hiker does not want to order the topographic map for the trail, various libraries throughout the state have Illinois topographic maps in their map sections for the public to view or borrow. Appendix F lists some libraries in Illinois which have Illinois topographic maps.

The U.S. Forest Service issues Sportsman's Maps for the Shawnee National Forest. These maps are the same scale as the topographic maps (1:24,000) but are arranged by township and ranges. The Sportsman's Maps have contour lines, roads, lakes, rivers, and buildings; Forest Service areas and private property are differentiated. These maps also have the locations of wildlife openings and ponds with their corresponding numbers. This proves to be very useful to the hiker because the wildlife openings and ponds are all marked on wooden posts next to the respective areas. When a hiker sees one of these posts next to a wildlife opening or pond, he may refer to the corresponding number on the map and then know his location.

All of the trails described for the Shawnee National Forest have the correct Shawnee Sportsman's Map listed for that trail. These maps are identified by township and range: for instance, T.12 S.–R.5 E. This means that the map is for Township 12 south, Range 5 east.

These maps may be obtained from the district Forest Service office that is listed at the end of the particular trail description. These maps will have to be purchased for a small fee. All U.S. Forest district offices for the Shawnee National Forest are listed in Appendix E.

In some instances, a trail in the Shawnee National Forest may cross the boundaries of two different Forest Service district offices. When this occurs one will have to order the appropriate Shawnee Sportsman's Maps from both offices. For instance, the River-to-River Trail crosses two Forest Service district boundaries. In this situation the hiker will have to request Sportsman's maps from two different district offices (Vienna and Elizabethtown).

While the maps in this book are accurate, they do not have any contour lines drawn on them. These maps were drawn as a general guide for the hiker. To supplement the maps in this book, the appropriate topographic map or Shawnee Sportsman's Map should be used to identify the elevations on the trail.

Weather Patterns in Illinois

Illinois lies midway between the Continental Divide and the Atlantic Ocean, some 500 miles north of the Gulf of

Mexico. The climate is continental, with cold winters, warm summers, and frequent fluctuations of temperature, humidity, cloudiness, and wind.

During the spring and summer months, storm systems are frequent, with precipitation averaging about 38 inches a year. The amounts of precipitation vary across the state and may fluctuate from year to year. Northern Illinois typically receives about 34 inches a year and southern Illinois about 46 inches a year.

During the fall, winter, and spring, precipitation tends to fall uniformly over large regions in the state. During the summer, precipitation occurs principally as brief thunderstorms, affecting relatively small areas.

Illinois is about 385 miles long from north to south and about 218 miles wide. Temperature variations between northern and southern Illinois exist because of latitude difference. Winter temperatures may show a contrast of approximately 14 degrees Fahrenheit between the northern and southern sections of the state. During July, the range of mean temperatures across the state is about 6 degrees as both temperature and sunshine are more uniform. Northern Illinois averages about twenty days a year when the temperature is over 90 degrees while the west-central and southern portions of the state average about fifty days of this temperature.

The length of the state causes the northern part of the state to average cooler and drier than the south. Annual precipitation is greater in the extreme south than further north, with most of the excess precipitation occurring during winter and early spring.

Snowfall also varies across Illinois, ranging from 9 inches in the south to more than 33 inches in the northern part of the state. Snowfalls of 1 inch or more occur on an average of ten to twelve days per year in the extreme north to three to four days in the southern part of the state.

Following are the average statewide temperatures in degrees fahrenheit:

January—27.5   July—76.0
February—31.1   August—74.9
March—40.2   September—67.1

April—53.5   October—56.7
May—63.3   November—42.4
June—72.6   December—31.0

Hikers should be concerned with and always aware of the current weather conditions. Many major metropolitan areas in the state have local phone numbers available for the current or extended weather conditions for that area. Appendix G lists telephone numbers for some of these areas in the state. The hiker may call any of these numbers to find out what the weather conditions may be for that area that day.

By closely observing the weather and developing weather patterns, the hiker can be prepared to keep warm and dry. The last thing the hiker needs to experience is hypothermia, or heat exhaustion. If you get wet, try to get into dry clothes as quickly as possible; if you get overheated, stop hiking, rest and cool down your body temperature.

When in doubt, always carry spare clothes in case the weather conditions change. Always be prepared for the worst! The next section outlines the clothing articles the hiker needs to take along while hiking.

Books listed in the bibliography discuss first-aid and outdoor survival skills.

Recommendations for Hiking

Many of the trails described in this book may be hiked in one day; some within two hours. Of course, trails such as the River-to-River, at 57 miles in length, will take a few days to hike.

Not every trail or park in Illinois has the same facilities available along the trail. Common sense tells us that restrooms will not be found every two miles along a trail; for that matter, neither will water pumps. Some of the trails described in this book have facilities available along the trail at strategic locations while other trails have no facilities at all.

The trail descriptions list what will be found along each trail, at the trailhead, and within the park itself.

Whether the hiker is out on the trail for a few hours or a few days, he will need to carry some essential items or supplies. This section identifies what the hiker needs to carry.

We have relied on our own years of hiking experience to compile the list of recommended items to carry when hiking. We believe the list provides the minimum items which the hiker should bring on every trail. We tried to structure the list so that the items listed would usually be on hand and would provide the hiker with a safe and comfortable outing.

In addition, we also will list optional equipment which the hiker may choose to carry, depending on the situation, trail and season. We also realize that this list is not mandatory; the hiker should feel free to carry additional items to suit his own personal needs.

The list that follows is geared towards the day-hiker, or the hiker who is not planning to camp overnight on the trail. Although there are trails in Illinois which are sufficiently long for backpacking purposes, the majority are used by day-hikers, or those who complete the trails that same day. Also, numerous books cover the topic of equipment needs for backpackers, and a few are listed in the bibliography.

The following list is divided into two categories: items which the hiker should carry at all times (essential items) and optional items.

Essential Items: The first essential item which the hiker will need to have will be something in which to put all of his supplies. This usually will be a rucksack or daypack. Most daypacks are made of lightweight material and are inexpensive. Almost every sporting goods store or department sporting goods section carries daypacks.

Proper footwear and clothing are also important items for the hiker to consider. Sometimes the shoe which the hiker wears while hiking may make the difference between a fabulous hiking experience and a disaster. A sturdy, lightweight boot is recommended for hiking, especially for any extended outings. Hiking boots available today are especially lightweight and extremely durable. And while it is difficult to list all the pieces of clothing the hiker should wear (depending on the season), we offer a few pointers. One of the most important things to remember when choosing the proper clothing is to wear clothing in layers. That is, wear loose clothing in a layering system. Should you become warm while hiking, you may shed a piece of your clothing.

An essential item of clothing that needs to be packed is a rain jacket or poncho. This piece of clothing is critical to have on the trail at all times, especially on long-distance hikes. Many times we have started hiking on a beautiful sunny morning only to be caught in a thunderstorm later that afternoon. Rain gear which is light, waterproof and breathable may be purchased.

Other items that the hiker should bring along include: identification, toilet paper, small shovel, sunglasses, hat (wide brim for the summer and wool for the winter), map(s), compass, lip balm, mosquito repellent (seasonal), knife, matches (preferably waterproof) or butane lighters, flashlight, pencil, paper, water bottle, water purifier tablets, sunburn lotion, snacks, space blanket, rope or string, salt tablets, biodegradable soap, mirror, garbage bag, sewing kit (scissors, needle and thread, safety pins), first-aid kit (aspirin, moleskin for blisters, antiseptic, tweezers, adhesive bandage strips, medicines for allergies, etc.), and whistle (should you become lost or in trouble).

Optional Items: Optional items include items or supplies that may be needed in a particular season of the year, or items the hiker may find important but which are not critical to carry on each and every trail. Optional items include: camera, binoculars, additional clothing, swim suit, gloves, guidebooks, (flowers, trees, animals, geology), fishing gear, cup, and vitamins.

PART II

Hiking Trails in Northern Illinois

NORTHERN ILLINOIS

1. Lake Le-Aqua-Na State Park
2. Pecatonica Prairie Path
3. Rock Cut State Park
4. Glacial Park — Nippersink Trail
5. Moraine Hills State Park
6. Des Plaines River Trail
   (Lake County)
7. Lakewood Forest Preserve
8. Daniel Wright Woods
9. Ryerson Conservation Area
10. Mississippi Palisades State Park
11. Des Plaines River Trail
    (Cook County)
12. Palatine Trail
13. Great Western Trail
14. Illinois Prairie Path
15. West Du Page Woods
16. Cantigny Park
17. Virgil L. Gilman Nature Trail
18. Roy C. Blackwell Preserve
19. Fox River Bike Trail
20. Herrick Lake Forest Preserve
21. The Morton Arboretum
22. Greene Valley Forest Preserve
23. Waterfall Glen Forest Preserve
24. Shabbona Lake State Park
25. Pilcher Park
26. Illinois-Michigan Canal
27. Starved Rock State Park
28. Matthiessen State Park

Figure 2. Hiking trails in northern Illinois

1. Lake Le-Aqua-Na State Park

Trail Length: 4.2 miles (6.7 kilometers)

Location: Lake Le-Aqua-Na State Park is located four miles north of Lena, and fifteen miles northwest of Freeport. To reach the park, take State Route 20 west out of Freeport to Route 73. Proceed north on Route 73 through the city of Lena and turn left on Lena Street. Proceed on Lena Street for five blocks to Lake Road. Turn right (north) and go on Lake Road for two miles to the park entrance.

County: Stephenson

Illinois Highway Map Coordinates: A-5

U.S.G.S. Topographical Map Name and Scale: Lena, 1:24,000

Hours Open: The park is open every day of the year except Christmas Day and New Year's Day. At certain times of the year, due to freezing and thawing, the park may be closed, and access to the park is by foot only. The shower building at Hickory Hill Campground is open from May 1 to November 1.

History and Trail Description: The name, Le-Aqua-Na, is derived from the nearby town of Lena and "aqua," the Latin word for water. The Stephenson County Sportsman's Club, one of the various groups sponsoring the park, conducted the contest that resulted in the naming of the park.

The State of Illinois initially acquired 614 acres of land here in 1949. In the years since then the state has acquired more land to bring the total figure to 715 acres. Lake Le-Aqua-Na was started in 1955 and was completed in 1956. The lake is 43 acres in size, ranges from 450 to 650 feet in width, and drains over 2,000

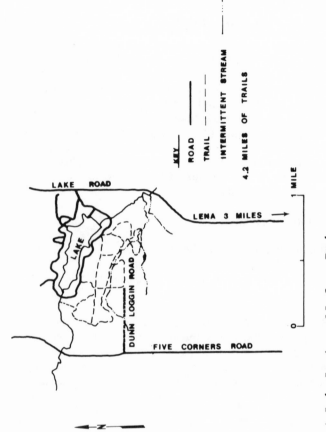

1. Lake Le-Aqua-Na State Park

acres. The maximum depth is 26 feet with a mile of shoreline.

The park has over 7 miles of trails available to the hiker, cross-country skier and horseback rider. The High Point Trail may be found north of the lake and measures 2.6 miles. The Sweet Gum Trail is located on the south side of the lake and measures 4.2 miles. The Sweet Gum Trail is the trail that will be discussed here.

The Sweet Gum Trail may be found by entering the park and heading west, passing the park dam. After ascending the hill you will find a parking area on the left side of the road. A large trailboard marked with the words "Sweet Gum Trail" can be seen from the parking lot. The trail starts at this point. Hikers, horseback riders and skiers are allowed to use the multi-purpose trail. The trail is really four loop trails that are interconnected for a total of 4.2 miles. The trail is generally about twelve feet wide, mowed and well kept. The trail should be followed in the direction outlined by the park trail map.

The trail is marked with wooden posts which have metal signs displaying either a skier, a backpacker, or a horseback rider on them. When a sign is covered with a red slash, it means that the specified trail activity is prohibited on that portion of the trail. When they are extremely wet and soft, the trails may be closed to equestrian activities. Consult park staff for trail conditions before riding.

The trail goes south from the trailhead, passing through a pine stand and then coming to a trail junction. The trail goes east at this point following the perimeter of the pine trees. The trail then starts heading west and comes to another trail junction. This is the second loop of the trail.

Turn left and go over a small bridge that crosses a creek. The trail then goes up a small hill and around an open field. Continuing east, the trail goes down a hill and soon parallels a small creek. The trail crosses another small bridge and heads west toward the trail junction again. Turn right and follow the trail as it parallels the creek again.

You will cross two unmarked trails that lead back to the trailhead. You may take these trails or continue following the main trail.

The main trail connects with a third loop. At this point you may follow this loop, which goes over the creek and parallels a pine stand for a short distance, or you may continue straight ahead. By following the loop, the hiker will come to Dunn Loggin Road and may then turn north to the equestrian area and the trail junction passed earlier.

The trail continues west through a small valley, paralleling the small creek. The trail then turns north and crosses the main trail again. The hiker can take the main trail back to the trailhead or hike the last loop trail.

The last loop trail, the gray loop, is fairly short. The gray loop trail joins another trail which goes down to the parking area and feeder creek for the lake. Continuing on the loop trail, the hiker will pass a pine stand. Turn right at the pine stand and follow this trail to a large open field, the equestrian area. There are tables, a water pump, restrooms and a shelter at this site. Here the hiker will meet the main trail which heads directly east back to the trailhead.

Facilities: Several picnic sites with shelters, restrooms, tables and water are scattered throughout the park. Campsites are available for recreation vehicles, primitive campers and for equestrian enthusiasts. A utility building with flush toilets and showers and a trailer dumping station are located at Hickory Hill Campground.

The equestrian area is accessible only by county roads bordering the park. Fishing and boating are allowed on the lake. All Illinois fishing rules and regulations are in effect. A concession stand is located on the lake and offers refreshments and boat rentals. A park office located on the grounds provides additional information.

Park Rules and Regulations: Fires are restricted to fire pads. Electric motors only are allowed on the lake.

Swimming is prohibited. The park is closed from 10:00 p.m. until 6:00 a.m. A maximum of four persons or a family per campsite is allowed. See Appendix A.

Mailing Address and Phone Number: Site Superintendent, Lake Le-Aqua-Na State Recreation Area, 8542 North Lake Road, Lena, Illinois 61048, 815/369–4282

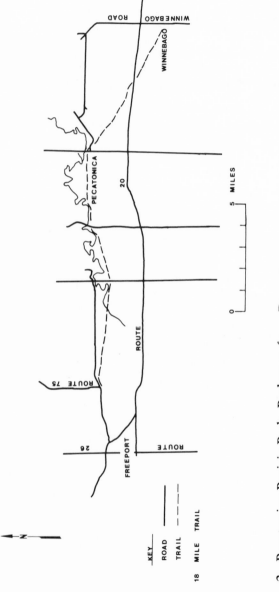

2. Pecatonica Prairie Path. Redrawn from Department of Transportation Highway Maps.

2. Pecatonica Prairie Path

Trail Length: 18 miles (29 kilometers)

Location: The Pecatonica Prairie Path is located in northwestern Illinois between Rockford and Freeport. The trail passes through Winnebago, Pecatonica, and Ridott and ends (or begins) at the eastern edge of Freeport. The western end of the trail begins just south of the East River Road and Illinois Route 75 at the east side of Freeport junction (look for a sign marked PRIVATE DRIVE, NO TRESPASSING and a trailboard with the trail name on it). Roadways leading to this westernmost point outside of Freeport include north-south Route 26 to Freeport and east-west Route 20.

The second trailhead is located at the easternmost point in Winnebago, Illinois. Winnebago is located just south of Route 20, about seven miles west of Rockford. From Winnebago Road go west on McNair Street to N. Swift Street, then south to the trailhead (three blocks). Limited parking is available at the trailhead; however, parking is allowed at the Winnebago High School parking lot at the intersection of Winnebago Road and McNair Street.

A third access is located in Pecatonica at Sumner Park. Traveling north or south on Pecatonica Road, turn west on First Street (the first east-west street south of the Pecatonica River). This access point is very convenient because it divides the trail into two approximately equal lengths, and also there is adequate parking along with water and restrooms at Sumner Park.

Route 51 is a major north-south route leading to Rockford, and from the east the major roadway is Northwest Tollroad Route 90. From Rockford follow Route 90 to Route 20 west to either of the three access points mentioned. The trail may be accessed from several other north-south roads; however, none provide any facilities other than the parking lot located at Farwell Bridge Road.

Counties: Stephenson, Winnebago

Illinois Highway Map Coordinates: B-6

U.S.G.S. Topographical Map Names and Scale: Winnebago, Ridott, Pecatonica, and Freeport East, all 1:24,000

Hours Open: The Prairie Path is open to the public year-round. For safety reasons use the trail during daylight hours only.

History and Trail Description: The Pecatonica Prairie Path follows the old right-of-way of the Chicago & Northwestern Railroad, presently owned by Commonwealth Edison Company. The path is leased to the Pecatonica Prairie Path, Inc., a nonprofit organization formed to develop and manage the Path for public use.

The Pecatonica Prairie Path passes through forests and villages, over rivers and creeks, past farms and across highways. Caution is necessary when crossing Route 20 since this is a four lane major highway. Other hazardous crossings include Pecatonica Road in Pecatonica and Rock City Road in Ridott.

Most of the trail is gravel and dirt and is very level; it is about ten feet wide. The only indicators or markers are trailboards located at major crossings.

The undisturbed land along the undeveloped sections of the path provides an excellent refuge for a variety of Illinois wildlife. Over sixty species of birds have been recorded. Also, deer, badger, fox, and raccoon are often seen.

The path parallels the Pecatonica River in an east-west direction, although the river is visible from only a few spots. Except at Ridott and Pecatonica, water or rest rooms are not available along the path. There is, however, one shelter with a picnic table and a roof available at the midway point between Sumner Park and Farwell Bridge Road.

Facilities: No camping or restroom facilities are available on the path. Parking is available at Ridott, in Sumner Park, at the Winnebago High School parking lot, at the Farwell Bridge crossing, and along county roads. Water is available at Sumner Park. Restroom facilities are available at Sumner Park and in Ridott.

Park Rules and Regulations: No motorized vehicles are allowed. Bicycles must have bells to warn hikers and other riders. No firearms. No bows and arrows. No kite flying. No model airplane flying. No horseback riding. Dogs must be on a leash. No alcoholic beverages. No fires.

Mailing Address and Phone Numbers: Pecatonica Prairie Path, P.O. Box 534, Pecatonica, Illinois 61063. Rockford: 815/987–2508; Freeport: 815/235–7267

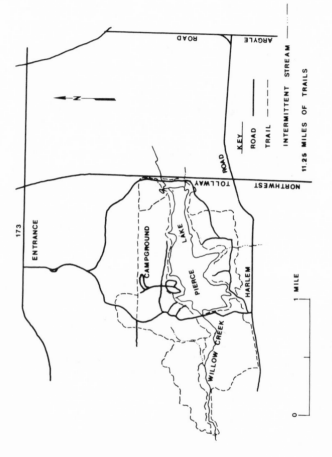

KEY

ROAD ————

TRAIL — — —

INTERMITTENT STREAM ·······

11.25 MILES OF TRAILS

0   1 MILE

3. Rock Cut State Park

3. Rock Cut State Park

Trail Length: 11.25 miles (18.1 kilometers)

Location: Rock Cut State Park is located seven miles northeast of Rockford, Illinois. The park can be reached from the south via Route 51 north to Rockford 251. Take Route 251 to Illinois Route 173, turn east and follow the road signs to the park. From western Illinois the park is reached by Route 251 north from Rockford, again to Illinois Route 173 east. From eastern Illinois, Rock Cut State Park is easily reached via Illinois 90, Northwest Tollway to Business Route 20 (west). From here, follow the road signs to the park entrance.

County: Winnebago

Illinois Highway Map Coordinates: B-7

U.S.G.S. Topographical Map Name and Scale: Caledonia, 1:24,000

Hours Open: The park is open every day of the year except on Christmas Day and New Year's Day. At certain times of the year, due to freezing and thawing periods, the roads may be closed and access to the park is by foot only.

History and Trail Description: Rock Cut State Park was first developed in 1957 when the Illinois Department of Conservation obtained over 13 acres. Pierce Lake, named after Representative William Pierce of the Illinois Legislative 10th District, was developed in 1962 when construction of a dam across Willow Creek was completed. The lake covers an area of slightly over 162 acres and has a four mile shoreline. Total acreage in the park today is 2,743 acres.

Rock Cut State Park reportedly was named for the abandoned rock quarrying operations from more than

100 years ago. Evidence of old quarry pits are visible at the northeast shore of Pierce Lake. These pits are now filled with water and are rearing ponds for migratory birds and local wildlife.

Good park maintenance is evident as all the trails are mowed in the grassy areas and kept clear-cut through the more dense areas. Foot bridges cross different waterways in the park. All of the hiking trails are also cross-country ski trails; these trails have symbols (brown background with figure of a hiker, and white background with a blue skier) located on all the trails in the park. Although most of the trail markers face north or east, the trails can be hiked in either direction from any access point. Additionally, the park has nature and interpretive trails (refer to the maps available at the park).

The campgrounds are a convenient place to start hiking. If day hiking is desired without camping, convenient parking locations include the three separate parking lanes south of Hickory Hills Campground and the parking area located directly north of the dam. The loop trail that circles the lake measures 3.5 miles; a good view of Pierce Lake can be had from most points along this trail. On the southeast side of Pierce Lake, and one-eighth mile west of the handicapped fishing pier, a relatively new trail is located. The new trail goes south and west along the park boundary. One mile from the trail junction, near the handicapped fishing pier, this trail crosses a paved road in the park. At the point where the trail meets the road, you can travel back northeast along the southern shore of the lake, shorten the trail by hiking a half mile north along the western shore and back to the dam and parking area, or continue the trail along the southern boundary of the park.

The trail along the southern boundary of the park is somewhat difficult and hazardous to hike. For example, beyond the first paved road the trail crosses a second paved road where there are no trail markers. You have to climb over the earthen mound created from road construction. Beyond the mound the trail is an abandoned asphalt road which continues for one eighth of a mile where another earthen mound is located. You must bypass this mound and continue for nearly a half mile west along Harlem Road to the entrance to Willow Creek Picnic and Youth Group Campground.

At the entrance to the Willow Creek area, the trail system follows the asphalt road to the road's end. The trail then becomes a footpath along the creek. You will then cross a ford over the creek and will come to a junction in the trail. During the wet season the hiker can expect to get wet feet crossing Willow Creek, but the ford is a safe crossing as it is level concrete about ten feet wide and nearly twenty feet across.

On the north side of the ford two trails are available. The first meanders directly east along Willow Creek for one mile back to the parking area at the dam; the second trail passes through more dense foliage and at higher elevations. The second trail follows a ridge which overlooks a meadow, Willow Creek, and the first trail (one and one-half miles to the parking area).

From the two trails, which make a loop north of Willow Creek, another trail section is available that is

A ford where the trail crosses Willow Creek, Rock Cut State Park

one-quarter mile from the dam and connects with the trail along the ridge that begins at the ford over Willow Creek. This additional section of the trail system meanders along the main park road for one-quarter mile to Hart Road (gravel road going west). The trail then splits and goes for a half-mile loop where it joins the main trail again; at the gravel road it goes directly east. The trail is clear-cut and marked as it passes by the Plum Grove Campground. The trail continues for one-quarter mile where it splits; one section borders the west boundary of the wildlife rearing ponds, and the other section continues around the north side of the rearing ponds. Both of the trail sections connect with the trail that circles Pierce Lake.

Facilities: Rock Cut State Park has five different camping areas with more than 200 class A sites. There are also five areas dedicated for picnicking only. Tables, outdoor stoves, drinking water, pit toilets and playground equipment are available. There is a shower building in the Plum Grove Campground and shelters at the Willow Creek area. The park also has two sanitary dump stations.

The park is open for winter sports including: ice skating, ice fishing, cross-country skiing, snowmobiling, and dog sledding.

Two fishing piers are accessible for the handicapped, and outdoor privies are available at the parking lots nearby.

Pierce Lake is annually stocked, and fishing is allowed with all Illinois fishing rules and regulations in effect. Boating is allowed on the lake, with two boat launch areas available. A concession stand is located at the boat launch area.

Permits Required: Permits are required for camping and for parking at the dog training area.

Park Rules and Regulations: No plants or parts of any tree may be removed or damaged. No swimming. The motor limit is 10 hp. All pets must be on a leash. Bi-cycles are not allowed on hiking trails. See Appendix A.

Mailing Address and Phone Number: Site Superinten-dent, Rock Cut State Park, R.R. 1, Box A-49, Cale-donia, Illinois 61011; 815/885–3311

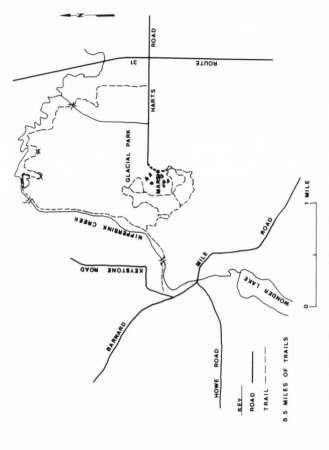

KEY

ROAD ——————

TRAIL - - - - -

8.5 MILES OF TRAILS

4. Glacial Park–Nippersink Trail

4. Glacial Park and Nippersink Trail

Trail Length: 8.5 miles (13.7 kilometers)

Location: Glacial Park is located in northeastern Illinois approximately sixty-five miles from Chicago. From central, southern, and eastern Illinois, Glacial Park is accessible via Illinois Tollroad 294 north to Route 120 west. In McHenry, Illinois, follow Route 31 north to the road sign for Glacial Park on Harts Road. From western Illinois, Glacial Park is accessible via Illinois Tollroad 5 east to 31 north, and from northern Illinois via 176 to Route 31 north or 173 to 31 south.

County: McHenry

Illinois Highway Map Coordinates: A-8

U.S.G.S. Topographical Map Name and Scale: Richmond, 1:24,000

Hours Open: 8:00 a.m. until sunset

History and Trail Description: Glacial Park was started with an initial land acquisition in 1975. In 1977, an additional 115 acres were added. In 1979, in conjunction with the Corporation for Open Lands and Northern Pump Company, a 168-acre parcel encompassing the Nippersink Creek was made available to the district for trail-related activities.

All of the trails are well marked and the trail intersections have signs with the title, length, and direction of the trail.

Within Glacial Park are two main nature trails, the Coyote Loop Trail and the Deerpath Trail. The Coyote Loop Trail is an excellent short-distance trail for students, families, and outdoor enthusiasts, as it has a wildlife observation platform, a windbreak demonstration plot, and examples of a songbird planting and northern wildlife plantings. In addition, the grassy path passes along a natural marsh and bog. Also visible along this .75-mile loop trail are old pastures and forests. There are also good examples of controlled prairie burns throughout the park.

The second loop trail, Deerpath Trail, measures two and a third miles. This trail also passes along the bog and marsh area and through more wooded areas, as well as through glacial ridges and the prairie management area. A .25-mile loop trail known as Broken Ski Extension allows the hiker to see controlled prairie burn remains, to hike up a glacial ridge, and to obtain a magnificent view from the trail junction on top of the ridge.

The Deerpath Trail has another scenic vista atop a ridge north of the prairie management area. Following this trail south, it connects with a half-mile loop trail along the base and on top of the glacial kame. The ridge of the kame provides excellent viewing.

From the Deerpath Trail, at the kame, there is a connecting trail from Glacial Park to Nippersink Trail, which goes around Glacial Park. By following the trail southeast and crossing the creek, the hiker ends the half-mile hike at the parking area and canoe landing; the northern branch of the trail meanders for four and one-half miles. Hikers must be cautious on this trail because more than half the length is also used by horseback riders, cross-country skiers, and snowmobilers.

About three-quarters of a mile north of the connecting trail to Glacial Park is a water pump located on top of a grassy sand kame. At the water pump there is a private road named Valley Road. North of Valley Road the trail becomes a gravel road several feet above the water level of Nippersink Creek. There is a shelter nearly one mile north of Valley Road, and pit toilets are accessible via a bridge and short connecting trail.

Beyond the shelter, Nippersink Trail meanders east away from the crop fields and passes a large pond. Many types of birds are visible along this northern tip of the trail. Southeast of the pond the trail meanders through a mostly marsh environment. For more than two miles past the pond, to the point where the trail parallels the railroad tracks, the trail may be impassable during the wet season, as this is mostly wetland. If the hiker wears proper footgear, this two-mile wetlands section can be very enjoyable as it offers the view of many plants and wildlife species common to wetland environments. Just before the railroad tracks, another water pump is available along the trail.

The trail ends at the parking lot along Harts Road. By taking Harts Road three-quarters of a mile west, the hiker will reach the main parking area at Glacial Park.

Facilities: Glacial Park has picnic facilities with fire grates, water and restrooms at the parking area. Nippersink Trail has a parking lot on Harts Road and at Keystone Road. Barnard Mill Road intersection has sanitary facilities and a canoe landing. The McHenry County Conservation District Headquarters is located at Glacial Park. Information, maps and books are available at the headquarters.

Permits Required: Permits are required for groups of twenty-five or more people.

Park Rules and Regulations: Camping is not allowed in Glacial Park or along Nippersink Creek. Fishing is allowed in Nippersink Creek with all Illinois fishing rules and regulations in effect.

Mailing Address and Phone Number: McHenry County Conservation District, 6512 Harts Road, Ringwood, Illinois 60072; 815/338–1405

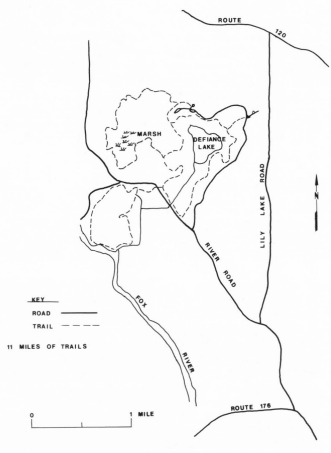

KEY

ROAD ——————

TRAIL — — — —

11 MILES OF TRAILS

0   1 MILE

5. Moraine Hills State Park

5. Moraine Hills State Park

Trail Length: 11 miles (17 kilometers)

Location: Moraine Hills State Park is located in north-eastern Illinois just south of McHenry. The park boundaries are centered between north-south Routes 31 and 12 and east-west Routes 120 and 176. Traveling on Route 176, turn north on River Road, and go two miles to the entrance; from McHenry and Route 120 turn south on River Road and go three miles to the entrance.

Other north-south roads which are nearby Moraine Hills State Park include Illinois Tollroad 94, Route 45, and Route 47.

County: McHenry

Illinois Highway Map Coordinates: B-8

U.S.G.S. Topographical Map Name and Scale: Wauconda, 1:24,000

Hours Open: The park is open year-round except on Christmas Day and New Year's Day. At certain times, due to freezing and thawing periods, the park is closed and access to the park is by foot only.

History and Trail Description: Moraine Hills State Park has 1,676 acres of upland and wetland environments. The rivers, lakes, marshes, prairies, and woodlands here are the result of the most recent glacial advance, the Wisconsin Glacier. At one time this area was occupied by several Indian tribes, including the Potawatomi, Sauk, and Fox. Construction of the McHenry Dam on the Fox River began in 1934 after several land acquisitions in the area.

Major land acquisition of the Lake Defiance area began in 1971. After a resource study and completion of a master plan, construction of the park facilities began in the spring of 1975.

The 11-mile trail system at Moraine Hills State Park consists of three main loops and includes the Lake Defiance Self-Guided Interpretive Trail as well as the Pike Marsh Interpretive Trail and connecting trails to several day-use areas. The trail system is designed to be hiked one way only and is very easy to follow. The two most centrally located parking areas are the Northern Lakes Day Use Area and the Pike Marsh Day Use Area. From the Northern Lakes Day Use Area, the Leather Leaf Bog Trail is located behind the comfort station, and the direction of travel is west (counterclockwise as you refer to the map).

Trailboards having maps and park rules and regulations are located at all day use areas (parking lots). Trail signs are located at all trail junctions indicating the name of the trail, direction of travel, and mileage.

The Leather Leaf Bog Trail measures 3.5 miles and represents an excellent example of kettlemoraine topography and supports very diverse plant communities. Plant species include marsh fern, marsh marigold, and several species of willow.

The Lake Defiance Trail which surrounds the 48-acre lake measures 4 miles. This trail connects the Northern Day Use Area with the Lake Defiance Day Use Area and the park office. Also, along the Lake Defiance Trail is the concession and interpretive center. As the trail meanders southward, paralleling the park road, connecting trails allow access from the Hickory Ridge Day Use Area, Pine Hills Day Use Area, Kettle Woods Day Use Area, and the Pike Marsh Day Use Area. At the southwesternmost point of this trail, there is a connecting trail going west under River Road. The connecting trail is for the Fox River Loop which also is designed for travel in one direction only.

This Fox River Trail passes through prairie areas adjacent to wetlands. A short trail leads to the parking area at McHenry Dam and to the concession area. The southern portion of this trail parallels the Fox River and the water drainage channel from Lake Defiance. The total length of this loop is 2.5 miles.

Additional trails in the park are the Lake Defiance Self-Guided Interpretive Trail, which measures nearly 0.5 miles, and the Pike Marsh Interpretive Trail.

The Lake Defiance Self-Guided Interpretive Trail is accessed from the Northern Lakes parking lot and from the Lake Defiance parking lot to the park office where the numbered posts begin.

The trail at Pike Marsh is accessed from the parking lot at Pike Marsh Day Use Area. Approximate length is 0.6 miles.

The diverse landscape in this area of McHenry County provides habitat for numerous forms of wildlife. Over 100 species of birds have been identified. The area is heavily used by mallard, teal, wood duck, Canada geese, and other migratory waterfowl.

Various mammals including red fox, eastern cottontail, mink, opossum, raccoon, and white-tail deer can be seen in the upland timber of oak, hickory, ash, cherry, dogwood, and hawthorn.

Facilities: Moraine Hills State Park has several parking areas. Picnic tables are available in all day use areas, along with water and comfort stations. A picnic shelter is available at the Pine Hills Day Use Area. Also, there are flush toilets at the McHenry Dam concession building and at the Park Office.

Playground equipment is available at the McHenry Dam area and at the Morainal Hills Day Use Area. Boats are available for public use on Lake Defiance.

In addition to the concession at McHenry Dam area there is a concession at the park office. An interpretive center is also located at the park office.

Permits Required: Groups of twenty-five persons or more require permission from the site superintendent.

Park Rules and Regulations: Groups of minors must have adequate supervision and at least one adult for every fifteen minors. All pets must be on a leash. There are no camping facilities available at Moraine Hills State Park. See Appendix A.

Mailing Address and Phone Number: Site Superintendent, Moraine Hills State Park, 914 S. River Road, McHenry, Illinois, 60050; 815/385–1624

6. Des Plaines River Trail (Lake County)

Trail Length: 6.3 miles (10.1 kilometers)

Location: The Des Plaines River Trail is located in northeastern Illinois along Route 41, just south of the Wisconsin border. The main trailhead at Sterling Lake is accessible from Route 41, one-eighth of a mile north of Route 173. A sharp right onto a paved road will lead to the parking area. The entrance to this parking lot may be closed at certain times of the year, depending upon the weather. However, additional access points to the trail are available.

A second access point may be reached north of the main entrance off of Route 41. Follow Route 41 north to Russell Road. Turn east on Russell Road, go a quarter mile, and turn south to the north entrance of Sterling Lake.

County: Lake

Illinois Highway Map Coordinates: A-9

U.S.G.S. Topographical Map Name and Scale: Wadsworth, 1:24,000

Hours Open: 8:00 a.m. to sunset

History and Trail Description: The trail and surrounding property are located along the floodplain of the Des Plaines River. The Lake County Forest Preserve District purchased the property in the area with the intention of developing a 40-mile recreation corridor.

Although the trailhead may be accessed from two areas from the north, probably the easiest place to begin the trail is at Van Patten Woods Forest Preserve. Van Patten Woods is located a half mile east of Route 41 off State Route 173. Van Patten Woods divides the trail into

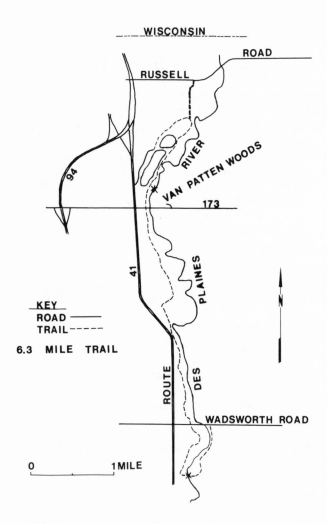

6. Des Plaines River Trail (Lake County)

two shorter sections: 4 miles to the south and 2 miles to the north.

A parking lot is available at Van Patten Woods. From the parking lot the hiker may go to the picnic area and to shelter A. From here a trail will be seen which goes to a 200-foot bridge over the Des Plaines River. Once the hiker crosses the bridge he may go north to the trailheads and Sterling Lake or south towards Route 173.

The trail north of 173 is ten to twelve feet wide and is a dirt lane. This area all the way to the trailhead and around Sterling Lake may be extremely muddy during wet weather.

The four-mile section of trail south of Route 173 is surfaced with crushed stone and is generally about twelve feet wide. This portion of the trail is well-maintained and is suitable for hiking, biking, horseback riding, cross-country skiing, and snowmobiling. The trail goes by open fields, prairie grass stands, and river floodplains. The trail also goes by some farm fields.

At about one and one-half miles south of Route 173 you will come across a water pump that can be used for drinking water. From the pump to Wadsworth Road, you will be here on a section of trail that is a

Water pump with hitching post, Des Plaines River Trail (Lake County)

prime viewing area for observing migratory birds such as long-neck geese.

South of Wadsworth Road, the trail meanders through more dense woodlands than those of the northern part of the trail. The southernmost portion of the trail then crosses over the Des Plaines River via a ninety-foot bridge. From here, the trail turns north and heads toward Wadsworth Road and Wadsworth Canoe Launch–Des Plaines River Trail Access. This is the end of the trail.

To return to the main trailhead or to Van Patten Woods, you must retrace your steps since this is not a loop trail.

Facilities: Water pumps, pit toilets, and car parking are located at the trailhead, at Van Patten Woods Forest Preserve, and at Wadsworth Canoe Launch. A canoe launch, fishing dock, observation platform, car and trailer parking, drinking water, and pit toilets are available at the Wadsworth Canoe Launch area. Van Patten Woods also has picnic grounds, shelters and playgrounds, first-aid stations, and public telephones. Fishing is allowed in the Des Plaines river and Sterling Lake with all Illinois fishing rules and regulations in effect.

Permits Required: Permits are required for horseback riding and snowmobiles and may be obtained at the general offices of the Lake County Forest Preserve District. Permits are also required for groups of twenty-five or more people. The shelters and playgrounds may be reserved at the district office.

Trail Rules and Regulations: No hunting, swimming, fires, or littering. Pets must be on a leash. No amplified music allowed. Parking in designated areas only. No consumption of alcoholic beverages in or within immediate vicinity of parking areas.

Mailing Address and Phone Number: Lake County Forest Preserve District, 2000 North Milwaukee Avenue, Libertyville, Illinois 60048; 312/367–6640

7. Lakewood Forest Preserve

Trail Length: 6 miles (9.6 kilometers)

Location: Lakewood Forest Preserve is located south of Wauconda, Illinois, off State Route 176. To get to the park, north and south traffic may take State Route 12 and exit onto Route 176 going east. Proceed for a few miles until just before intersecting Fairfield Road. Before Fairfield Road there will be a park sign. Turn right (south) into the park.

County: Lake

Illinois Highway Map Coordinates: B-9

U.S.G.S. Topographical Map Names and Scale: Lake Zurich and Grayslake, 1:24,000

Hours Open: The preserve is open from 8:00 a.m. to sunset. The museum is open every day from 1:00 p.m. to 4:00 p.m.

History and Trail Description: Lakewood Forest Preserve, an area rich in history, attracted settlers from the earliest times, with weathered stone foundations as symbols of those farmsteads. The preserve contains over 1,400 acres of rolling countryside dotted with woods, small lakes, meadows and wetlands.

The trail system consists of a combination hiking/horseback trail that meanders through the south side of the park and covers over 6 miles.

The trailhead may be reached by proceeding into the park and going past the museum and ranger station to a T junction in the road. This is Ivanhoe Road. Turn left (east) and go for a half block to a metal sign with a symbol of a hiker on it. Turn right on this road and drive down to the small parking lot that is available. During

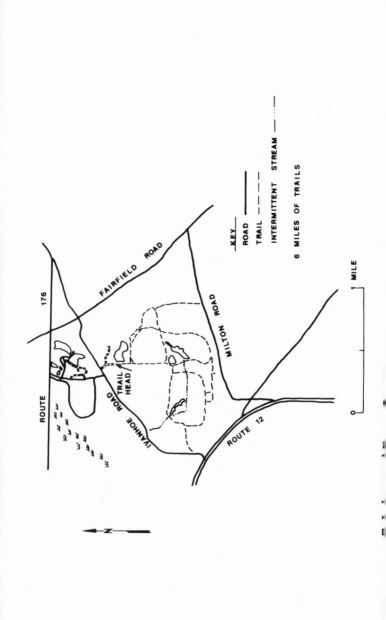

KEY

ROAD _____

TRAIL _ _ _ _

INTERMITTENT STREAM ....

6 MILES OF TRAILS

ROUTE 176

FAIRFIELD ROAD

IVANHOE ROAD

TRAIL HEAD

MILTON ROAD

ROUTE 12

N

0   1 MILE

the winter season this road may be closed; if so, continue down Ivanhoe Road to a larger parking lot on the north side of the road.

At the parking lot, you will find rest rooms, water, and a small lake where fishing is permitted. In addition, restrooms are available for the hiker about a mile from the trailhead. The trail starts just south of the parking lot. You will have to go around a gate that is set up to prevent motorized vehicles from entering the trails. Trailboards are set up at different locations on the trail. The trailboards have a map of the trail showing the hiker's exact location at the time. You may hike the trails in any direction and may hike the entire trail length or just a few loop trails.

The trail is very wide and is an old gravel/dirt road. The trail goes by and through open fields, around three small lakes, through the woods and onto the backside of a neighboring subdivision. At some spots the trail goes up and down some rolling hills and offers some good views of the surrounding area. The easternmost part of the trail goes by a horse stable. At this point the trail markers on the trail show that the trail ends. The gravel road actually keeps winding south of the horse stable area, and you could continue hiking. There is also access for the public on this trail off of Milton Road. The easternmost edge of the park borders a subdivision, and there is a small opening where the public may follow a trail that connects with the trail system in the park.

Facilities: The preserve has a small museum, a ranger station, and an animal warden station on the grounds. There are many picnic areas in the park that have tables, restrooms, water and shelters. The preserve also has a winter recreation area on the east side of Fairfield Road. There is also a snowmobile trail and a physical fitness trail in the park. Skiers are free to ski any of the trails in the park. There is also a tent camping area for groups of fewer than 100 persons. Fishing is allowed in the lakes with all Illinois fishing rules and regulations applying.

Permits Required: A permit is required for groups of twenty-five or more persons and for reserved shelters. In addition, snowmobile and horseback permits are required. Permits may be obtained in person at the main park office in Libertyville. A permit is also required for camping.

Park Rules and Regulations: No dogs are allowed on the horse trail. No swimming in the lakes or motorcycles on the trails. No hunting, ice fishing, or ice skating allowed.

Mailing Address and Phone Number: Lake County Forest Preserve District, 2000 North Milwaukee Avenue, Libertyville, Illinois 60048; 312/367–6640

8. Captain Daniel Wright Woods

Trail Length: 4 miles (6.4 kilometers)

Location: Wright Woods is located five miles north of Ryerson Conservation Area and can be reached off of Riverwoods road. To reach the park, Interstate 94 southbound and northbound traffic may exit onto State Route 22. Proceed west for one-half mile to Riverwoods Road. Turn right (north) on Riverwoods Road and proceed for one and a half miles to Everett Road. Turn left (west) on Everett Road and go for two miles until the road comes to a T. Turn left at the T junction and proceed straight ahead into the park.

County: Lake

Illinois Highway Map Coordinates: B-9

U.S.G.S. Topographical Map Name and Scale: Wheeling, 1:24,000

Hours Open: The park is open all year and closes at sunset every evening.

History and Trail Description: Captain Daniel Wright was the first white settler in Lake County. Pottawattomi Chief Metama and his tribe helped Wright build his cabin near Half Day in 1834.

The trail system at Wright Woods consists of interconnecting loop trails which total 4 miles. The trails are also used by horseback riders and skiers. The trail may be started from the parking area near the park building. A trailboard is located right by the building and contains the trail layout. The trail is located north of the building, along the entrance road. A small horse marker will be seen along the road at the trail intersection with the road. The trail may be hiked in either direction at this point.

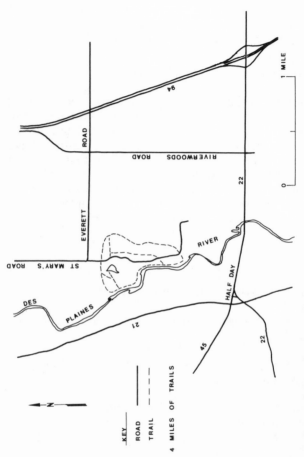

KEY

ROAD ——————

TRAIL – – – –

4 MILES OF TRAILS

8. Daniel Wright Woods

If you go west, the trail will soon come to the Des Plaines River. The trail then goes south, paralleling the river. You will soon reach a trail intersection where you will see a trail sign. This sign says "River Trail" and refers to the other trail as the Nature Trail. The Nature Trail goes back to the small lake and picnic area. If you continue along the River Trail you will go over the small creek that comes out of the lake and goes into the Des Plaines River. Shortly after that another trail intersects with the River Trail. This trail may be hiked back to the parking lot area. The River Trail then continues south and will cross a park road. You will see physical fitness trail signposts all along this part of the trail. There are eighteen physical fitness stations set up along this part of the trail.

The trail then comes to another intersecting trail. You can either continue straight ahead or go left (west). If you go straight, the trail will lead you back to where you started. By going left you will come upon another section of the park road. This road connects with the parking lot and you can hike back to it. The physical fitness trail starts at the junction of these trails. By following the road southward, you will see and may use the physical fitness stations.

Facilities: Wright Woods contains numerous picnic areas with picnic tables, grills, water, restrooms, shelters, and playground equipment available. A first aid station, public telephone and other information may be obtained at the ranger station. A small pond located here permits fishing. All appropriate Illinois fishing rules and regulations apply for the pond and the Des Plaines River.

Permits Required: A permit is required for horseback riding and may be obtained from the park district headquarters. A permit is also required for groups of twenty-five or more persons for reserved shelters.

Park Rules and Regulations: All pets must be on a leash. No alcoholic beverages in or within immediate vicinity of parking areas. No snowmobiles are allowed. Parking only in designated areas.

Mailing Address and Phone Number: Lake County Forest Preserve District, 2000 North Milwaukee Avenue, Libertyville, Illinois 60048; 312/367–6640

9. Edward L. Ryerson Conservation Area

Trail Length: 6.5 miles (10.4 kilometers)

Location: Ryerson Conservation Area is located north-west of Deerfield, Illinois. To reach the park, north-bound traffic may take Interstate 94 and exit at Deer-field Road. Go west on Deerfield Road for a few blocks to Riverwoods Road. Turn right on Riverwoods Road (north) and proceed for two miles to the park entrance. Turn left onto the park road and follow the signs to the education center parking lot. Interstate 94 southbound traffic may exit onto State Route 22 and go west to Riv-erwoods. Turn left (south) and proceed a few miles to the park entrance.

County: Lake

Illinois Highway Map Coordinates: B-9

U.S.G.S. Topographical Map Name and Scale: Wheel-ing, 1:24,000

Hours Open: March until October–9:00 a.m. to 5:00 p.m., November until February–8:30 a.m. to 4:30 p.m.

History and Trail Description: The Edward L. Ryerson Conservation Area, a part of the Illinois Nature Pre-serves system, is known for its wildflowers, virgin for-ests and animal life. The park borders the Des Plaines River on the east.

The trail system consists of many interconnecting trails that total 6.5 miles. The trails may be started in the parking lot near the education center. The education center has a ranger on duty where you can request maps and other information. The trail system has trail signs set up throughout the park that show your exact loca-tion. You may hike the trails in any direction and for

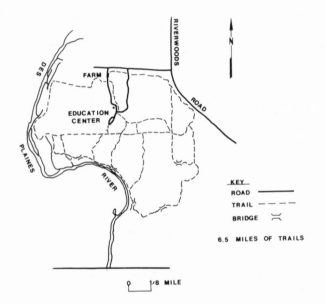

9. Ryerson Conservation Area. Redrawn from park map.

any length. Some trails may be closed at times, to protect the animals in the park.

The trails go through open fields, along the Des Plaines River, along a farm field, and by the farm itself. As you hike the trail along the Des Plaines River, you will observe many abandoned houses. These houses were homes and summer cottages prior to when the park district bought this land. There are some small bridges that you must cross, and the trail also crosses the park road two times. At one point along the river the hiker will see a small dam. A house is located by the dam and provides a nice resting area.

The trail by the farm may be confusing, and you should be cautious in this area. You will walk through the center of the farm and see a trailboard set up close to the fence. You must follow this fence eastward all the way to the river. Once you reach the river, the trail turns south and parallels the river for a short distance.

All of the trails are fairly flat and are excellent for cross-country skiing.

Facilities: An education center located on the grounds provides the hiker with information, trail maps, and other materials. The education center offers a variety of school and adult group programs throughout the year. Many special winter programs, including animal tracking, skiing, and using a compass, are also offered at the park. A newsletter is also distributed by the Ryerson Conservation Area and may be of value to the hiker. A small farm is also located on the grounds. Water and restrooms are available at the education center and at the farm.

Permits Required: Permits are required for all groups of ten or more persons and may be obtained at the education center.

Park Rules and Regulations: No collecting of any animals or plants in the park. Walk only on the trails. No releasing of animals. Fishing, swimming, pets and boat access are not allowed. Vehicles and bicycles are not permitted on the trails. No picnics allowed. No alcohol, taped music, ball playing or frisbee. See Appendix C.

Mailing Address and Phone Numbers: Lake County Forest Preserve District, 2000 N. Milwaukee Avenue, Libertyville, Illinois 60048, 312/367–6640, or Edward L. Ryerson Conservation Area, Lake County Forest Preserve District, 21950 Riverwoods Road, Deerfield, Illinois 60015; 312/948–7750

10. Mississippi Palisades State Park

Trail Length: 11 miles of trails (17.7 kilometers)

Location: Mississippi Palisades State Park is located three miles north of Savanna on State Route 84. The traveler may enter the park from the north or south entrance. The park office is located at the north park entrance, so the hiker may want to go there to find out the trail conditions or to request more information.

County: Carroll

Illinois Highway Map Coordinates: B-4

U.S.G.S. Topographical Map Names and Scale: Blackhawk and Savanna, both 1:24,000

Hours Open: The park is open year-round except on Christmas Day and New Year's Day. At certain times of the year, due to freezing and thawing, the park may close and access to the park is by foot only.

History and Trail Description: The area known as Mississippi Palisades State Park was once inhabited by a considerable Indian population which left remnants of its culture upon the landscape. Numerous burial mounds are located within the park boundary. These mounds are easily accessible via well-marked hiking trails.

The park is located near the confluence of the Apple and Mississippi rivers. The name Palisades was given to the steep limestone bluffs along the Mississippi River because of their resemblance to similar geological formations on the Hudson River.

In 1929, the State of Illinois acquired 376 acres of land here to preserve the natural beauty and historic sites. The park now has over 1,717 acres.

The trail system consists of over 11 miles of hiking

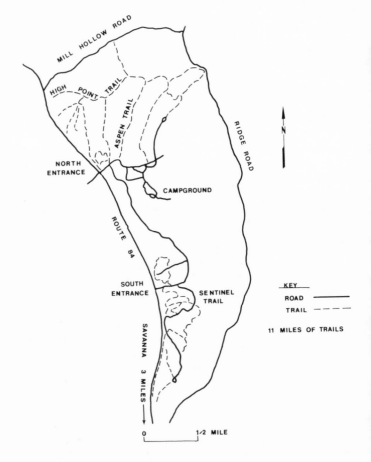

10. Mississippi Palisades State Park. Redrawn from park trail map.

trails located at both the northern and southern ends of the park. The trailheads of the major trails are well marked by trailboards; likewise, all trail junctions are marked by metal trail signs. The trail signs display the trail layout which is marked by a red dot showing your exact location. The trailboards show only the trail that you are hiking. All of the trails are color-coded on the trail signs.

There are six major trails located at the north area and four major trails at the south end of the park. Over 7 miles of trails wind their way through the hills at the north end of the park and over 4 miles at the south end.

The trails at the north end of the park may be started north of the park office. Vehicles may be left at the parking area by the park camping area. The Rocktop Trail, High Point Trail and the Aspen Trail are accessible from the parking lot.

The Rocktop Trail is a short loop trail that makes its way around the top of the bluffs, offering beautiful views of the Mississippi River and its valley. There is an overlook along the trail where one may view the river. A trailboard is set up at the head of this trail, which measures 0.6 miles. The end of this trail connects with the High Point Trail.

The High Point Trail starts out as an old paved road that slowly turns to a dirt lane. The trail is about twelve feet wide and is very easy to follow once the hiker reaches the top of the ridge. The trail immediately starts climbing uphill, following the ridge line. At the top of the hill the trail continues to follow the major ridges. You will soon reach a trail intersection marked by a sign for the Goldenrod Trail. From here you may go east and follow the Goldenrod Trail, or go west and continue following the High Point Trail.

West from the Goldenrod Trail intersection, the High Point Trail continues to follow the ridge lines and intersects another trail. The trail to the north leads to a shelter overlook offering a beautiful view of the river valley below. The trail to the south leads to four sections of the High Point Trail. There is a trail sign at this point to help you determine your exact location.

The trail to the extreme right goes to the bluffs. The next trail to the right follows the valley floor to the road below. The third trail goes to the top of the hill, and the trail to the extreme left goes down through the valley, coming out near the trailhead. From here, you can follow the road to the head of the Aspen Trail.

The Aspen Trail follows the ridgetops of the hills in the area. The Aspen Trail connects with the Goldenrod Trail and also with the Deer and Bittersweet Trails. The Goldenrod Trail has a branch that leads down to Mill Hollow Road while the second branch goes to the High Point Trail.

One primitive campsite is found on each of the Goldenrod, Bittersweet, and Aspen Trails. A marker along the trail will point to the camping area.

From the Aspen Trail you can follow the Deer Trail or the Bittersweet Trail or continue following the Aspen Trail to the end. The Deer Trail is a loop trail that branches off to areas of the Aspen Trail, goes by Ridge Road, and follows an open field for a short distance. The end of the Aspen Trail is at the end of the park road. Picnic and camping areas are available. The Bittersweet Trail takes you along the ridge top and then down to the camping area; the road will lead you back to the trailhead.

After hiking the trails at the north end, you can drive on the park road to the south end where the other trails are located.

The trails at the south end offer more spectacular views of the river valley than the trails at the north end of the park. In addition, many rock formations and 200-foot cliffs are seen along some of the trails here.

The trails at the south end of the park may be started in a few areas along the park road or along State Route 84.

The Sunset Trail is a short loop trail that may be started off the south park entrance road. The trail ascends a ridge line, follows the ridges in a loop going over another road, and passes a lookout point. From the lookout point the trail goes south again to the trailhead. From here you may walk along the park road or reach the parking area by the shelter close to Route 84. The Sentinel Trail starts here.

The Sentinel Trail begins climbing the slope of the hill right away. The trail divides into two sections. The branch to the west leads to the bluffs. From here, you will see more spectacular views of rock formations and the river valley. The trail then meets again, crosses the road, and connects with the Pine Trail.

The Pine Trail ascends and descends through some beautiful valleys. You will cross a bridge, climb hills, and come to another overlook. Two large vertical rock formations are seen at the overlook area. These rock formations are referred to as "Twin Sisters' Rocks." The trail crosses the park road again and joins with Upton's Trail. Upton's Trail goes past some of the largest bluffs in the park and passes by Indian Head Rock.

Upton's Trail parallels Route 84, following the base of the bluffs the entire length. The Mississippi River is visible along the entire hike. The trail passes by Upton's Cave, which can be seen from the trail itself. You can go inside this cave for a short distance. From here the hiker can retrace his footsteps along the trails to the trail start, or he can follow Route 84 back to the starting point.

Extreme caution must be used while hiking the trails in the park. Many of the trails pass by and may follow the bluffs' edge and may descend steep rock ledges.

The trails at the north end of the park are also used for cross-country skiing in the winter. Some of the trails may not be skied and are marked accordingly. The trails at the south end of the park are extremely steep, rocky, and narrow and are unsafe for skiing.

Facilities: Numerous picnic tables, water faucets, and restrooms are located throughout the park. Shelter houses and playground equipment are located at the main entrance and camping areas. Tent and trailer facilities, including a utility building with showers and flush toilets, are available. Electric hook-ups and a sanitary dump station are provided for contained areas. There are free launching ramps and two boat docks at the river

Upton's Cave, Mississippi Palisades State Park

access area. Boat rentals are available from a private concessionaire, and there are no motor size limits. A park office on the grounds offers additional information. Limited horse trails are located in the park; no horse rentals are available.

Permits Required: A camping permit is required.

Park Rules and Regulations: Park closes at sundown. Quiet hours from 10:00 p.m. until 7:00 a.m. No chain saws are permitted in the park and loud mufflers are prohibited. See Appendix A.

Mailing Address and Phone Number: Site Superintendent, Mississippi Palisades State Park, 4577 Route 84 North, Savanna, Illinois 61074; 815/273–2731

11. Des Plaines River Trail (Cook County)

Trail Length: 27 miles (43.4 kilometers)

Location: The Des Plaines River Trail is located in northeastern Illinois along the eastern bank of the Des Plaines River. From Madison Street in Forest Park the trail passes through many suburbs of Chicago north to the Lake–Cook County border, Lake Cook Road.

Major access points include the Potawatomi Woods and Dam No. 1 Woods off of Dundee Road, Allison Woods and the River Trail Nature Center off of Milwaukee Avenue at Winkelman Road, Camp Pine Woods off of Euclid Avenue, Big Bend Lake off of East River Road and Golf Road in Des Plaines, Illinois. All of the aforementioned areas are considered part of the Des Plaines Division of the Forest Preserve District of Cook County.

Major access points between Touhy Avenue in Park Ridge and Madison Street in Forest Park include: Axehead Lake off of Touhy Avenue, Dam No. 4 east off of Dee Road or Devon Avenue, Robinson Woods South off of Lawrence Avenue, Schiller Woods North off of East River Road–Montrose Avenue or Irving Park Road in Schiller Park, Evans Field off of Thatcher Avenue, and Thatcher Woods and Thatcher Woods Glen off of Chicago Avenue in River Forest. All of these areas are considered part of the Indian Boundary Division of the Forest Preserve District of Cook County.

County: Cook

Illinois Highway Map Coordinates: B-9 to C-9

U.S.G.S. Topographical Map Names and Scale: Wheeling, Arlington Heights, Park Ridge and River Forest, all 1:24,000

Hours Open: For safety reasons, use the trail during daylight hours only. The Forest Preserve District picnic grounds and parking areas close at sunset.

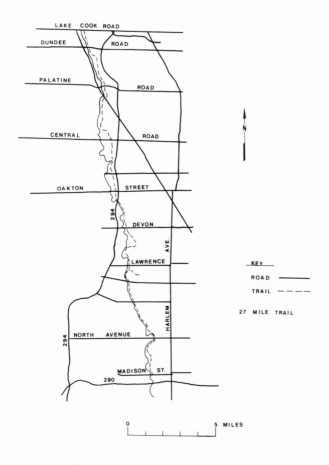

11. Des Plaines River Trail (Cook County). Redrawn from IDOT Cook County Highway
Map.

History and Trail Description: The Des Plaines River Trail passes through the narrow band of native landscape along the eastern bank of the Des Plaines River in Cook County. The area is rich with the history of the many Indians who once settled here.

Evans Field is the site of an Indian village; east of Evans Field, five mounds were built by prehistoric Indians. The Indian Boundary Line, which crosses the trail just east of Grand Avenue in River Grove, is the north line of a strip of land twenty miles wide from Lake Michigan to Ottawa ceded to the whites by the Potawatomi in 1816. Big Bend Lake is the site of an old Indian village; Camp Pine Woods is the site of a pioneer cabin.

The Des Plaines River Trail (Cook County) is the longest of two trails established along the Des Plaines River which are part of a proposal to make a 40-mile recreation corridor from the trailhead at Sterling Lake, which is south of Russell Road in Lake County, to the River Trail in Cook County. A third section, the newest, is still under construction and is not desirable for use at this time (refer to phone number at the end of this description for an update on the trail completion).

The majority of the trail is a gravel and dirt path. Native trees and wildflowers are seen all along the trail. There are many species of birds visible in this area, including many migratory birds. Many deer and rabbit can be seen at different times of the year as the Des Plaines River and surrounding preserve are an excellent refuge for all forms of wildlife.

The Des Plaines River Trail is part of two different divisions of ten divisions in Cook County. The Cook County Forest Preserve District has some 150 miles of multi-purpose trails available for hikers, bikers, horseback riders, and cross-country skiers. The two divisions of this trail are the Indian Boundary Division from Touhy Avenue in Park Ridge to Madison Street in Forest Park, and the Des Plaines Division from Touhy Avenue north to the Lake–Cook County border.

Because the majority of trails in Cook County are maintained but are not appropriately marked, we have excluded them from our trail descriptions; however, these other trails are listed in trail maps available from the Forest Preserve General Headquarters (address listed under the heading "Mailing Address and Phone Number").

The Des Plaines River Trail is marked only by symbols of horses attached to posts at major road crossings (white figure on a brown background). The north end of the trail ends at Lake Cook Road, which is a four-lane road. The south end stops at Madison Street. You will see a cemetery and cannot continue south of Madison Street.

Horses are allowed on this multi-purpose trail; however, the majority of horseback riders are seen between Golf Road and Lake–Cook Road. One section of the trail that is a bit confusing is at the Allison Woods section. From the east, finish the gravel path at Allison Woods parking area and follow the entrance to Milwaukee Avenue. Cross Milwaukee Avenue and follow the blacktop road (Winkelman Road) beside the Holiday Inn for one-eighth of a mile. The trail then goes west (left). Opposite directions are appropriate if you are traveling from west to east.

Another confusing section of the trail is between Rand Road and the crossing at Algonquin Road. Going north, cross Algonquin Road, go north on Campground Road past the Banner Day-Care Center and then the Methodist Camp. Continuing on this road you will pass the Northwestern Woods. This part of the road is known as Joseph Schwab Road. Follow the Joseph Schwab Road under the viaduct to Northwest Highway. Turn right (east), follow the sidewalk crossing the Busse Highway Intersection, and then continue for two blocks to Garland Place. Turn left (north) onto Garland Place and follow for one block to Rand Road. The trail is very visible directly across Rand Road. Be cautious as you cross the street because Rand Road is a hazardous crossing.

South of Lawrence Avenue the trail becomes narrower, almost a footpath in parts, and is much closer to the bank of the river. In fact, much of the trail between

Lawrence Avenue and North Avenue is the floodplain of the Des Plaines River. During wet seasons these sections may be impassable; one section that is difficult almost year-round is between Grand Avenue and Belmont. This section is very low and is often flooded. A good alternate route is to go west from either Grand or Belmont Avenue to Des Plaines River Road. Then go north or south to your desired intersection, east again over the river and continue the trail.

From the north crossing Belmont Avenue, the trail is hard to locate. Crossing Belmont, you will notice a cemetery. Continue south behind the guardrail and follow the iron fence toward the river. Upon reaching the last fencepost follow the narrow path around it, and continue the trail south along the fence and cemetery property.

Another difficult section is near Fullerton Woods East. The main trail goes left (east) while the connecting trail goes along the river, past a dam and a bridge, finally crossing the river. Follow the main trail to the left for about one-quarter mile where another trail junction is reached. Again, follow the left trail, and you will find yourself at the water pump at Evans Field.

If you missed the turn off for the main trail and do not desire to cross over the river (the trail would then end at First Avenue), there is a trail on the east side of the river at the foot of the bridge. This trail meanders through some floodplains and meets with the main trail to form the aforementioned junction. Follow the right trail and, again, you will find yourself at the water pump at Evans Field.

From Evans Field follow the entrance out to Thatcher Avenue and continue south on Thatcher Avenue. Cross North Avenue and continue south about 100 yards where a section of guardrail is separated (about four feet wide). A new shelter should be visible just yards behind the guardrail. The trail continues past the shelter and along the river.

The remainder of the trail is but a footpath which passes through some densely wooded areas. At Chicago Avenue the trail becomes an asphalt path for a short distance past a lagoon and behind the Trailside Museum.

The Trailside Museum is an excellent place to stop and view a variety of birds and mammals native to this area. Many of the wildlife on display are reestablishing themselves at this wildlife shelter; staff members are available for assistance.

South of the Trailside Museum the trail divides into two sections which meet again and form a loop. The shorter route follows Thatcher Avenue south again just beyond the Chicago & Northwestern Railroad where it turns into the woods and goes west. The longer route goes west through the woods, follows the bank of the river beyond the railroad tracks, and then moves east again to where the trails meet and form a loop just beside a trail shelter.

Facilities: There are many trail shelters located along this trail; however, many have been destroyed or are being eliminated and others are being replaced with new ones. Contact the Forest Preserve to find the exact locations of those available for use.

Water and restrooms are available at most of the forest preserve lands that have picnic areas; also, shelters and parking areas may be found at these forest preserves. A youth group campground is available at Camp Baden Powell on Des Plaines River Road south of the headquarters on Foundry Road in Mount Prospect.

Permits Required: Permits are required for the youth group campground. Horseback riders must have a license. Each group of twenty-five people or more must obtain permits for picnicking at any of the established areas. For picnic permits, you may contact the following in person: Permit Clerk, Forest Preserve District Office, Daley Center, 50 W. Washington, Room 406, Chicago.

Park Rules and Regulations: Use receptacles for garbage and trash. Report any fires. No alcoholic beverages allowed.

Mailing Address and Phone Numbers: For additional facilities maps and maps of the ten divisions of forest preserve districts in Cook County contact: Forest Preserve General Headquarters, 536 North Harlem Avenue, River Forest, Illinois; 312/261–8400 (city), 312/366–9420 (suburban). Des Plaines Division Headquarters, River Road at Foundry Road, Mount Prospect, Illinois; 312/824–1900 or 824–1883

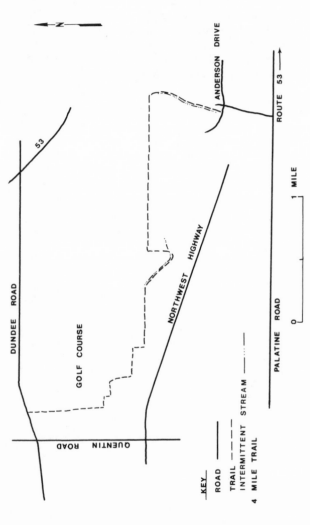

12. The Palatine Trail

12. The Palatine Trail

Trail Length: 4 miles (6.4 kilometers)

Location: The Palatine Trail is located in Palatine. The trail may be reached by north- and southbound traffic by taking State Route 53 and exiting west onto Palatine Road. Go on Palatine Road for eight blocks until Winston Drive. Turn right (north) on Winston Drive and proceed for about four blocks to Maple Park. The trailhead is found at Maple Park.

County: Cook

Illinois Highway Map Coordinates: B-9

U.S.G.S. Topographical Map Names and Scale: Lake Zurich and Palatine, both 1:24,000

Hours Open: The trail is open year-round.

History and Trail Description: The idea for the construction of a multi-purpose hiking, biking, and nature trail was initially presented to the Board of Commissioners of the Palatine Park District in 1963 during the preparation of a Master Plan for Parks and Recreation for Palatine. A portion of an abandoned railroad right-of-way was acquired in 1966. Funds for the construction of the trail were provided by the sale of general obligation bonds as approved in a referendum in 1972.

The Palatine Trail system is a paved asphalt trail which extends through an open corridor, going by numerous parks, schools, and residential neighborhoods.

The trail is indicated with metal posts marked "Palatine Trail." These signs are seen at the intersections of several roads that must be crossed.

The trail may be started across the street from Maple Park, on the north side of Anderson Drive. The trailhead at Maple Park goes northward, passing by a small creek, Doug Lindberg Park, and Lake Louise School. The trail then turns west and follows the power lines. Jane Adams School and Sycamore Park can be seen while hiking this section, where a few roads are also crossed.

As soon as you come to Hicks Highway, continue south to a small creek. The trail goes underneath the road at this point and comes up on the west side of Hicks Highway. The trail then crosses three small wooden bridges, goes by a large apartment complex, and then parallels the power lines again. You will pass Salt Creek Nature Study Area, Ashwood Park, and a water retention area.

You will cross Smith Road, following the trail behind some housing units. The trail borders the south side of Palatine Hills Golf Course and Recreation Area. From here, the trail follows the road that goes into the golf course, and then continues west through another gate and into a stretch of forest. The trail goes north at this point, passing through the woods all the way to Dundee Road, where the trail ends.

Facilities: Various recreation facilities may be found at the parks along the route of the trail.

Mailing Address and Phone Number: Palatine Park District, 250 East Wood Street, Palatine, Illinois 60067; 312/991–0333.

13. The Great Western Nature Trail

Trail Length: 17 miles (27 kilometers)

Location: The Great Western Nature Trail is located in northeastern Illinois two miles west of St. Charles. The east trailhead is located on the south side of Dean Street opposite the entrance for LeRoy Oakes Forest Preserve. Traveling east or west on State Route 64, signs for LeRoy Oakes Forest Preserve can be seen. From Route 64 follow Randall Road north to Dean Street. Go west on Dean Street for one-half mile and turn south, across from the entrance for LeRoy Oakes Forest Preserve.

The west trailhead is located in Sycamore at the intersection of Route 64, Old State Road, and Airport Road. Sycamore is located at the intersection of Route 23 and Route 64, five miles north of De Kalb.

Counties: De Kalb and Kane

Illinois Highway Map Coordinates: C-8

U.S.G.S. Topographical Map Names and Scale: Geneva, Elburn, Maple Park, and Sycamore, all 1:24,000

Hours Open: The preserve is open from 8:00 a.m. to 9:00 p.m. Monday through Friday and from 7:00 a.m. to 9:00 p.m. Saturdays and Sundays. Trail users are urged to complete their journeys by sundown.

History and Trail Description: The Great Western Nature Trail is a crushed stone path about ten feet wide which parallels the north side of Route 64 for seventeen miles. Previously, the trail was a railroad bed, and evidence of the old railroad ties and markers are seen.

The right-of-way of the Great Western Trail was developed into a railroad in 1887 by the Minnesota and Northwestern Railroad. Later that same year the Chi-

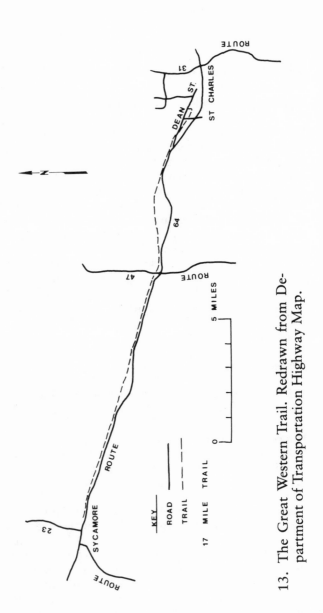

13. The Great Western Trail. Redrawn from Department of Transportation Highway Map.

cago, St Paul and Kansas Railway purchased all property of the Minnesota and Northwestern Railroad. At its peak, the Chicago Great Western operated fifteen-hundred miles of track connecting Illinois, Iowa, Kansas, Minnesota, Missouri, and Nebraska.

Along the 17-mile path are several prairie sites, marshes, wetlands resembling bogs, and several short, densely wooded areas. The trail also passes along several active farms and through the small communities of Wasco, Lily Lake, Virgil, Richardson, and Sycamore.

At several points along the trail adjoining woodlands have been developed into subdivisions. Mile markers are located on either side of the trail; these markers are wooden posts about one foot high, with red numbers on them, and are located one to two feet off the crushed stone path.

Additionally, the trail has stop signs at all road crossings, and there is a stop signal at Burlington Road, a hazardous crossing.

Wildlife in the area includes deer, racoon, opossum, beaver, fox, skunk, rabbit, and woodchucks. Also, a great variety of birds can be seen, including ducks, coot, and the great blue heron.

Primary users of the trail are bicyclists, mostly because of the trail length and because there are no camping facilities along the trail. The trail is also popular for cross-country skiers. Although LeRoy Oakes Forest Preserve and the Sycamore Community Park are the only established parking areas on the trail, there are many intersecting roads from which shuttles can be arranged for hikers if they wish to complete shorter lengths of the trail.

The Great Western Nature Trail is a National Recreation Trail. See Appendix D.

Facilities: Restrooms are available at the trailhead (LeRoy Oakes Forest Preserve), at the Wasco Crossing, and at Sycamore Community Park. Water is available at LeRoy Oakes Forest Preserve, Wasco, Virgil, and Sycamore Community Park.

Three picnic tables and two shelters are located

along the trail. Picnic tables are located between LeRoy Oakes and Wasco, one mile west of Route 47, just west of County Line Road, and at both trailheads. Shelters are available at Virgil, Lily Lake, and the trailhead opposite LeRoy Oakes Forest Preserve.

Trail Rules and Regulations: No horseback riding and no motorized vehicles. Hunting is not allowed and pets must be on a leash.

Mailing Address and Phone Number: Kane County Forest Preserve District, 719 Batavia Avenue, Geneva, Illinois 60134; 312/232–1242

14. The Illinois Prairie Path

Trail Length: 40 miles (64 kilometers)

Location: The Illinois Prairie Path is located in northeastern Illinois. The trail is shaped like the letter Y; one part goes northwest to Elgin, the second segment goes southwest to Aurora and Batavia, and the third part goes east to Bellwood. The great length and course of the trail make access and desired distances very accommodating since the trail goes through many communities. Communities from which the trail may be accessed include Bellwood, Berkeley, Elmhurst, Villa Park, Lombard, Glen Ellyn, Wheaton, Warrenville, Aurora, Winfield, Wayne, South Elgin, and Elgin.

The three sections of the trail join at Carlton Avenue and Liberty Street in Wheaton, the mid-point of the trail. Access and parking is available near all trail crossings; however, some community parks and forest preserves are convenient for access to the Prairie Path. One such park is the Elmer J. Hoffman in Wheaton which is on Prospect Road (north-south), off Hill Avenue, just one-half block east of where Hill Avenue crosses the railroad tracks.

In Warrenville, the Roy C. Blackwell Preserve, on Butterfield Road between Batavia and Winfield roads, has parking facilities. There is a $2.00 day-use fee for Du Page County residents and a $4.00 fee for nonresidents.

In Wayne, parking is available at Pratts Wayne Woods. Access is south on Powis Road from Stearns Road. From the east, Stearns Road intersects Route 59, and from the west Stearns Road is accessible from Dunham Road junction. To reach the Prairie Path from Pratts Wayne Woods, follow the Boy Scout's trail signs for the Red Caboose Trail for one mile.

Illinois roadways to the trail include north-south routes 31, 25, 59, 53, and 83, and tollroad 294. The

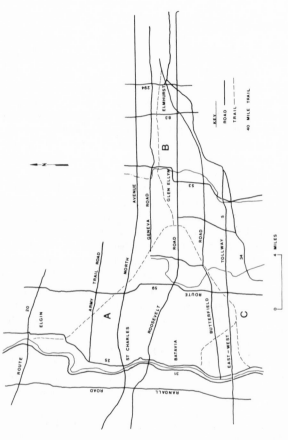

14. The Illinois Prairie Path. Redrawn from Illinois Prairie Path Map.

east-west roads for access to surrounding communities of the Prairie Path include Illinois Tollway 90 to Elgin, routes 20 and 64 (North Avenue), Route 38 (Roosevelt Road), Route 56 (Butterfield Road), and east-west toll-road (Illinois 5).

Counties: Kane, Du Page, Cook

Illinois Highway Map Coordinates: C-8 and C-9

U.S.G.S. Topographical Map Names and Scale: Elmhurst, Lombard, Wheaton, Naperville, West Chicago, Geneva, and Elgin, all 1:24,000

Hours Open: Year-round. No restricted hours, but daylight hours are standard for safety reasons.

History and Trail Description: The Illinois Prairie Path is a 40-mile multi-purpose trail available for hiking, biking and horseback riding. The trail is divided into three sections, A, B and C. Section A is from the Historic Bridge at Carlton and Liberty Streets in Wheaton to Raymond Street in Elgin; section B is from the Historic Bridge in Wheaton to Butterfield Road (Route 56) in Bellwood; section C is from the Historic Bridge to Route 25 and Hankes Avenue in Aurora, and includes a spur section which is the connecting trail to the Fox River Trail. The Illinois Prairie Path follows the route of the former Chicago, Aurora and Elgin Railway.

The Illinois Prairie Path was the idea of Mrs. May Theilgoord Watts, distinguished naturalist, teacher, and author. In addition, local responses and cooperation by utility companies, civic leaders, and state, county, and local officials played a vital role in path development.

In 1966, the Path, a not-for-profit corporation, was formally established under a lease granted by Du Page County, owner of the rights-of-way. On June 2, 1971, the major portion of the path was designated a Recreation Trail of the National Trails System, becoming the first trail in Illinois to be designated as a National Recreation Trail. (See Appendix D.) In 1972, the Illinois Department of Conservation purchased the Kane County segments of the rights-of-way and leased the property to the forest preserve district for use as part of the path. In 1979, the state acquired four and a half miles of right-of-way in Cook County to First Avenue in Maywood.

From the Historic Bridge over the Chicago & Northwestern Railway in Wheaton, section A passes through wooded areas, such as the Lincoln Marsh (one mile from the bridge) and Timber Ridge Preserve. The Lincoln Marsh has a connecting trail to the short nature trail in this wetland ecosystem. Further northeast the trail passes through residential communities and also through rural communities, many times bordering farm fields. This section is generally about five feet wide and made of crushed limestone.

Wooden posts with yellow numbers are the mile markers along the trail. Most crossings have the name of the road and show the Prairie Path emblem, a green oval with three railroad spikes forming an inverted Y. Also, within the oval are the symbols for footprints, a horseshoe, and a bicycle wheel.

Near the western border of Du Page County, the trail borders Pratts Wayne Woods where the Boy Scout trail ends. The Boy Scout trail is known as the Red Caboose Trail, which begins at Gary Road and Geneva Road and meets and becomes the Prairie Path at the Jewel Road crossing.

At Kenyan Road, where the Model Railroad Club is housed, is the Clintonville station of the Chicago, Aurora, and Elgin Railway. The trail becomes a footpath at this point and heads north to Elgin. Although the trail ends at Prairie Street near the Fox River, for practical purposes the trail ends at Raymond Street at the railroad crossing. The section north of the railroad is not marked and becomes the sidewalks along city streets.

Section B of the Prairie Path is the most used portion because it passes through many developed areas. From Wheaton going east, the Path passes through Glen Ellyn, Lombard, Villa Park, Elmhurst, Berkeley and Bellwood. An extension to First Avenue in Maywood is planned, but has not been developed yet. Many of the communities have taken advantage of the railroad rights-of-way by developing parks along the path. These parks often have benches and water available.

Section B is marked the same as section A and is also of crushed limestone. Some points of interest along section B include the Villa Avenue CA & E Station, the Elmer J. Hoffman Park in Wheaton, and Wheaton College.

Section C is constructed much the same as A and B; however, it passes through more rural areas and through some very new subdivisions. From the Historic Bridge follow Carlton Avenue two blocks south to Roosevelt Road where the trail begins. Just south of Roosevelt Road is the Prairie Path Park owned by Wheaton Park District (the other Prairie Path park is in Glen Ellyn).

One area of section C passes near the Roy C. Blackwell Preserve. A parking area and camping facilities are available at this preserve. The Roy C. Blackwell Preserve is accessed from Batavia Road in Warrenville; proceed east one-eighth mile on Butterfield Road to the entrance.

At Eola Road the trail separates; one path goes to Aurora, and the other to Batavia and the Fox River Trail. To continue to Aurora, cross Eola Road and follow the left side of the Y junction; this section ends at Indian Trail Road near Route 25. The section west of Eola Road to Aurora becomes a dirt and gravel path sometimes narrowing to a footpath.

To continue toward Batavia, go north over the tollroad via an overpass and then west on Bilten Road. On Bilten Road you will see a new subdivision; follow Prairie Lane through the subdivision. Prairie Lane intersects the old Bilten Road; at this point, continue west two blocks to the trail junction.

Between Bilten Road and Butterfield Road (Route 56) the Prairie Path ends; near the geographic border of Du Page and Kane counties, a connecting trail continues northwest to the Fox River trail.

Section A and Section C have a greater variety of

wildlife since there are more wetlands and wooded areas along the trail.

Facilities: Most access points along the trail have adequate parking facilities. Water fountains are located in various parks along the trail. Restaurants, gas stations, and other businesses are located in almost all the communities through which the path travels. For camping areas contact the Du Page and Kane County Forest Preserves listed below.

Trail Rules and Regulations: No motorized vehicles, alcoholic beverages or firearms. No kite or model airplane flying allowed. No camping or cookouts allowed.

Mailing Address and Phone Numbers: Illinois Prairie Path, P.O. Box 1086, 616 Delles Road, Wheaton, Illinois 60187, or Forest Preserve District of Du Page County, 881 West Charles Road, Lombard, Illinois 60148, 312/620–3800, or Forest Preserve District of Kane County, 719 Batavia Avenue, Building A, Geneva, Illinois 60134; 312/232–1242

15. West Du Page Woods Forest Preserve

Trail Length: 4 miles (6.4 kilometers)

Location: West Du Page Woods is located in Winfield. The preserve may be reached by east—and westbound traffic by taking Roosevelt Road (Route 38). One mile west of the intersection of Roosevelt Road and Winfield Road is Gary's Mill Road. Turn east onto Gary's Mill Road and proceed for about five blocks to the parking area.

County: Du Page

Illinois Highway Map Coordinates: C-9

U.S.G.S. Topographical Map Name and Scale: Naperville, 1:24,000

Hours Open: The preserve is open every day of the year. The preserve opens one hour after sunrise and closes one hour after sunset.

History and Trail Description: West Du Page Woods was acquired in 1919 and is one of the oldest of the Forest Preserve District of Du Page County's thirty-six preserves. West Du Page Woods has 470 acres of upland woods and has one of the few fens in Du Page County.
   The trail system at West Du Page Woods consists of three interconnecting loops that total four miles. The trail system may be started north of the parking area by the small pond. An information board which contains a trail map is set up at the north end of the parking lot.
   The trail system here is a six-foot wide, multi-purpose trail used by hikers, horseback riders and skiers. These trails may be hiked in any direction. The trails are marked with wooden posts that have red rectangles on them. A white triangle in the rectangle which

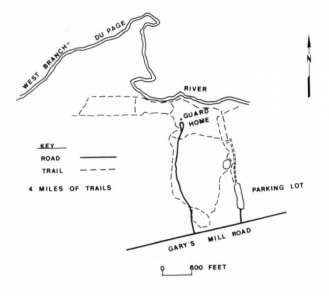

15. West Du Page Woods Forest Preserve. Redrawn from park trail map.

points upwards means that the trail is going away from the trailhead while a white triangle which is pointing downward means that the trail is inward bound.

Most of the trails go through upland forest, passing residential homes on the west side of the park and paralleling the west branch of the Du Page River on the north. As you hike west on the green loop, you will soon come to a small pond. You can hike around this pond in either direction since the hiking paths converge again at the service road. This service road dead-ends, leading back to the site superintendent's residence.

The trail crosses this service road and continues into the woods. Soon you will come to a trail junction close to the site superintendent's home. Go west back toward the parking area or go east towards the blue loop.

The blue loop goes through open fields on the south, paralleling residential homes to the south. From here the trail descends to the river, where the trail goes through the woods again. The blue trail leads to the orange loop, which heads back north toward the parking area.

Facilities: West Du Page Woods has an information board, water, restrooms, sled runs, a youth camping area and a site superintendent's home.

Permits Required: A camping permit is required for group camping. Annual permits are required for horseback riding. One of the picnic areas is reservable. All permits may be obtained at the district headquarters.

Park Rules and Regulations: Pets must be on a leash. Alcoholic beverages are prohibited.

Mailing Address and Phone Number: Forest Preserve District of Du Page County, P.O. Box 2339, Glen Ellyn, Illinois 60138; 312/620–3800

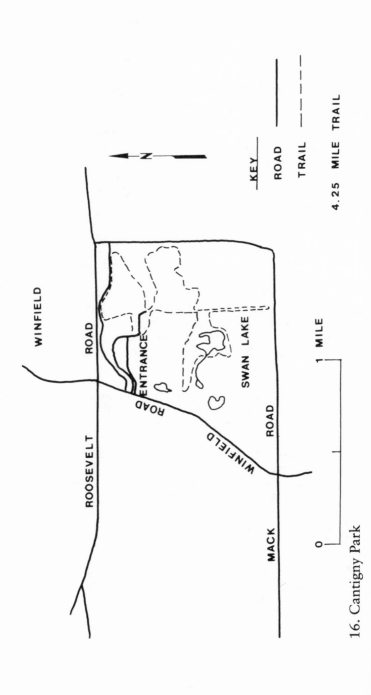

WINFIELD

ROOSEVELT ROAD

MACK

WINFIELD ROAD

ENTRANCE

ROAD

SWAN LAKE

ROAD

N

KEY

ROAD

TRAIL

4.25 MILE TRAIL

0   1 MILE

16. Cantigny Park

16. Cantigny Park and War Memorial Museum and Gardens

Trail Length: 4.25 miles (6.8 kilometers)

Location: Cantigny Park is located thirty miles west of the Chicago Loop and may be reached via the East-West Tollway (Illinois Route 5) or the Eisenhower Expressway. When exiting off of Route 5, turn off on Naperville Road and go north. Turn left at the first stoplight (Aurora Road), and then go west to Winfield Road. Turn right on Winfield Road and proceed to the park entrance. From the north and south, Cantigny Park is accessible via State Route 59. From Route 59, turn east on Roosevelt Road and proceed to Winfield Road. Turn right (south) on Winfield Road and go for two blocks to the park entrance.

County: Du Page

Illinois Highway Map Coordinates: C-9

U.S.G.S. Topographical Map Name and Scale: Naperville, 1:24,000

Hours Open: The grounds are open daily and are available for hiking from 9:00 a.m. to 5:00 p.m. from October through April, and 9:00 a.m. to 6:00 p.m., May through September. The McCormick Museum is open noon to 5:00 p.m. every day from Memorial Day through Labor Day; the remainder of the year, it is open noon to 4:00 p.m. Wednesday through Sunday. The McCormick Museum is closed in January.

The 1st Division Museum is open 9:00 a.m. to 5:00 p.m. every day from Memorial Day through Labor Day; the remainder of the year, it is open 10:00 a.m. to 4:00 p.m., except Monday.

History and Trail Description: Cantigny Park is a 500-acre county estate of the late Colonel Robert R. Mc-Cormick and his grandfather, Joseph Medill. The park consists of the R. R. McCormick Museum and Gardens, 1st Division Museum, tanks, and picnic areas.

The trail system at Cantigny grounds consists of a 4-mile and a 2-mile trail that are interconnected. The 4-mile trail is known as the Colonel Robert R. Mc-Cormick Trail, and the 2-mile trail is known as the Freedom of the Press Trail.

The trail system was originally developed and used as a scout training trail; however, the trail is now available for use by the public.

It is recommended that the trail be hiked in one direction only because the markers are numbered from 1 to 60. These numbered markers begin north of the campgrounds. All the markers are shaped like an Army arm patch and have a red number, directional arrow, and the number of the marker.

The trail begins south of the 1st Division Museum. A trail post at the trailhead is inscribed with both the words "five miler" and an arrow, the symbol of the trail. The trail is generally about eight feet wide and starts out on grass, then changes to dirt, a gravel road, and finally back to a dirt trail.

The trail passes by the campgrounds, around an open field, and through woodlands following the shores of Swan Lake. The trail around Swan Lake is generally muddy, especially during the wet season.

Beyond Swan Lake the trail becomes a gravel road. The hiker will go east on this gravel road until it meets a wide lane that heads south; follow this lane to Mack Road. At Mack Road the hiker will make a U-turn and then head north on the east side of the same lane. The entire lane is lined with trees on both sides.

From here the trail meanders around an open field and on the edge of the woods. It continues along a small creek where the trail separates into several poorly marked footpaths. Trail marker 60 directs the hiker back to the McCormick Museum and the parking area.

Facilities: Two museums, the R. R. McCormick Museum and the 1st Division Museum, are located on the grounds. The 1st Division Museum is a war memorial museum and tells the story of this famous division in the two world wars and in Viet Nam. Picnic areas, restrooms and water are available at the museums. There is a small campground for scouts and other organized groups. Ten acres of gardens are also located on the grounds. There is also a small tank park that has a few tanks available for viewing. Sunday afternoon concerts are held at the McCormick Museum Library, and art exhibits are displayed in the long corridor of the museum.

Permits Required: All individuals interested in hiking the trails must check in with the grounds control officer in the 1st Division Museum. Youth groups need camping reservations, which can be made at the museum.

Park Rules and Regulations: Food is not permitted on the trails. No fires allowed, except by groups in the campground. No pets or bicycles allowed on the grounds.

Mailing Address and Phone Number: Cantigny, 1 S 151 Winfield Road, Wheaton, Illinois 60187; 312/668–5161

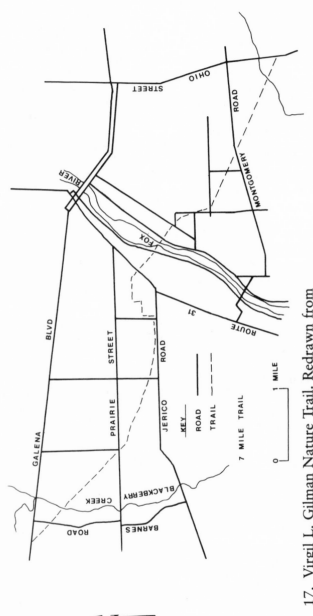

17. Virgil L. Gilman Nature Trail. Redrawn from Fox Valley Park District map.

17. Virgil L. Gilman Nature Trail

Trail Length: 7 miles (11.3 kilometers)

Location: The Virgil L. Gilman Nature Trail is located in northeastern Illinois, beginning south of Aurora in Montgomery. From Chicago and the east, the trailhead is reached via Illinois Tollway 5 to State Route 31 south. Follow Route 31 south through Aurora into Montgomery to Montgomery Road. Go one and three-tenths of a mile east on Montgomery Road to Hill Avenue (four way stop signal) and turn south for seven-tenths of a mile to the trailhead. The trailhead is on the west side of Hill Avenue and has a small parking area and trail information board. The parking area and trailhead are easily recognized; the parking area is immediately across (north) from the sign for Consolidated Freightways and just west of the Skelgas Distribution Center. The trail can be traveled in either direction as there are several access points. Refer to "Facilities" for the access points with parking available.

County: Kane

Illinois Highway Map Coordinates: C-8

U.S.G.S. Topographical Map Names and Scale: Aurora South, Sugar Grove and Aurora North, all 1:24,000

Hours Open: Sunrise to Sunset

History and Trail Description: The Virgil L. Gilman Nature Trail follows the railroad rights-of-way of the Elgin, Joliet and Eastern Railroad, and the Chicago, Milwaukee, St. Paul and Pacific Railroad.

The Virgil L. Gilman Trail is a smooth, crushed-stone path about six feet wide with one exception, that being an unmaintained section between the trailhead at

Hill Avenue and a point just west of Waubausee Creek; this one-eighth mile section is an uneven dirt path.

Most of the path is easy to follow from any access point; however, one section in Aurora is somewhat difficult to follow. Between Terry Avenue and Lake Street (Route 31) the trail actually becomes the sidewalks winding through this residential and industrial neighborhood. There are signs (white arrows on a brown background) indicating travel direction for the path, but only a few are scattered along this six block section.

Traveling east, the path at Terry Avenue goes one-quarter block north to the first intersection then east to Elmwood Drive. Go north on Elmwood Drive for one block, then east for one block. At the stop sign, turn right (south) one block to the parking lot where the trail is located. The opposite directions are appropriate for going westbound.

The trail passes through rural, suburban, and urban areas. Some sections offer a view of farmlands; other sections pass through residential areas as well as some commercial/industrial areas. One section near Waubausee Creek has a marsh adjacent to the trail.

Native plants and wildlife of Illinois can be seen along most sections of the trail. Some of the trees that can be seen include cottonwoods, white poplars, sycamores, and oak. Birds seen along the trail include duck, heron, redwing blackbirds, woodpeckers, cardinals, and bluejays.

Probably the most interesting section of the trail is west of Terry Avenue where the trail passes through its most densely wooded section. Another interesting section is the crossing of the truss bridge spanning the Fox River.

The Virgil L. Gilman Nature Trail is considered a National Recreation Trail. See Appendix D.

Facilities: Parking is available at the trailhead off Hill Avenue (Lincoln Highway), Montgomery Road, Ashland Avenue, Route 25, River Street, Lake Street (Route 31), Terry Avenue at Jerviko Road, Edgelawn Drive, Orchard Road, Barnes Road, and Galena Boulevard.

Restrooms and shelters are available at Lebanon Park on Douglas Avenue, at Copley #1 Park, and along the trail just west of Orchard Road. Water is also available at the shelter and restroom area east of Orchard Road.

Picnic areas are available at the south Broadway Avenue Park and at the end of the trail at Galena Boulevard.

Trail Rules and Regulations: No camping, fires, dumping or littering, and no hunting.

Mailing Address and Phone Number: Fox Valley Park District, 712 South River Street, Aurora, Illinois 60506; 312/897–0516

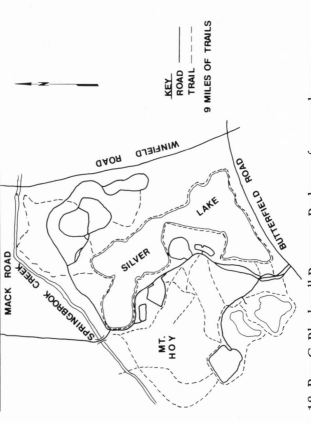

KEY
ROAD ――――
TRAIL ― ― ―

9 MILES OF TRAILS

MACK ROAD

SPRINGBROOK CREEK

WINFIELD ROAD

BUTTERFIELD ROAD

SILVER

LAKE

MT. HOY

18. Roy C. Blackwell Preserve. Redrawn from park map.

18. Roy C. Blackwell Forest Preserve

Trail Length: 9 miles (14.8 kilometers)

Location: The Roy C. Blackwell Forest Preserve is located three miles south of Winfield. The Preserve is three miles west of Herrick Lake Forest Preserve and may be reached via Butterfield Road (Route 56). The Preserve borders Butterfield Road and Winfield Road, with the main park entrance off Butterfield Road.

County: Du Page

Illinois Highway Map Coordinates: C-9

U.S.G.S. Topographical Map Name and Scale: Naperville, 1:24,000

Hours Open: The Preserve is open every day of the year. The Preserve is open one hour after sunrise and is closed one hour after sunset.

History and Trail Description: Early in 1960 the Forest Preserve District of Du Page County purchased a worked-out gravel pit as their land reclamation program. The district believed that the gravel pit had excellent potential as a multiple-use recreation area. The gravel pit could be transformed into a large recreational lake and serve as a major rainwater retention basin. In order for this idea to come true, the gravel pit needed to be deeper and larger.

At the same time that the lakes were being excavated, the county leaders were concerned about the growing problem of solid waste disposal in Du Page County. The district developed a plan that would solve the problems of waste disposal and clay disposal from the construction of the lake.

A hill constructed of garbage and refuse was built

next to the lake. Clay removed from the lake was used to cover the refuse, which was deposited every day. When the hill was completed, it was transformed into a winter sports area. This hill, now known as Mt. Hoy, rises more than 150 feet above its surroundings, making it the highest point in Du Page County.

The district purchased adjacent forest and meadowland to increase the size of the preserve to more than 1,200 acres. The preserve is named in honor of a former board president, Roy C. Blackwell.

Blackwell Preserve consists of two tracts: North Blackwell and South Blackwell. South Blackwell encompasses the recreation facilities while North Blackwell remains virtually undeveloped.

The trail system at South Blackwell Forest Preserve consists of many interconnected trails that wind their way around Mt. Hoy, Silver Lake, and the other recreation sites. In addition, some 13 miles of unmarked but mowed hiking trails meander through North Blackwell.

Mt. Hoy, the main landmark in the park, will be seen constantly by the hiker as he wanders throughout the park on the trails.

The trails at South Blackwell are marked with wooden posts inscribed with a symbol of a hiker. These posts are located at the trailheads and at various sections of the trails. There are numerous areas throughout the park where the trail may be started. These trails may be hiked in any direction.

The longest continuous trail in the park is the trail that winds its way around the shoreline of Silver Lake. The southern part of this trail parallels Butterfield Road and is on top of a steep ridge that leads down to the lake. There are also some stairs that go down to the lake. From this trail, other trails, such as the one which winds its way through the campground, may be reached.

A few trails, including one that is paved, wind their way to the top of Mt. Hoy. From here you have a good view of the park and the surrounding area. A tubing run is set up on the northeast side of this hill for winter enthusiasts. As you hike up the side of the hill, you will

Two small lakes and beach area, as seen from Mt. Hoy, Blackwell Forest Preserve

see many metal vent poles that protrude from the hill. These vent methane gas, which is produced by the decomposing garbage.

A horse trail also winds its way south of the park maintenance center and west of Mt. Hoy. This trail crosses Springbrook Creek and leads into the section north of Springbrook Creek.

Cross-country skiing is allowed on any of the trails in the park.

Facilities: Blackwell Forest Preserve has campgrounds, a swimming beach, a boat launch, a tubing run, and numerous picnic sites which have picnic tables, restrooms, water, and shelters. A gate house is set up at the entrance to South Blackwell Preserve where, during the summer season and during part of the winter season, residents of the county as well as visitors have to pay a daily entry fee. Fishing is allowed in Silver Lake contingent upon all Illinois fishing rules and regulations.

Permits Required: Permits are required for boating on Silver Lake. Annual permits may be obtained from the district headquarters while daily passes may be obtained at the entrance gatehouse. A camping permit is required at the family campground. Annual permits are required for horseback riding.

Park Rules and Regulations: Pets must be on a leash. No boat shall be more than twenty feet in length. No motors are allowed and no inflatable crafts, rafts, pontoons, or wind-surfers are allowed.

Mailing Address and Phone Number: Forest Preserve District of Du Page County, P.O. Box 2339, Glen Ellyn, Illinois 60138; 312/620–3800

19. Fox River Bike Trail

Trail Length: 6.5 miles + 3.0 miles of connecting trail to the Illinois Prairie Path (15.3 kilometers)

Location: The Fox River Trail is located in northeastern Illinois along the Fox River between Route 64 in St. Charles and the Kane–Du Page County line just south of Butterfield Road (Route 56).

Major north-south roads for access include Routes 25 and 31. The major east-west roadways include Illinois Tollroad 5 and routes 56, 38, and 64. The trail is on the east side of the Fox River. Access is obtained at any east-west road reaching the Fox River in St. Charles, Geneva, and Batavia. Refer to "Facilities" for parking areas.

County: Kane

Illinois Highway Map Coordinates: C-8

U.S.G.S. Topographical Map Names and Scale: Geneva and Aurora North, both 1:24,000

Hours Open: Daylight hours

Trail Description: The Fox River Trail is a multi-purpose trail designated for hikers, bikers, joggers, cross-country skiers, and skateboarders. The trail has two parts, one from Route 64 in St. Charles to Batavia, and the second from the north side of the Fox Valley Country Club and Archery range to the Kane–Du Page County line just south of Butterfield Road (Route 56).

The first 6.5 miles is made of paved asphalt and has a yellow line down the middle for right-lane usage. This section of the trail passes through St. Charles, Geneva, and Batavia. As it meanders along the bank of the Fox River, the trail passes through commercial, residential,

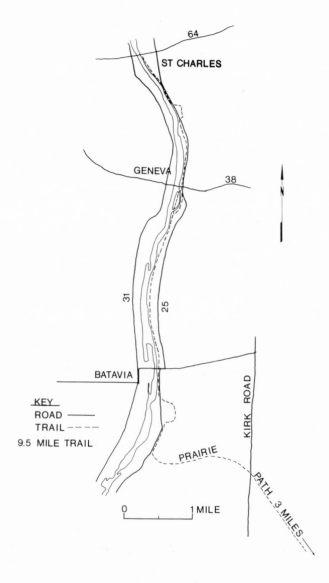

64

ST CHARLES

GENEVA

38

N

31

25

BATAVIA

KEY
ROAD ——
TRAIL ----
9.5 MILE TRAIL

PRAIRIE

KIRK ROAD

PATH 3 MILES

0   1 MILE

19. Fox River Bike Trail

and undeveloped wooded areas. Along this section of the trail a great variety of birds can be seen, especially migratory birds.

In St. Charles the path passes along Langum Park, Riverside Park, Good Templar Park, Bennett Park, Island Park, Old Mill Park, and Fabyan Forest Preserve. In Geneva a spur trail connects with Island Park via two bridges. Either section can be hiked; take a bridge to the island or remain on the main trail along the river bank.

This section is marked primarily by symbols, such as a bicycle and an arrow, on wooden posts indicating usage and direction. At the south side of Batavia the trail is lost to construction and land reclamation along the river, but if you travel directly south or north (depending where you come from) past the BMX bicycle race track and bike shop, you can find either section of the trail.

The section south of Batavia and north of the Fox Valley Country Club and Archery Range is all gravel as it travels southeasterly toward Du Page County. This three-mile section of gravel path is marked with white symbols on a brown background and mounted on wooden posts. The wooden posts are very visible all along the trail.

All along this 3-mile gravel trail you will see many species of birds. This section passes through newly developed subdivisions, and through rural and protected forest areas. On the south side of Butterfield Road at the Kane–Du Page County line, the connecting trail to the Fox River Trail ends and becomes the Illinois Prairie Path.

Facilities: There are no established facilities available on the trail, but in St. Charles, Geneva, and Batavia, water, restaurants, and restrooms are available. Parking is available at parks and along most streets in these communities.

Trail Rules and Regulations: No snowmobiles, motorcycles or motorized vehicles of any type. No alcoholic beverages. Picnicking is allowed in designated sites only.

Fishing is not allowed along the trail. Pedestrians and joggers have the right-of-way. Users should remain on the right hand side of the trail.

Mailing Address and Phone Numbers: Geneva Park District, 1250 South Street, Geneva, Illinois, 60134; 312/232–4542; or, Kane County Forest Preserve District, 719 Batavia Avenue-Bldg. A, Geneva, Illinois, 60134; 312/232–1242

20. Herrick Lake Forest Preserve

Trail Length: 4 miles (6.4 kilometers)

Location: Herrick Lake Forest Preserve is located in Wheaton, Illinois. The park may be reached by east— or westbound traffic by taking Butterfield Road (Route 56). The park is two miles west of Naperville Road and one mile east of Winfield Road. The main entrance to the park is off Butterfield Road but access to the trail is from Herrick Road. Herrick Road is located just west of the main entrance. Turn south on Herrick Road and proceed for a few blocks to the parking area.

County: Du Page

Illinois Highway Map Coordinates: C-9

U.S.G.S. Topographical Map Name and Scale: Naperville, 1:24,000

Hours Open: The preserve is open every day of the year. The preserve is open one hour after sunrise and is closed one hour after sunset.

History and Trail Description: Herrick Lake Forest Preserve consists of 760 acres of woodlands including a 22-acre lake. The lake is natural and was formed when the Wisconsin Glacier retreated fourteen thousand years ago.

The trail system consists of two loop trails which total 4 miles. The trailhead may be accessed from the parking lot off Herrick Road. At the south end of the parking lot there is a water pump. The trail goes east to the main trail.

The trails may be hiked in either direction and are multi-purpose trails used by hikers, skiers, and horseback riders. The trails are marked with wooden posts which have red rectangles on them. A triangle in the

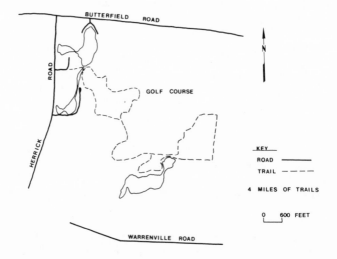

20. Herrick Lake Forest Preserve. Redrawn from
    park map.

rectangle which points up means that the trail is going away from the trailhead, and a white triangle which is pointing down means that the trail is inward bound.

Shortly past the water pump there is a trail post with the words "trailhead" written on it. From here the trail may be hiked either north or south. If you hike south you will soon reach a group camping area on the west side of the trail. From here the trail goes by a stand of young trees and to a trail junction. At the trail junction you can continue hiking the loop northwards back to the trailhead or south to the other loop.

As you hike the trail south to the other loop, you will pass through an open field and will be able to see the southern tip of the golf course. The trail continues through a small stand of trees, by a small marsh, and finally to another open field. The trail at this point goes around the open field following the forest boundary. The trail goes by the golf course, some residential homes, a fenced pond, a small water detention lake, and finally back to the original trail. You can hike the trail back to the first loop and then back to the trailhead.

Facilities: Herrick Lake Forest Preserve has picnic areas with shelters, picnic tables, restrooms, and water available. On the northern shore of the lake, a concessionaire sells snacks and rents rowboats, sailboats and canoes. A youth camping area is also available in the preserve.

Permits Required: A camping permit is required for youth camping. Annual permits are required for horseback riding. The two shelters and two of the picnic areas may be reserved. All permits may be obtained at district headquarters.

Park Rules and Regulations: Pets must be on a leash. Alcoholic beverages are prohibited. Private boating is prohibited and motorized vehicles are prohibited on the grounds.

Mailing Address and Phone Number: Forest Preserve District of Du Page County, P.O. Box 2339, Glen Ellyn, Illinois 60138; 312/620–3800

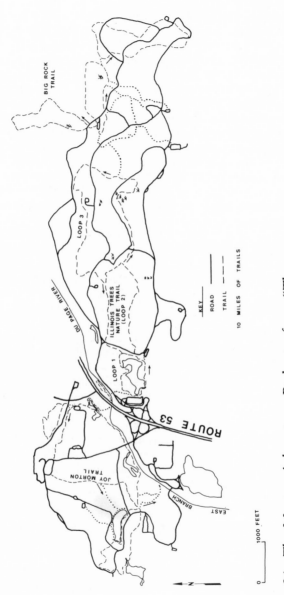

BIG ROCK TRAIL

DU PAGE RIVER

LOOP 3

ILLINOIS TREES
NATURE TRAIL
(LOOP 2)

LOOP 1

ROUTE 53

JOY MORTON TRAIL

EAST BRANCH

KEY
ROAD
TRAIL

10 MILES OF TRAILS

N

1000 FEET
0

21. The Morton Arboretum. Redrawn from "The Walking Trails of the Morton Arboretum."

21. The Morton Arboretum

Trail Length: 10 miles (16 kilometers)

Location: Morton Arboretum is located just north of Lisle and the East-West Tollway (Illinois 5) and twenty-five miles west of Chicago. Exit north onto Route 53 off Illinois 5. Entrances to the Arboretum are accessible from either northbound or southbound State Route 53, which bisects the park. From Chicago and the suburbs, Morton Arboretum is easily reached via the Eisenhower Expressway (290) to Illinois 5, or from the Tri-State Tollway (294) to Illinois 5 then west to Route 53.

County: Du Page

Illinois Highway Map Coordinates: C-9

U.S.G.S. Topographical Map Name and Scale: Wheaton, 1:24,000

Hours Open: Grounds open every day, weather permitting, Standard Time 9:00 a.m. to 5:00 p.m. and Daylight Time 9:00 a.m. to 7:00 p.m. The Visitors' Center is open April through November, Monday to Saturday 9:30 a.m. to 5:00 p.m., and on Sundays from 12 noon to 5:00 p.m. From December to March the Visitors' Center is open Monday to Saturday 9:30 a.m. to 4:00 p.m. and on Sundays from 12 noon to 4:00 p.m.

History and Trail Description: The Morton Arboretum was established in 1922 by Jay Morton, founder of the Morton Salt Company, on the grounds of his estate near Lisle. The grounds consist of 1,500 acres devoted to cultivated plants and natural vegetation displayed outdoors for people to study and enjoy.

The Arboretum is a privately endowed, not-for-profit educational foundation administered by a board of nine trustees.

The majority of the trails are on the east side of the

Arboretum. Loops 1, 2, and 3 of the Illinois Trees Nature Trail begin at the Visitors' Center and main parking area. These loops are identified on trailboards as you hike northwest away from Meadow Lake and the Visitors' Center. The trails alternate from dirt to wood-chip footpaths. East of the Illinois Trees Nature Trail are the Big Rock, Forest, and East Woods Trails.

None of the trails is marked, but all are fairly easy to follow. All secondary/connecting trails are well maintained and may or may not be as wide as the main trails.

The trails on the east side of Morton Arboretum have the greatest amount of diversity, as the trails are rugged and hilly. These trails meander through dense woodlands, around marshes and along perennial streams. The Forest and East Woods Trails can be extremely difficult during the wet seasons, especially the north section of the Forest Trail which can become very muddy in parts.

A newer trail connects the northern corner of the Forest Trail with the most easterly point of the Big Rock Trail. The connecting trail is a good alternate route that bypasses the northern portion of the Forest Trail and creates a shorter loop if less hiking is desirable.

The trail around Meadow Lake (at the Visitors' Center) is a crushed stone path. At the main parking area a trailboard indicates the Illinois Trees Nature Trail and the secondary trail connecting the west side trails.

North of the main parking area a connecting trail from the Viburnam Path follows the Du Page River under the bridge (Route 53) to Sunfish Pond and to the trails on the west side of the Arboretum. This is the only footpath connecting the east and west sides.

The Joy Morton Trail (Joy Path) is a rough asphalt lane starting at the Thornhill Conference Center. The Joy Path crosses Lake Road, where it becomes a dirt path. A secondary trail connects the Joy Path with Lake Marmo which then connects with the Evergreen Trail, a wood-chip path which passes through tall stands of evergreens.

South of Lake Road, the Joy Morton Trail becomes difficult to follow as it is not very well maintained. This trail then parallels the Du Page River and runs north to where it meets the connecting trail back east to the Visitors' Center.

Generally the west side of the Arboretum has large gardens and the east side a great variety of trees. All of the trails can be hiked in one day.

Birds represent the most abundant wildlife within the Arboretum boundaries. Many ducks and other large birds are present at Meadow Lake by the Visitors' Center.

Currently the Morton Arboretum is receiving pressure from Du Page County and the State of Illinois to give up parts of its properties for the construction of a new tollway. Although not all the property is under proposal, the remaining wildlife and plant life would be greatly reduced; some claim that the wildlife in the area would disappear and plant life would be of much lesser variety and quality.

Facilities: The Visitors' Center is located on the east side of the Arboretum. An information building, theater, and restaurant are also located there. The administration building contains the education department, library, research laboratories, and a climate and map room.

On the west side of the park is the Thornhill Conference Center Outpost, which houses the classrooms for the education department.

Parking is available at the Visitors' Center and throughout the Arboretum. There are restrooms at the Visitors' Center and the Outpost. A public telephone is located in the foyer of the restaurant. The entry fee is $2.00 per car; there is no fee for pedestrians or senior citizens who drive themselves.

Rules and Regulations: There are no camping or picnic grounds at the Arboretum. Collecting of specimens of any kind is prohibited. No pets, bicycles, motorcycles, snowmobiles, intoxicants, or littering allowed. No excessive noise or parking along the roads.

Mailing Address and Phone Number: The Morton Arboretum, Lisle, Illinois; 312/968–0074

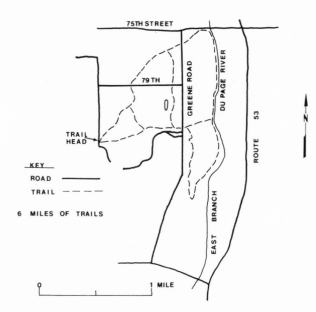

22. Green Valley Forest Preserve

22. Greene Valley Forest Preserve

Trail Length: 6 miles (9.6 kilometers)

Location: Greene Valley Forest Preserve is located three miles west of Woodridge. To reach the park, State Route 53 may be taken by north—or southbound traffic. Turn west onto 75th Street and proceed for five blocks to Greene Road. Turn south onto Greene Road and go for another five blocks to 79th Street. Turn right (west) on 79th Street and go for a few blocks until reaching a forest preserve sign which reads "West Access Area." Turn left (south) on this road and proceed to the trailhead.

County: Du Page

Illinois Highway Map Coordinates: C-9

U.S.G.S. Topographical Map Name and Scale: Romeoville, 1:24,000

Hours Open: The preserve is open every day of the year. The preserve is open one hour after sunrise and is closed one hour after sunset.

History and Trail Description: Greene Valley Forest Preserve is named after the Greene family who settled and farmed the area. The site consists of 1,441 acres.

The trail system consists of four interconnecting color-coded trails 6 miles in length. The trail system is multi-purpose, with hiking, skiing, and horseback riding allowed.

A trailhead post and information board is found at the parking lot in the west access area. A trail map and park rules are encased in the information board, and the trail markings are shown on the trailhead post.

The trails may be hiked in any direction and on any of the four loops. The trail is marked with wooden posts that have red metal rectangles on them. A white triangle pointed up means that the trail is outward bound and a downward-pointed triangle means that the trail is homeward bound.

The trail system consists of a mowed grass path about twelve feet wide. The trails on the park trail map are referred to as the red, green, orange, and blue loops.

The trail from the parking area heads due east, going by a little red shed and the site superintendent's home. This part of the trail is part of the green loop, which basically goes through open fields and connects with the orange loop. To the south of the trail there is a landfill operation. This landfill can be seen throughout the hike.

From the green loop, the orange loop can be accessed. The orange loop winds its way on the west side of Greene Road, going by a small pond, through woodlands, open fields, along power lines, and over 79th Street twice. The red loop may be accessed at the south end of the orange loop, on the east side of Greene Road.

The red loop heads in a southerly direction through an open field, with the landfill to the west. The trail then heads back north, going into woods and then coming to the east branch of the Du Page River. The trail parallels the river for a short distance and meets up with a branch of the red loop that heads back to Greene Road and with a section of the blue loop. The blue loop continues north, paralleling the east branch of the Du Page River. The trail goes all the way to 75th Street where it starts going west, paralleling the power lines. The trail then crosses Greene Road again and the hiker will soon run into the orange loop, which he may follow back to the trailhead.

Facilities: Greene Valley Forest Preserve has an information board, restrooms, drinking water, telephone, and seventeen campsites set up for youth camping only.

Permits Required: A camping permit is required for group camping. Annual permits are required for horseback riding.

Park Rules and Regulations: Pets must be on a leash. No trespassing around the landfill site. Alcoholic beverages are prohibited.

Mailing Address and Phone Number: Forest Preserve District of Du Page County, P.O. Box 2339, Glen Ellyn, Illinois 60138; 312/620–3800

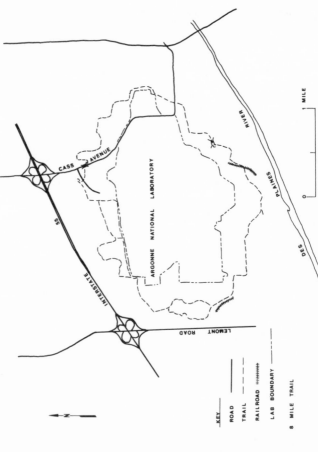

23. Waterfall Glen Nature Preserve

KEY

ROAD ————
TRAIL —————
RAILROAD ++++++++
LAB BOUNDARY —·—·—·—
8 MILE TRAIL ———————

ARGONNE NATIONAL LABORATORY

CASS AVENUE

INTERSTATE 55

LEMONT ROAD

DES PLAINES RIVER

0   1 MILE

23. Waterfall Glen Nature Preserve

Trail Length: 8 mile loop trail (12.8 kilometers)

Location: Waterfall Glen Nature Preserve is located in northeastern Illinois approximately twenty-five miles southwest of Chicago. The most direct route to the parking area and trailhead is via Interstate 55 to Cass Avenue South. About one-eighth mile south of Interstate 55 one will find the entrance to the frontage road where the parking area and information building can be seen. Just beyond the information building is Northgate Road, where you turn west to the main parking area and trailhead.

Waterfall Glen Nature Preserve surrounds Argonne National Laboratory, which is centered between north-south routes 53 and 83, just south of Interstate 55.

County: Du Page

Illinois Highway Map Coordinates: C-9

U.S.G.S. Topographical Map Names and Scale: Sag Bridge and Romeoville, both 1:24,000

Hours Open: One hour after sunrise to one hour after sunset.

History and Trail Description: The trail system at Waterfall Glen Nature Preserve surrounds Argonne National Laboratory. This area is a glacial till deposited by the Wisconsin Glacier.

At the trailhead an information board with a map displays the trails and identifies the other facilities available at Waterfall Glen. There are four different loop trails, each color-coded.

The trail system is designed as a multi-purpose trail and is used by hikers, horseback riders, cross-country skiers, and those interested in orienteering. The most-used sections of the trails include the green, orange, and blue loops; a round trip is 6 miles. The colors correspond with the trail markers, which are round circles painted on wooden posts. Also, on the same posts are triangles (white on red background) either pointing up—indicating travel away from the trailhead/parking area—or pointing down—indicating return.

Most of the trails at Waterfall Glen are wide grassy lanes thirty to forty feet wide; however, the red loop from the campground to the blue loop is a combination of crushed stone paths and gravel roads. Additionally, there are some shorter sections that range from small footpaths to trail widths of eight feet.

At the south end of the blue loop, adjacent to a marsh, the trail connects to the red loop, which goes around the southern boundary of Argonne National Laboratory, thus forming the largest loop of the trail system (8 miles).

The red loop is marked by a fluorescent orange circle on brown plastic posts; also, there are white arrows on a brown background indicating direction of travel with respect to the trailhead.

All of the trails are designed for hiking in either direction. The green, orange, and blue loops pass through tall stands of evergreens, occasionally along bogs, and in several locations either right through or right next to a marsh. One side of the green and orange loops follows along the nine-foot fence surrounding Argonne Laboratory. The connecting trail from the orange to the blue loop crosses a road and guardpost at the west gate entrance for Argonne National Laboratory. About one-eighth mile further, the trail becomes the shoulder of the paved road to the west gate entrance; therefore, for this one-eighth mile section hikers must beware.

The longer loop, the red loop, offers more variety than the shorter loop trails as it passes along marshes, bogs, and prairies and through densely wooded areas. A great variety of wildlife may be observed along the marshes of the red loop trail. A model airplane field is located along this trail segment.

On a high ridge at the southernmost point of the red loop is a scenic area which overlooks the Des Plaines River Valley. Another scenic view may be had from the iron footbridge. Here the trail crosses over the creek (there is a ford for horses) and offers a fine view of the V-shaped valley. A third attraction, probably the highlight of this trail, is the waterfall located a half mile west of the campground.

All along this trail system are footpaths, intersecting roads, and other wide lanes which intersect the main trail. The hiker must stay on the established trail since some of the surrounding property is privately owned.

A variety of wildlife can be seen at Waterfall Glen. The most frequently seen animals are the native white-tail deer and the white fallow deer imported from Asia. Also, many migratory birds can be seen.

Facilities: Restrooms, parking, and drinking water are available at the trailhead and campground. East of the blue loop, one-quarter mile south along the red loop, is a model airplane field. Orienteering courses are established along the northeast corner of Waterfall Glen.

Permits Required: Reservations are required for the model airplane field as well as for the campground; the parking area at the campground is reserved for people with camping permits.

Park Rules and Regulations: No alcohol is allowed on Preserve grounds. No collecting or hunting of trees, shrubs, flowers or wildlife, except mushrooms, is permitted.

Fires must be contained in fireplaces and grills provided, or in a burner. Cutting and gathering firewood is not permitted. Pets are allowed, but must be on a leash at all times.

Mailing Address and Phone Number: Forest Preserve District of Du Page County, P.O. Box 2339, Glen Ellyn, Illinois, 60138; 312/790–4900

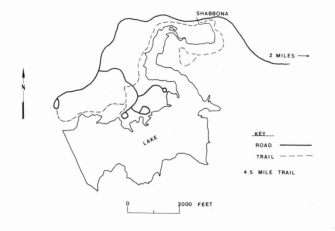

24. Shabbona Lake Recreation Area. Redrawn
from park trail map.

24. Shabbona Lake State Recreation Area

Trail Length: 4.5 miles (7.2 kilometers)

Location: Shabbona Lake State Recreation Area is located one mile south of Shabbona off of State Route 30. To reach the park, State Route 30 can be taken to the town of Shabbona. In town there will be a sign pointing in the direction of the recreation area; this street is Shabbona Street. Turn south on Shabbona Street and proceed for one-half mile. Turn left (east) on another gravel road and follow the sign one-half mile to the park entrance.

County: De Kalb

Illinois Highway Map Coordinates: C-7

U.S.G.S. Topographical Map Names and Scale: Shabbona Grove and Waterman, both 1:24,000

Hours Open: The park is open year-round except on Christmas Day and New Year's Day. During the summer the park is open from 6:00 a.m. until 10:00 p.m. and in the winter from 8:00 a.m. until sundown.

History and Trail Description: Shabbona Lake State Recreation Area is a 1,500-acre recreation complex. The site development began in 1973 with a lake basin clearing program which included tree removal in selected areas, shoreline modification, and construction of earthen fishing piers. In 1974 the three-thousand foot long earthen dam and associated concrete spillway structure was started. The dam was completed in the fall of 1975, and the lake is now 318 acres in size. Day-use area development began in 1976 and is continuing today.

The 4.5-mile hiking trail follows the lake shore.

The trail may be started at the Shabbona Grove Picnic Area or by Three Fires Picnic Area. The trail is called the Arrowhead Trail and is marked with two-foot wooden markers which have red arrowheads painted on them. At both starting points of the trail trailboards have been set up showing the trail layout.

The trail is about eight feet wide and goes by wildlife food plots, up and down gently rolling hills, through open fields and through wooded areas. The trail goes over three small wooden bridges and by many bird feeders. The trail crosses the park road once. Shortly after crossing the road you will come to a sign pointing to a wildlife viewing blind. You may go inside the blind to view the refuge area on the lake. This area is a resting area for waterfowl and allows you to see several rare species of birds. The trail then continues paralleling the lake, with a steep drop of about thirty feet down to the lake from the trail.

The northern part of the trail becomes a loop going past the lake, up a small hill, and then back to the original trail again. You must retrace your path back to the starting point.

The trail is also used by cross-country skiers.

Viewing blind, Shabbona Lake State Recreation Area

Facilities: A ranger station located on the grounds offers additional information. There are also various picnic areas with tables, grills, shelters, restrooms, playground equipment, and water faucets. A boat ramp and a concession stand are also available, with boats for rent. A 7-mile snowmobile trail has been constructed and may be used by the hikers. Dove hunting is allowed during the appointed hunting season. A softball diamond and horsepits are also available.

Permits Required: A dog training area permit is available upon request. Snowmobilers must register at the park office.

Park Rules and Regulations: No camping or overnight accommodations are allowed. Swimming and/or wading is prohibited at Shabbona Lake. There is a 10 horsepower limit on the lake. See Appendix A.

Mailing Address and Phone Number: Site Superintendent, Shabbona Lake State Recreation Area, Route 1, Box 121, Shabbona, Illinois 60550; 815/824–2106

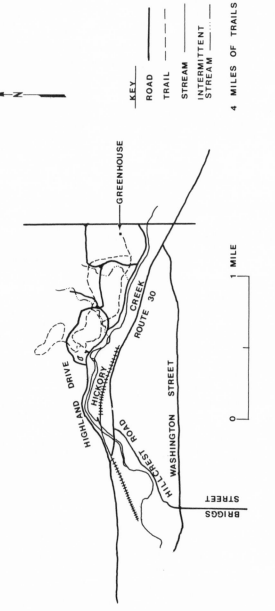

N

KEY

ROAD —————
TRAIL — — —
STREAM ∼∼∼
INTERMITTENT
STREAM ·········

4 MILES OF TRAILS

GREENHOUSE

HIGHLAND DRIVE

HICKORY

HILLCREST ROAD

CREEK

ROUTE 30

WASHINGTON STREET

BRIGGS STREET

0   1 MILE

25. Pilcher Park

25. Pilcher Park

Trail Length: 4 miles (6.4 kilometers)

Location: Pilcher Park may be reached from either Interstate 55 or Interstate 80. Interstate 55 travelers may exit onto Interstate 80 and go east for eight miles to Briggs Street. Turn north on Briggs Street and proceed for about one mile until the road turns into Hillcrest Road. Follow Hillcrest Road east for one-half mile to State Route 30. Turn left (west) on Route 30, proceed one block and go under the railroad tracks. Turn right onto the first street (Highland Drive) and proceed to the park entrance.

Westbound Interstate 80 traffic may exit at State Route 30 and proceed north for three miles to Highland Drive. From here, follow the same directions as described above.

County: Will

Illinois Highway Map Coordinates: D-9

U.S.G.S. Topographical Map Name and Scale: Joliet, 1:24,000

Hours Open: Pilcher Park Nature Center is open Monday through Friday from 9:00 a.m. until 4:30 p.m. and on Saturday and Sunday from 10:00 a.m. until 4:30 p.m.

History and Trail Description: During the turn of the century, Pilcher Park was a private arboretum. The park was bought by Robert Pilcher and its 327 acres were given to the City of Joliet in 1921. The park is now operated by the Joliet Park District.

The trails at Pilcher Park consist of four interconnecting trails that total over 4 miles. All of the trails may be started at the Nature Center and at the small zoo.

The High Trail starts near the back door of the Nature Center and winds its way northward for one mile through the upland woods. The trail goes over a small bridge and creek and then crosses the bicycle trail and park road. At this point you will see orange paint blazes on the trees. Do not pay attention to these markings for they were painted by a horse stable operator who used them on the horse trails in the park. Very shortly after this, the trail splits, and you may go north or east. If you go east the trail continues through a stand of large old trees, crosses the bicycle trail two more times, then parallels a steep stream valley. From here the trail turns west and will connect with the original trail again. This can be followed back to the Nature Center and to other trails.

Back at the Nature Center you can walk to the zoo which is situated directly behind the center. The zoo currently does not have any animals because the animals were killed a few years ago by some vandals. A short trail called the Walk in the Woods Trail begins at the zoo. At various points along the trail, information boards attached to wooden posts describe the animals, trees, and natural systems that can be observed in the forest.

At the halfway point the Trail of the Oaks joins the Walk in the Woods Trail. You may stay on the Walk in the Woods Trail or hike eastward on the Trail of the Oaks. There is a wooden trail marker at this point. Continuing on the Walk in the Woods Trail, you will return to the Nature Center area where you can hike the Sensory Trail which connects with the Walk in the Woods Trail.

The Sensory Trail is a short asphalt trail which goes through the woods. There is a large wooden sign at the start of the Sensory Trail. Hiking this trail you will go over a small bridge and see a trail sign that points in the direction of Trail of the Oaks. The Trail of the Oaks goes in an easterly direction, crossing the park road twice and traversing small bridges and creeks. As you go across the park road the second time, you will reach a junction in the trail and a trail marker will be visible.

You can continue straight on the trail, proceeding ahead to the greenhouse, or you can turn left (north) and follow the trail as it joins the Walk in the Woods Trail.

Heading north on the trail, you will come across some horse stables and a cement water well. From here the trail crosses the park road and continues through the woods on a wooden walkway which was constructed above a low, wet area. The trail then crosses the park road again and joins another trail. At this point, you can continue on the Trail of the Oaks or follow the trail branch southward back to the southern part of the Trail of the Oaks and finally back to the Nature Center.

All of the trails are easily distinguishable and are fairly easy to follow. The park also has cross-country skiing and bicycle trails. The hiker may also hike on these trails. Horseback riding is allowed in the park on some of the bicycle trails and part of the High Trail.

Facilities: A Nature Center is located on the grounds where one may request trail maps and other general information from the ranger on hand. The Nature Center has many displays of animals and plants. Water and restrooms are located at the Nature Center and at the water well. A greenhouse is located on the grounds where flowers may be seen year-round; the greenhouse also offers seasonal flower shows. The park offers many special programs and special events, such as spring wildflower walks, fall color walks, and instruction in gathering maple syrup. A small creek flows by the park where one may go fishing. All Illinois fishing rules and regulations are in effect.

Permits Required: No horseback riding except by permit.

Park Rules and Regulations: All dogs must be on a leash. No ice skating allowed on the creek.

Mailing Address and Phone Number: Joliet Park District, 1301 Hosmer Street, Joliet, Illinois 60435; 815/727–1011

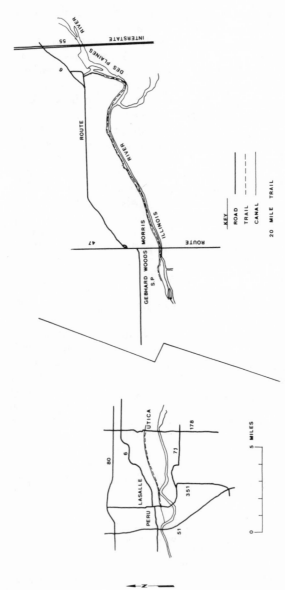

26. Illinois and Michigan Canal Trail. Redrawn from IDOT highway maps.

26. Illinois and Michigan Canal Trail

Trail Lengths: 5 and 15 miles (8 and 24 kilometers)

Location: The Illinois and Michigan Canal Corridor has two areas with marked, multi-purpose trails. One 15-mile segment goes from Channahon State Park to Gebhard Woods State Park. The second segment goes from La Salle to Utica and is about 5 miles long.

To reach Channahon State Park, take Interstate 55 from the north and south. Southwest of Joliet you meet State Route 6. Turn west onto Route 6 and go to the town of Channahon. Turn left onto Canal Street in Channahon and proceed a half mile until you see the park signs. Turn right and proceed one block to the entrance.

To reach Gebhard Woods State Park, take Interstate 80 or Route 6 from the west or east. The motorist may then go to the intersection of routes 6 and 47 in Morris. Proceed west on Route 6 for five blocks to Union Street. Turn south on Union Street and follow the signs to the park entrance.

To reach the trail in La Salle follow Route 351 through La Salle. When you see Canal Street on the north side of the Canal, turn west and go about 100 feet to a parking area on the south side of Canal Street.

The trailhead in Utica may be reached by taking Route 178 into Utica. South of the canal, turn west onto Johnson Street and go three blocks to Morton Street. Turn north on Morton Street and proceed to the parking area.

Counties: Will, Grundy and La Salle

Illinois Highway Map Coordinates: D-7 and D-8

U.S.G.S. Topographical Map Names and Scale: Channahon, Minooka, Morris, Coal City, and La Salle, all 1:24,000

Hours Open: Gebhard Woods and Channahon State Park are both open year-round, except on Christmas Day and New Year's Day. When weather conditions necessitate the closing of the roads during freezing and thawing periods, access to the park or facilities is by foot only.

History and Trail Description: The Illinois–Michigan Canal was the impetus for the settlement and development of northeastern Illinois. The canal was directly responsible for the beginning of Chicago's growth as well as the cause for the development of Lockport, Joliet, Morris, Seneca, Marseilles, Ottawa, Utica and La Salle–Peru.

The Illinois–Michigan Canal actually had its origin with the Indians at the Chicago Portage, the low divide between the waters of Lake Michigan and the Des Plaines River. The Indians used it as a carrying place long before the advent of the white man. This portage was also recorded in the annals of the French explorers Joliet and Marquette in 1673. It was also noted in 1790 by the French military engineer Victor Collot and in 1807 by U.S. Secretary of the Treasury Albert Gallatin in his report on roads and canals.

The original boundaries of Illinois were moved about fifty miles in order to give Illinois a coast on Lake Michigan and to ensure that Chicago, the point at which the canal would connect with Lake Michigan, would be in Illinois.

Construction of the canal was started by the State of Illinois in 1836 and was completed in 1848. The canal cost about $9.5 million, stretched ninety-six miles, and linked Lake Michigan with the Illinois River at La Salle, the two bodies of water from which the canal took its name. When the canal was originally built, it was 36 feet wide at the bottom, 60 feet wide at water level, and had a 15-foot wide towpath. The canal included fifteen locks, three dams, and four aqueducts. Several feeder streams, two with aqueducts, once fed the canal. Today, some of the locks and aqueducts may be seen while hiking.

On January 1, 1974, the canal was transferred to the Department of Conservation for the development of a hiking and biking trail. In addition, about twenty-eight miles of the canal are filled with water for canoeing.

In February 1984, Congress established the Illinois and Michigan Canal Heritage Corridor. The Act created a 100-mile linear historical park system with a commission to oversee that the corridor is preserved. The goals are to protect and enhance the cultural, natural and recreational resources along the Illinois and Michigan Canal Corridor. The National Park Service plans to produce guides and will market the Corridor's resources to encourage economic development.

Currently two areas have marked hiking trails along the canal towpath. Hiking, biking, and canoeing are open from Channahon to Gebhard Woods State Park and from Utica to La Salle. Ten miles of hiking are also available between Gebhard Woods and Seneca, but this trail is not currently marked. In addition, 44 miles of snowmobile trails have been developed along the old towpath. Both trail segments are flat along the entire lengths and are the width of a single-lane road. The trails are marked with orange paint blazes that are usually painted at the trailheads and at all intersections with roads. In addition, small blue and white signs have the words "Illinois and Michigan Canal State Trail" written on them.

Both trail segments are one-way, so you would have to backtrack on the trail or set up a ride at the other end of the trail.

The 15-mile trail between Channahon and Gebhard Woods State Parks may be started at either end. The trailhead at Channahon State Park is located just south of the park off of Bridge Street. Lock 7 is on the north side of Bridge Street, and a parking area is found right next to the canal. A trailboard set up at the parking area gives the trail distances for four locations: McKinley Woods—2.8 miles; Dresden Access—5.8 miles; Aux Sable Access—8.1 miles; and Gebhard Woods—14.8 miles.

Lock tender's house and lock and dam no. 6, Channahon State Park

The trail starts heading south with the canal on the right and the Des Plaines River appearing on the left side. At McKinley Woods you will see a small wooden bridge that goes over the canal, leading to the woods. Picnic tables, car parking, and a shelter are found at McKinley Woods.

From here, the trail goes west. Prior to reaching Dresden Lock and Dam, you will see a sign for a camping and picnic area on the left side of the trail. There you will see some picnic tables, a small wooden shelter with a fireplace in it, and restrooms.

Just beyond the camping area you will pass Dresden Lock and Dam, which has a rest bench. Approximately two miles later you will arrive at Aux Sable Access. Before reaching this access point you will pass another camping area. Beyond the camping area the trail crosses a road and then comes to the access area. Another lock and dam and an aqueduct can be seen at this access. A parking lot, water pump, and restrooms are also available at this access. In addition, a small wooden bridge, which allows you to view the lock and dam system, goes over the lock and dam.

Past the Aux Sable Access Area you will cross a bridge over the canal and will follow the towpath on the south side again. In a few miles you will see many residential homes on the north side of the canal. At this point, the trail is at the outskirts of Morris.

The trail goes by William G. Stratton State Park and then crosses a bridge to the north side of the canal.

Prior to reaching Gebhard Woods State Park, you will see the Nettle Creek Aqueduct. From this point you may continue following the towpath a short distance to the park, or you may follow the trail and paint blazes away from the canal to the camping and picnic areas within the park.

The second trail segment along the Illinois and Michigan Canal may also be started at either end, Utica or La Salle. If you start at La Salle you will have to climb down some stairs from the parking area where you will see Lock 14. This lock was restored in 1981–82. Continue across the lock on a small bridge and then follow the towpath on the south side.

The trail goes east towards Utica and passes by Illinois River backwaters on the right side. Bluffs are seen along the trail, on the left side of the canal. A wooden bench is also available about half way along the trail. At the trail end in Utica you will come to a gate and a small parking area.

Facilities: Gebhard Woods State Park has picnic facilities with tables, grills, water, restrooms, and a shelter. A baseball diamond and horseshoe pits are also available. Children may fish in the four ponds in the park. Youth camping sites are also available.

Channahon State Park has picnic tables, shelters, restrooms, water, grills, and playground equipment. Tent camping is also available. Locks 6 and 7 and the locktender's house at lock 6 are at Channahon State Park. Fishing is allowed in the canal, and in the Du Page, Illinois and Des Plaines rivers, contingent upon all Illinois fishing rules and regulations.

Permits Required: A camping permit is required.

Park Rules and Regulations: See Appendix A.

Mailing Address and Phone Numbers: Site Superintendent, Gebhard Woods State Park, Box 272, Morris, Illinois 60450; 815/942–0796; or, Channahon State Park, Box 54, Channahon, Illinois 60410; 815/462–4271

27. Starved Rock State Park

Trail Length: 15 miles (24 kilometers)

Location: Starved Rock State Park is located in north central Illinois one mile south of Utica. Travelers coming from west, east, and north can reach the park by exiting off Interstate 80 south onto State Route 178, which leads directly to the park entrance. Starved Rock can be reached from the south by taking State Route 51. From Route 51 follow State Route 351 through Oglesby to State Route 71. Travel east on Route 71 to the park entrance.

County: La Salle

Illinois Highway Map Coordinates: D-7

U.S.G.S. Topographical Map Names and Scale: La Salle and Starved Rock, both 1:24,000

Hours Open: The park is open year-round except on Christmas Day and New Year's Day. At certain times, due to freezing and thawing periods, the park may be closed and access to the park is by foot only.

History and Trail Description: Indian tribes were known to live in this area and the name Starved Rock was derived from an Indian legend which states that the Illiniwek tribe who took refuge on top of the 125-foot sandstone butte were surrounded by the Ottawa and Potawatomi tribes and eventually starved. A series of battles which led to this event occured during the 1760s. About a hundred years earlier the French had built a chain of forts along the Illinois River. Fort St. Louis was constructed on top of Starved Rock and was used by traders, trappers, and local Indians. It was destroyed by fire in the early 1700s.

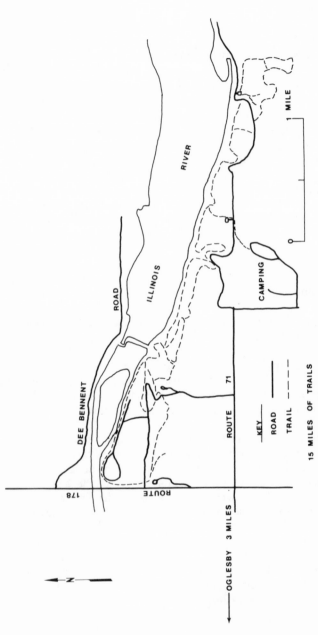

27. Starved Rock State Park. Redrawn from park map.

The trails in the park consist primarily of short connecting trails. Trailboards are available at most trail junctions and some parking areas. You will find the trails on the west side, near the lodge, to be the most populated.

The trails wind through canyons, on top of bluffs, and along the Illinois River bank. Throughout the park the hiker can observe the rock formations in the area. The bluff trails are developed along the high ridges of the canyons in the area and offer hard-to-moderate hiking. The bluff trails lead the hiker through the woods and offer frequent scenic overlooks. These trails are marked with brown blazes on the trees. Along the river, on top of the bluffs, there are several viewing platforms developed by the Youth Conservation Corp.

The River Trail begins at the west end of the park where most of the facilities are located. The connecting trail leading to the rock formation "Starved Rock" is also located here.

At several points the river trails connect with the bluff trails, and some of these connecting trails include a steep staircase climb.

Starved Rock State Park also has established trails which allow the hikers to view the many beautiful canyons in the area. These interior canyon trails allow one to view the rock formations created by natural forces. Streams, waterfalls, and pools may be seen in many of the canyons.

In addition, there are many connecting trails which lead from parking lots to major trails. Also, a trail begins at campsite E16 and E17, at the campground on the southeast side of the park, and connects Route 71 to parking lot G. This connecting trail measures approximately three-quarters of a mile.

Overall, the trails are well maintained and clearly marked and offer a challenging hike. Individual trails (bluff, river, or canyon) are color-coded with blazes on the trees. The trails are generally about three feet wide.

Permits Required: A camping permit is required.

Park Rules and Regulations: No swimming, climbing or rapelling anywhere in the park. All pets must be on a leash. See appendixes A and D.

Facilities: A park office and interpretive center are located in the park. A lodge is located here and has a dining room, refreshments hall and twelve year-round cabins surrounding it. There are 135 campsites in the park with electricity, restrooms and water available. Near the lodge there are picnic tables, restrooms, shelters, water, and a boat landing.

Mailing Address and Phone Number: Site Superintendent, Starved Rock State Park, Box 116, Utica, Illinois 61373; 815/667–4726

28. Matthiessen State Park

Trail Length: 6.25 miles (10 kilometers)

Location: Matthiessen State Park is located along the Vermilion River three miles east of Oglesby. It can be reached from State Route 51 from the north and south, and Interstate 80 from east or west. The park is just three miles from the campground at the south end of Starved Rock State Park. The northern boundary is Route 71, and the eastern boundary is Route 178.

Illinois Highway Map Coordinates: D-7

County: La Salle

U.S.G.S. Topographical Map Name and Scale: La Salle, 1:24,000

Hours Open: The park is open year-round except on Christmas Day and New Year's Day. At certain times, due to freezing and thawing periods, the park is closed and access to the park is by foot only.

History and Trail Description: Prior to 1943 this area was known as Deer Park and was under the private ownership of Frederick William Matthiessen. In 1943 the state took over the property and renamed the park in honor of Matthiessen.

Matthiessen State Park is quite similar to Starved Rock State Park in geological features. The main canyon in the park was formed by stream erosion; it consists of two sections, the upper and lower dells. The entire area is a series of beautiful canyons and wooded bluffs carved out of sandstone.

The 6.25 miles of hiking trails are made up of six trails. In the dells area the trails loop around the canyons and bluffs, allowing the hiker to view the natural features in both the upper and lower dells.

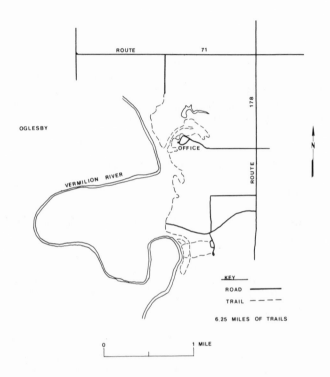

ROUTE 71

178

OGLESBY

ROUTE

VERMILION RIVER

OFFICE

N

KEY

ROAD ⎯⎯⎯

TRAIL ⎯ ⎯ ⎯

6.25 MILES OF TRAILS

0   1 MILE

28. Matthiessen State Park

The lower canyon trail which winds through the upper and lower dells measures a little over 1 mile. The Bluff Trail in the upper dells, which begins at the concession stand, loops around the east side and measures about 1 mile. Some sites seen while hiking the Upper Bluff Trail include the dam, a private lake, Giants' Bathtub, Cascade Falls, and most of the lower canyon which includes Sandy Point.

From Cascade Falls, a bluff trail loops around the lower dells; it measures less than 1 mile. Along this trail the "Wishing Well," the "Paint Box," and "The Strawberry Rock" can be seen in the lower canyon. A connecting trail meanders northward from this trail to the archery range and eventually out of the park. The connecting trail which leads to the archery range appears to be an abandoned one-lane road. This section passes through open fields and also through dense woods. Much of this section is overgrown. As you near the parking area for the archery range, you will parallel a private drive and the road for Deer Park Country Club (golf course). Beyond the archery range you can follow the road north to Route 71, to the nature preserve, and to Starved Rock State Park on the north side of Route 71.

Another connecting trail winds southward to the section of the park known as the Vermilion River Area. This southbound trail measures approximately 2 miles. The trail goes through woods, above the bluffs, through open fields and by a viewing platform, which is located a little over one mile from the lower dells area.

Shortly after passing the viewing platform you will cross over the park blacktop road. After crossing the blacktop road, the trail heads east as a one-way dirt road known as the Township Road. Following the road, you head south past the shelters and picnic areas. To your right (west) is a dirt path which leads down to the lower area trail along the river. As you near the river you will cross a bridge over a feeder creek; you can go north, where the trail becomes a loop and joins with the same trail near the Township Road you just left, or you can go south along the river. If you go south, you have the option of cutting the trail short and hiking the middle staircase/trail, or you can follow the river trail to the end and climb the third flight back to the bluff trail.

Within the Vermilion Area are several short connecting trails, all of which lead down to the lower canyon trail along the east bank of the river. This trail is connected to the upper bluff trails via bridges and steps.

In periods of high water, the interior canyon trails and low-lying trails are impractical to hike because of flooding. Eight miles of horseback, cross-country skiing, and snow-shoe trails are also available in the park.

Facilities: The Dells Area has a concession stand, shelter, toilets, park office, parking and picnic facilities. The Vermilion Area has shelters and restrooms.

Park Rules and Regulations: No camping, rapelling, rock or ice climbing allowed. Hiking allowed only on marked trails. All pets must be on a leash. See Appendix A.

Mailing Address and Phone Number: Site Superintendent, Matthiessen State Park, Box 381, Utica, Illinois 61373; 815/667–4868

PART III

Hiking Trails in Central Illinois

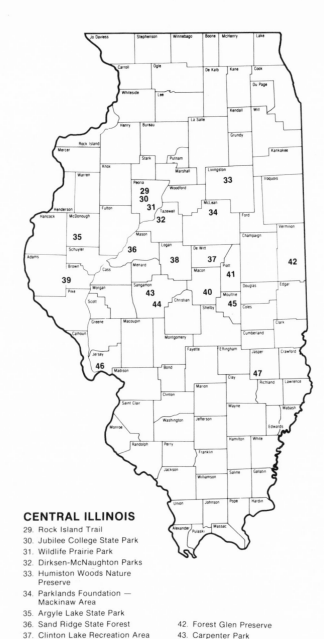

CENTRAL ILLINOIS

29. Rock Island Trail
30. Jubilee College State Park
31. Wildlife Prairie Park
32. Dirksen-McNaughton Parks
33. Humiston Woods Nature Preserve
34. Parklands Foundation — Mackinaw Area
35. Argyle Lake State Park
36. Sand Ridge State Forest
37. Clinton Lake Recreation Area
38. Railsplitter State Park
39. Siloam Springs State Park
40. Rock Springs Center
41. Allerton Park
42. Forest Glen Preserve
43. Carpenter Park
44. Lincoln Memorial Garden
45. Fishhook Waterfowl Area
46. Pere Marquette State Park
47. Newton Lake Conservation Area

Figure 3. Hiking trails in central Illinois

29. Rock Island Trail

Trail Length: 5 miles (8 kilometers)

Location: Currently three segments of the Rock Island Trail are open for hiking. One trail segment starts in Alta and measures about 2.5 miles. The second trail may be started in either Dunlap or Princeville and measures 5 miles, and the third segment may be started in Wyoming and measures 3.5 miles. The Dunlap segment is described here.

To reach the trailhead at Dunlap, the hiker may take Interstate 74 west out of Peoria to Interstate 6. Turn north on Interstate 6 and proceed to Route 91. Turn north on Route 91 and go six miles to Dunlap. At the north end of Dunlap the hiker will see a sign for Parks School Road. Turn left (west) and go about a quarter mile, then turn right into a small parking lot. You will see a sign at the trailhead that has the words "Rock Island Trail" written on it.

To access the trail in Princeville, the hiker may take Route 91 into Princeville. Turn south at Walnut Avenue. Proceed south for about one mile, go over a set of railroad tracks, and turn left on the first dirt road past the railroad tracks. Follow this dirt road for a few blocks until it comes to a dead end and parking area.

County: Peoria

Illinois Highway Map Coordinates: E-5 and F-5

U.S.G.S. Topographical Map Names and Scale: Dunlap, Edelstein and Princeville, all 1:24,000

Hours Open: The trail is open year-round.

History and Trail Description: In the late 1950s the Chicago, Rock Island and Pacific Railroad ceased operation

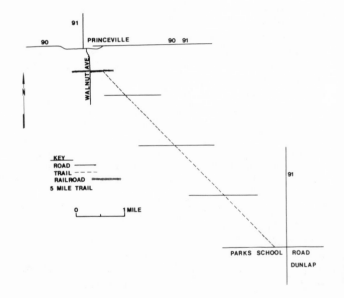

29. Rock Island Trail

along its track running from Peoria to Toulon. In subsequent years the tracks, ties, some ballasts, drainage structures, and bridge components were salvaged and removed from the right-of-way.

In 1965 the Forest Park Foundation of Peoria obtained title to the right-of-way, and it subsequently became known as the Rock Island Forest Park Trail. In addition, the Forest Park Foundation purchased approximately 160 acres of land adjacent to the railroad between Alta and Dunlap. Sixty acres were given to the Illinois Youth Commission in return for a promise to provide maintenance and development services at Jubilee College State Park and along the right-of-way. One hundred acres known as the Mayer Tract, north of Alta, were given to the Department of Conservation along with the right-of-way to be developed as a wildlife refuge and linear recreational corridor.

The Department of Conservation undertook a study to evaluate the potential of the Rock Island Trail as a multiple-use linear recreation corridor. It was determined that the Rock Island Trail would provide needed recreational opportunities for the region and the state. Plans called for opening over 27 miles of bicycle, hiking, and associated camping facilities along the old Rock Island Trail. But many obstacles have impeded the achievement of this goal. Some of these obstacles include: adjoining landowners objecting to any development; legislative resolutions prohibiting the Department of Conservation from proceeding with further work on this project; and in recent years a legislative resolution prohibiting volunteers from working on the trail. Therefore, up to this date only about 13 miles of trails have been developed.

The trail segment from Dunlap to Princeville measures 5 miles. This section, marked with "Rock Island Trail" signs every mile, goes by farms and through some wooded areas.

The trail is generally flat the entire length and can be easily hiked or biked.

The trail crosses a few farm and country roads, and ends at some railroad tracks and a small parking area at the outskirts of Princeville. A small parking area and garbage can are available here.

Facilities: There are no facilities along the trail. Food, water, and restrooms are available in Dunlap and Princeville.

Park Rules and Regulations: No motorized vehicles allowed. See Appendix A.

Mailing Address and Phone Number: Site Superintendent, Jubilee College State Park, R.R. 2, Box 72, Brimfield, Illinois 61517; 309/243-7683

30. Jubilee College State Park

Trail Length: 4.5 miles (7.3 kilometers)

Location: Jubilee College State Park is located in central Illinois approximately fifteen miles northwest of Peoria. The major access road is Interstate 74. Road signs both west of the park and east of the park along Route 74 indicate the proper exit ramp for access to the park.

Major access roads to Peoria include east-west Route 24 and north-south Route 121, along with Interstate 74.

County: Peoria

Illinois Highway Map Coordinates: F-5

U.S.G.S. Topographical Map Name and Scale: Oak Hill, 1:24,000

Hours Open: The park is open year-round, except on Christmas Day and New Year's Day. When weather conditions necessitate the closing of roads during freezing and thawing periods, access to facilities is by foot only.

History and Trail Description: The site is known for the Jubilee College which operated from 1840 to 1862, one of Illinois' earliest educational enterprises.

The founder of Jubilee College was Bishop Philander Chase, who was called to Illinois to assume jurisdiction of the newly formed Episcopal diocese, one of his many duties. In 1933 the college and grounds consisted of 96 acres which were presented to the State of Illinois as a memorial. Today Jubilee College State Park totals more than 3,500 acres.

The trail system at Jubilee College State Park includes 4.5 miles of established hiking trails and approximately 30 miles of equestrian trails. Hikers are allowed

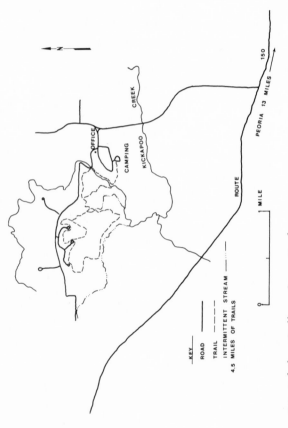

KEY
ROAD
TRAIL
INTERMITTENT STREAM
4.5 MILES OF TRAILS

N

OFFICE
CAMPING
KICKAPOO CREEK
ROUTE
PEORIA 13 MILES
150
MILE
0

30. Jubilee College State Park

to use the equestrian trails; however, these trails have been excluded from this description because we found them to be inaccurately and poorly marked, or not marked at all.

The 4.5 miles of hiking trails are marked with a combination of symbols to identify the trail. There are white figures of a skier on a blue background, white figures of a hiker on a brown background, and for those portions which follow the equestrian trail, a white horse on brown background.

A trailboard is set up at the west edge of the tent camping area, signifying the start of the trail. The first section of trail meanders southwest until it meets the Jubilee Creek. The trail formerly crossed the creek via a suspension bridge; however, a new trail is located along the eastern bank of the creek, and crossing is made farther north at the ford. There are plans to install a suspension bridge at the ford.

The trail along the eastern side of Jubilee Creek is hazardous even though it is fairly new. Water bars and steps have been placed where necessary; however, several places warrant extra caution as the trail follows the sloping shoreline.

Most of the trail system is on the west side of the ford. After crossing the ford, the trail goes west and becomes part of the equestrian trail. Less than fifty yards from the ford is a trail marked with a symbol of a skier. This trail, the alternate for hikers, travels northwesterly until it crosses the equestrian trail again. Also, before the equestrian trail there is a connecting trail that meanders in a southeasterly direction. This trail leads back to Jubilee Creek and the old suspension bridge crossing.

Upon reaching the equestrian trail again, go south to a major trail junction. At the junction, follow the connecting trail that goes northwest until you come to another junction. This trail junction has a bench and a trail sign indicating direction and travel to the other sections of the park. The trail to the right meanders northwesterly to the Bow Wood Glen Picnic Area, past the Milkweed Meadow Picnic Area, and south to the Prairie Drift Lane Picnic Area. Here, south of the Prairie

Drift Lane Picnic Area, is the end of the trail that goes to the left at the junction mentioned above.

A newer trail connects the Prairie Drift Lane Picnic Area with the Cone Flower Cove Picnic Area. From the Cone Flower Cove Picnic Area, the trail goes west until it joins the equestrian trail once again. By following the equestrian trail southeast, a hiker will eventually join the same trail junction that goes west to the second trail junction already mentioned.

Wildlife is abundant; many species can be seen at Jubilee College State Park. The large acreage and waterways also support a variety of trees and vegetation as well.

Facilities: Tent and trailer camping is available, some with electricity. An equestrian camping area is located at the north end of the park. There are several picnic areas which have tables, shelters, water, charcoal grills, restrooms, and litter receptacles.

Permits Required: Use of the equestrian area must be approved by park staff. Camping permits are also required.

Park Rules and Regulations: Groups of twenty-five persons must obtain permission from the site superintendent. Groups of minors must have adequate supervision and at least one adult for each group of fifteen minors. All pets must be on a leash. See Appendix A.

Mailing Address and Phone Number: Site Superintendent, Jubilee College State Park, R.R. 2, Box 72, Brimfield, Illinois, 61517; 309/243-7683

31. Wildlife Prairie Park

Trail Length: 4 miles (6.4 kilometers)

Location: Wildlife Prairie Park is located ten miles west of Peoria and one mile south of Edwards. Travelers from the west and east may take Interstate 74 to Exit 82 (Edwards Road). Turn south on Edwards Road and proceed four miles to Edwards. South of Edward, the road is known as Taylor Road; the entrance is on the east side of Taylor Road.

County: Peoria

Illinois Highway Map Coordinates: F-5

U.S.G.S. Topographical Map Name and Scale: Peoria West, 1:24,000

Hours Open: First weekend in May until Memorial Day: Weekdays 9:00 a.m. to 4:30 p.m. and on Weekends 9:00 a.m. to 6:30 p.m. Memorial Day to Labor Day: Daily 9:00 a.m. to 6:30 p.m. Labor Day to October 31: Weekdays 9:00 a.m. to 4:30 p.m. and on Weekends 9:00 a.m. to 6:30 p.m. In addition, the Banquet Hall is open every Sunday year-round for breakfast and the park is open in the winter on weekends for cross-country skiing.

History and Trail Description: Wildlife Prairie Park was developed and opened in 1978 to provide educational, conservational, and recreational activities for the citizens of central Illinois. The park consists of over 1,600 acres of grazing land, rolling hills, lakes, floodplains, and hardwood forests. Currently, 150 acres have been developed; the remaining 1,450 acres serve as natural buffers to protect the native wildlife.

The park, operated by a private nonprofit founda-

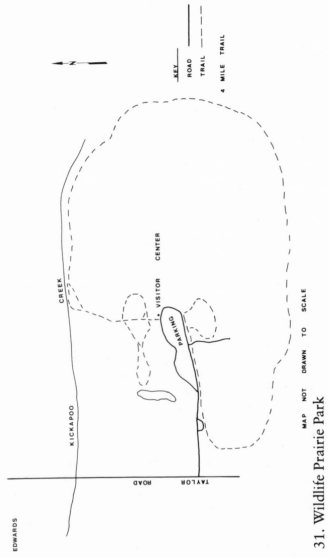

31. Wildlife Prairie Park

tion, relies on contributions, such as fees for membership, admissions and services, sales in the store and gift shop, and thousands of volunteer hours for its development, construction, and operation.

The park is a small wildlife sanctuary and zoo. Many animals roam in their natural settings, with short hiking trails taking the hiker past all of the wildlife in the park. Some of the animals at the park include bison, black bear, coyotes, bobcat, cougar, wolves, bald eagle, deer, and badgers. The animals are all fenced in, making it safe for the hiker.

The trail system at Wildlife Prairie Park consists of short trails which meander past many of the animals and waterfowl in the park. In addition, the main 4-mile hiking trail in the park takes the hiker through the floodplain of the Kickapoo Creek and around the park.

The short trails may be started at the Visitors' Center. Maps of the trail are available inside the center. All of the trails are well marked with trail maps found along the trails, showing your exact location. In addition, wooden trail signs point to the direction of other trails. All of the trails are about six feet wide and are very easy to follow.

The Merrill Woods Trail passes many of the animals in the park. A black bear, puma, and wolves are some of the animals that can be seen from this trail. The Helligae Trail and Linder Trail connect with the Merril Woods Trail. The Helligae Trail takes you to the waterfowl blind while the Linder Trail takes you to a wildlife viewing deck.

The Linder Trail goes into the Old Wagon Trail and passes by a large eagle-viewing area. From here a short trail connects with this trail and takes you to the pioneer farmstead. A small barn with animals, a restored cabin, and a school are located in this area. Close to the cabin you will access the main trail of the park.

The main trail of the park, appropriately known as the Floodplain Trail, measures about 4 miles. As the trail lies within a floodplain, it may at times be inundated. You may check with the Visitors' Center or call the park to find out the condition of the trail. The trail varies in width, starting out as a small footpath by the cabin and becoming a large gravel road towards the end of the trail on the other side of the park.

At the trailhead by the cabin, you will see a trailboard identifying the trail. From here you will descend the hill and will come to a Y in the trail. You may go in either direction; both parts of the trail meet farther down. We recommend the left trail because the trail to the right is very wet and muddy at times. You will see wooden boards, nailed onto trees, with white painted arrows signifying the trail direction. In addition, you will see a few trail maps and wooden posts which have a symbol of a cross-country skier on them.

Beyond this point the trail follows the Kickapoo Creek for almost one mile. The trail then crosses a small hill, eventually following and traversing a small creek. You will then climb another small hill and will be in a large open field. Looking west, you will be able to see the Visitors' Center.

Soon you will come to the area in the park where strip-mining took place. You will walk on top of the strip-mined area, go by a lake that resulted from the strip-mining, and will come down to a gravel road.

This gravel road leads back to the parking area that you passed when first entering the park. Another trailboard will be seen at this parking area.

Past the parking area, the trail becomes a wood chip path. The trail passes by a few picnic areas, playground equipment, and the large sliding board. The trail parallels the park road for a short distance, taking you to the Banquet Hall. Another trail joins the Floodplain Trail close to the Banquet Hall. This trail, known as the South Bison Trail, is a short loop trail.

Facilities: A Visitors' Center is located on the grounds and has a small gift shop, restrooms, and animal and plant displays inside. Food and drinks may be bought at the Banquet Hall. A small country store and a ranger first-aid station are also located at the park. Numerous picnic areas and playground equipment are located here. A small railroad in the park takes visitors past some of the areas in the park. In addition, many wild animals that are native to Illinois will be seen in their natural habitats. Restrooms are available in the Visitors' Center and the Pioneer Pavilion.

Park Rules and Regulations: No pets and no alcoholic beverages are allowed.

Mailing Address and Phone Number: Wildlife Prairie Park, R.R. 2, Taylor Road, Hanna City, Illinois 61536; 309/676-0998

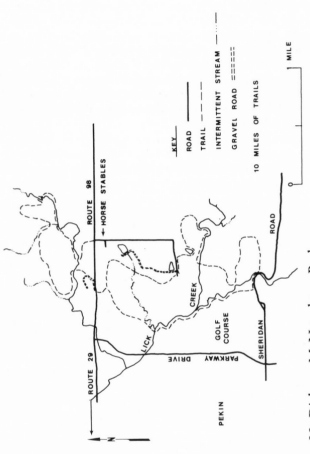

32. Dirksen-McNaughton Parks

32. Dirksen and McNaughton Parks

Trail Lengths: McNaughton Park, 6 miles (9.6 kilometers); Dirksen Park, 4 miles (6.4 kilometers)

Location: Dirksen and McNaughton Parks are both located in Pekin. To reach the parks, take State Route 29 from the north or the south. Turn right (east) at State Route 98 and proceed two miles to the park entrance. The park road turns south into McNaughton Park. McNaughton Park is located on the south side of Route 98 and Dirksen Park on the north side. Follow this road either to the horse stables area or to the end of the road where there is a turnaround.

County: Tazewell

Illinois Highway Map Coordinates: F-5

U.S.G.S. Topographical Map Name and Scale: Marquette Heights, 1:24,000

Hours Open: 6:00 a.m. until 10:00 p.m.

History and Trail Description: McNaughton Park was named after John T. McNaughton, who once owned the *Pekin Times* newspaper. Dirksen Park was named after the late Senator Everett Dirksen, a resident of Pekin. The development of the trail in McNaughton Park was started in the summer of 1970 and was completed in the spring of 1971. The trail was completed with the help of hikers, Boy Scout Troop 194, and the Pekin Park District.

The trail in McNaughton Park, called the Potawatomi Trail, measures 6 miles, while the trail in Dirksen Park, the Running Deer Trail, measures 4 miles. Both of the trails are blazed very well with spray paint on the trees. The Potawatomi Trail is marked with red paint; the Running Deer Trail, with yellow paint.

Both trails may be started near the horse stables right off of Route 98, or you may begin at the end of the road where there is a turnaround for vehicles. There is also a little parking area at the horse stables. The horse stables are run by a private firm, the land being leased to them by the Pekin Park District.

From the parking area, walk due west past the stables, through a few gates, and then continue onward to a small picnic area and shelter. From this spot both the Running Deer Trail and the Potawatomi Trail may be reached. A wooden trail marker behind the shelter shows the direction of the Running Deer Trail. The Potawatomi Trail is found by hiking west until red trail blazes are seen on the trees.

The Running Deer Trail slowly starts heading downhill and passes a small creek before approaching Route 98. From this point the trail crosses the road and follows it east for the short distance until it reaches the archery range. From here the trail follows the road and then branches off into the woods. Soon you will cross a creek. Follow this creek west for a short distance. The trail will start to follow another creek valley, and then it starts heading in a westerly direction, going by open fields. The trail crosses another small creek and comes out of the woods at the edge of an open field. The trail then goes around the open field and starts back into the woods again. Following the natural topography, the trail comes down to cross another creek, then climbs another small hill. From here the trail follows the edge of a cliff for a short distance before dropping off to the creek valley again, where it crosses the creek once more.

After reaching the highest point in the park (639 feet in elevation) you descend to the main creek that was crossed earlier. After crossing the creek, you head west toward private homes. The trail turns south toward Route 98 and the road that leads into the park. From here you follow the road back to the trailhead.

Passing the stables you will reach the Potawatomi Trail. You also have the option of taking the car to the turnaround area to start hiking the trail beginning north of the parking area.

The trail is clearly marked with red blazes. The trail

goes downhill over a small creek and over small bridges. The trail then follows some power lines for a short distance. From here the trail heads back into the woods, paralleling the open fields. The trail bridges another creek and comes to the picnic areas just west of the stables. From here the trail heads west, goes under the power lines again, and then turns south moving downhill. Shortly, the trail crosses Lick Creek, which may be quite high during the wet season.

From here the trail parallels the creek for a long time, going up and down the small hills in the area. The trail then passes a golf course and starts south, coming finally to Sheridan Road. Follow this road eastward for a short distance and, as soon as you pass the creek, start north into the woods. From here the trail soon skirts an open field and then heads west until it reaches the creek again. You will see a platform overlooking the creek. The trail continues paralleling the creek, going by a forty-foot eroded stream bank, and moving uphill to another open field. The trail parallels this open field for a short distance, then crosses another creek. The trail parallels this creek for a short distance, starts north and then west, passing an old house foundation. Finally it comes to some restrooms that are east of Joseph Zurcher Lake. The trail goes around the south end of the lake and up a small hill to the car turnaround area.

Facilities: There are picnic facilities with picnic tables and restrooms available by the turnaround. A small shelter and observation are also at the Joseph Zurcher Lake. Picnic facilities are also available west of the horse stables.

Permits Required: Camping is by permit only. A permit may be obtained by contacting the Pekin Park District.

Park Rules and Regulations: No alcoholic beverages, hunting, trapping or swimming allowed. No vehicles on the grass and no one allowed on the ice.

Mailing Address and Phone Number: Pekin Park District, 1701 Court Street, Pekin, Illinois 61554; 309/347-3178

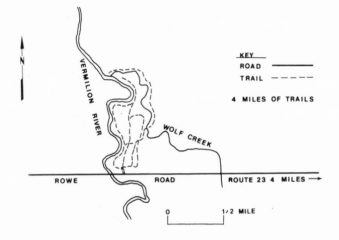

KEY
ROAD ———
TRAIL — — — —

4 MILES OF TRAILS

VERMILION RIVER

WOLF CREEK

ROWE   ROAD   ROUTE 23 4 MILES →

0   1/2 MILE

33. Humiston Woods Nature Preserve

33. Humiston Woods Nature Preserve

Trail Length: 4 miles (6.4 kilometers)

Location: Humiston Woods Nature Preserve is located six miles northwest of Pontiac. To reach the park, motorists may take Interstate 55 and exit onto State Route 23 (exit 201). Proceed north about two blocks and turn left (west) onto Rowe Road. A sign on Route 23 points to Humiston Woods Nature Preserve. Proceed on Rowe Road for four miles to the park entrance, which is located on the north side of the road. You must leave your car parked out in front of the park on Rowe Road because the gates to the park are kept locked.

County: Livingston

Illinois Highway Map Coordinates: E-7

U.S.G.S. Topographical Map Name and Scale: Northwest Pontiac, 1:24,000

Hours Open: The park is open all year.

History and Trail Description: Humiston Woods Nature Preserve is owned and administered by Pontiac Parks and Recreation Department.

At the front of the park, there is a gate and a small opening that you pass through. From here you will see a trailboard that shows the layouts of the six interconnected trails in the park. Each trail is identified by an appropriate name and symbol. The beginning of each trail is identified by wooden trail markers. Four trails may be started at the main trailboard. At all four of these trailheads are gates which were built to keep motorized vehicles from entering the park and the trails. You may hike the trails in any direction you want. At some trail intersections there are trail signs to identify the trail. Just to the east of the trailboard is a small pond; two of the trails go past this pond.

The River Trail may be started just west of the main trailboard and basically parallels the Vermilion River. The trail starts going down toward the river where you will see a sign which says "Fishing Hole." From here you will reach a pavilion and picnic area that has picnic tables and small grills, all overlooking the Vermilion River. Also a small platform offers a beautiful view of the river valley. From here the trail continues paralleling the river and soon joins another branch of the trail. At this point the trail may be followed north to the junction of the Vermilion River and Wolf Creek. The trail can then be followed back to the pavilion, or you may start hiking on the Deer Trail which intersects the trail before the pavilion.

The Deer Trail basically stays on top of a ridge, parallels Wolf Creek for a short distance, follows the park fence, and comes around to the east side of the parking area and trailboard. The Pioneer Trail may be hiked northward over the Deer Trail and then over Wolf Creek. The Pioneer Trail then parallels Wolf Creek until it joins the Vermilion River. During the winter, when the

Observation platform overlooking the Vermilion River, Humiston Woods Nature Preserve

ice is thick enough, you may cross the Vermilion River and hike along its west side back to the road. From here you may take the road back to the park entrance.

All of the trails are fairly easy to walk and may be enjoyed by the entire family. During the wet season, the River Trail and part of the Pioneer Trail are inundated and are impossible to hike.

Facilities: Maps are available at the main trailboard. Restrooms and a small picnic area are also found by the main trailboard. A pavilion, overlook platform, grills, picnic tables and restrooms may also be found along the River Trail.

Park Rules and Regulations: No hunting.

Mailing Address and Phone Number: Pontiac Parks and Recreation Department, P.O. Box 91, Pontiac, Illinois 61764; 815/844-6818

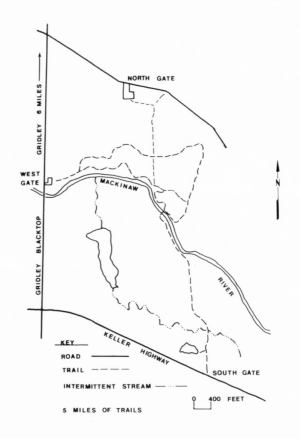

34. Parklands Foundation–Mackinaw Area. Redrawn from Parklands Foundation map.

34. Parklands Foundation–Mackinaw Area

Trail Length: 5 miles (8 kilometers)

Location: Mackinaw Area is located twenty miles northwest of Bloomington. To reach the site, take Interstate 55 from either the south or north. Turn off at the Lexington exit (exit 178) and proceed west on this road, which is also known as Keller Blacktop or Highway. Proceed on Keller Blacktop for about seven miles to Gridley Blacktop. Turn right (north) on Gridley Blacktop and proceed for about one-half mile to the Mackinaw River. Past the river there is a small parking area and sign which says "Parklands Foundation, Mackinaw Area." This parking area is referred to as the west gate.

You can also access this park at two other gates, the north and south gate. The south gate is located off Keller Highway. To reach the north gate, continue on Gridley Blacktop past the west gate. Turn right (east) at the first road and follow it for approximately three-quarters of a mile to a small parking area on the south side of the road.

County: McLean

Illinois Highway Map Coordinates: F-7

U.S.G.S Topographical Map Name and Scale: Gridley, 1:24,000

Hours Open: The park is open all year, and closes every day at dark.

History and Trail Description: The Mackinaw Area park is owned by the Parklands Foundation. The Parklands Foundation is a private, not-for-profit corporation which acquires land in central Illinois for recreation and nature study, and preserves the land in its natural state for wildlife habitat. Parklands Foundation solicits gifts of land and money to purchase various units of land.

The trail system at Mackinaw Area consists of about 5 miles of trails found on the north and south sides of the Mackinaw River, with 2.5 miles of these trails marked by twenty numbered posts located along the entire length of the trail. These numbers correspond to trail descriptions in a nature trail guide provided by the Parklands Foundation. The trail system may be started at either of the three access gates to the park, but the numbering of the nature trail starts close to the west gate. The trail is about four feet wide and well defined.

At the west gate parking area there is a wooden board with "Parklands Foundation" written on it; the board states the park rules. The trail heads east into the woods to a junction marked with a trailboard. Soon you start seeing the numbered posts along the trail and come close to the bluffs, which offer scenic views of the river. The trail then parallels the river for a while. Prior to reaching post number eight, you will see a sign which has "loop trail to bridge" written on it. If you follow the trail toward the bridge, you will head down the bluff to the river valley below, where you will reach a suspension bridge.

You may cross the bridge and follow the trail south

Suspension bridge over the Mackinaw River, Parklands Foundation–Mackinaw Area

toward the south gate, or you may continue following the marked nature trail to the north. Caution must be used when crossing the bridge since it tends to swing from side to side.

The south branch of the trail to the south gate is not marked well but is fairly well defined. The trail goes up a small hill away from the bridge and into the woods. From here the trail parallels an open field and becomes wider since it is now part of an old road. This part of the trail is referred to as the Elizabeth Stein Trail, named by the Parklands board for a donor to the corporation. The trail continues heading south, crossing a small wooden bridge over a creek, passing a wooden post which has "trail" written on it, passing a small shed and Rediger Pond, and finally exiting by the south gate.

The south gate has a parking space off Keller Blacktop where a sign, "Parklands Nature Preserve," will be seen. Retrace your steps back to the suspension bridge and continue following the nature trail through the park.

The nature trail east of the suspension bridge goes by creeks, up small hills, and through woodland openings and the floodplain forest. Another trail from the north gate parking area intersects the nature trail and may also be hiked. When you reach post 20 on the nature trail, you will be near the end of the loop and will come back to the original trail intersection where you started.

Many small bird houses can be seen along the trail. Deer, owls and rabbits may be seen in the park also. Wooden park benches are available along the trail at various locations and make nice resting stops for the hiker.

The trails are also used by cross-country skiers in the winter.

Facilities: No facilities available at this site.

Park Rules and Regulations: No dogs are allowed in the park. Only foot traffic is allowed on the trails. All plants and animals are protected.

Mailing Address: Parklands Foundation, Box 261, Bloomington, Illinois 61702

KEY
ROAD ——————
TRAIL — — — —

6 MILES OF TRAILS

N

ARGYLE LAKE

COLCHESTER 2 MILES

LAMOINE RIVER

0   1 MILE

35. Argyle Lake State Park

35. Argyle Lake State Park

Trail Length: 6 miles (9.6 kilometers)

Location: Argyle Lake State Park is located seven miles west of Macomb and two miles north of Colchester. To reach the park take State Route 136 seven miles out of Macomb. In Colchester you will see a sign for Argyle Lake State Park. This road is known as Coal Street. Turn north on Coal Street and proceed two miles to the park entrance.

Illinois Highway Map Coordinates: G-3

County: McDonough

U.S.G.S. Topographical Map Name and Scale: Colchester, 1:24,000

Hours Open: The park is open year-round except on Christmas Day and New Year's Day. At certain times, due to freezing and thawing periods, the park is closed and access to the park is by foot only.

History and Trail Description: A group of early settlers of McDonough County began the first Cumberland Presbyterian Church which met at the residence of John McCord. In 1854, the congregation moved to the Argyle Presbyterian Church near the west side of the park. The church founder, of Scottish descent, gave the community its name from Scotland's famous county of Argyle, for which the park was also named.

   The initial land acquisition for Argyle Lake State Park was 1,052 acres in 1948, and soon afterwards lake construction started on a tributary of the east fork of the LaMoine River. The lake, completed in 1949, consists of 95 acres and has a drainage of approximately 3,800 acres. The park currently has over 1,149 acres.

The trail system in Argyle Lake State Park comprises many interconnecting trails which wind their way around the park's main road for over 6 miles. These trails have various names; most of them are marked at their starting points.

The trails can be started at numerous areas in the park. At certain trailheads, trailboards outline the trail layout. The trails are about six feet wide, although some parts of the trails may be the width of a one-lane road.

While hiking the trails you will see numerous signs marked "Foot Trail" or "Horse Trail." In many cases the horse trails in the park join the hiking trail for a short distance and then branch off.

The trails are moderately rough as they go up and down along numerous small hills and some steep banks close to the lake. There are many stairs and several small creeks to cross via small wooden bridges. One section of the trail takes you past the dam and spillway. You will have to cross the spillway on the concrete apron or over rocks. During periods of high water this area may be impossible to cross by foot. The trails also have water bars to help divert the water off the trails; during the wet times of the year, the trails can become very muddy and difficult to walk.

In the future the park is planning to change all of the trail signs to one new name. The site superintendent thought that one name would be less confusing to hikers than the numerous trail names currently used.

One designated camping area along the trail may be used by the backpacker. The camping area is found on the eastern part of the trail.

Certain areas of the trail have restrooms, benches or picnic tables.

Facilities: The park has picnic facilities, such as tables and stoves, grills, water, restrooms, playground equipment, tent and trailer camping (electricity), and a summer interpretive program. In addition, a concession stand located on the lake offers a variety of refreshments during the summer months. Boats and pontoons may be rented at the concession stand. At the site superintendent's office located in the park, hikers may request maps and get camping permits. Fishing is also allowed on the lake, contingent upon Illinois fishing rules and regulations.

Permits Required: A camping permit is required.

Park Rules and Regulations: Motor limit is 10 hp. See Appendix A.

Mailing Address and Phone Number: Site Superintendent, Argyle Lake State Park, R.R. 2, Colchester, Illinois 62326; 309/776-3422

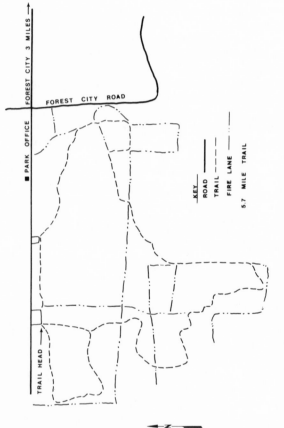

36. Sand Ridge State Forest. Redrawn from Sand Ridge trail guide.

36. Sand Ridge State Forest

Trail Length: 5.7 miles (9.2 kilometers)

Location: Sand Ridge State Forest is located twelve miles northeast of Havana off State Route 136. To reach the park, take Route 136 east out of Havana and turn north onto a gravel road when you see the sign for Forest City and Sand Ridge State Forest. Proceed six miles on this road to the park entrance.

County: Mason

Illinois Highway Map Coordinates: G-5

Illinois Topographical Map Names and Scale: Manito and Duck Island, both 1:24,000

Hours Open: The park is open all year except Christmas Day and New Year's Day.

History and Trail Description: Sand Ridge State Forest was initially acquired by the state in 1939 when 5,504 acres were purchased. The forest at that time consisted of small lots of natural hardwood timber and abandoned farms. After the state purchased the land, the forest was managed as a total forest ecosystem. The forest, formerly called Mason State Forest, was renamed Sand Ridge State Forest in 1971. Currently the forest has over 7,180 acres.

Two marked hiking trails are located in Sand Ridge State Forest. The first trail, a 2.2-mile loop trail, is located north of the forest headquarters. The second trail is also a loop trail, consisting of two trails totaling 5.7 miles. In addition there are over 9 miles of bridle trails, 37 miles of marked snowmobile trails, and over 150 miles of fire lanes in the forest that may be hiked.

The 5.7-mile trail described here is formally known as the Oak Trail. The Oak Trail is actually two trails which are combined for a total length of 5.7 miles. The short loop is 1.6 miles and is marked by red colored dots on the trees; the 4.7-mile trail is marked by yellow colored dots.

The trailhead can be reached by going west past the forest headquarters a few miles until you come to a horse campground. At the horse campground a trail sign points to the trailhead. The Oak Trail is generally about ten feet wide and is underlain by sand. In addition, prickly pear cactus and sand burs grow on the entire length of the trail and may make hiking somewhat miserable. We recommend wearing long pants while hiking this trail.

The trail goes up and down the gently rolling hills in the forest. No streams or bridges have to be crossed on the trail, but many times the trail crosses and at times may become a part of the fire lane. If you want to reduce the trail length, you could easily hike one of the fire lanes that connect with the trail at another spot.

After one mile there is a trail marker. At this point, you can proceed back to the trailhead or proceed on and hike the remaining four miles. The rest of the trail goes through the forest, passing through a pine stand, crossing several fire lanes, and paralleling the park road heading back towards the trailhead.

Restrooms and water pumps are found at the trailhead or about one mile before the trail ends, at a car parking area. The trail may also be used for cross-country skiing or for horseback riding.

Facilities: Sand Ridge State Forest has a park office where you may request additional information. Picnic sites are scattered in the park and have water, picnic tables and restrooms. Camping is available here with a group camping area, a family area, a horse area and a walk-in campground available. There are twenty-four campsites at the family area and three sites for the walk-in campground. Hunting is allowed in the forest during open season and with applicable rules and regulations applying. A fish hatchery is also located here. The hatchery encompasses 160 acres and raises forty-two million fish annually. Nature study groups, school classes, scout groups, insect collectors, and bird watchers also use the forest.

Required Permits: A camping permit is required and may be obtained from the ranger.

Park Rules and Regulations: All motorized vehicles are prohibited from the trails and fire lanes. See Appendix A.

Mailing Address and Phone Number: Site Superintendent, Sand Ridge State Forest, P.O. Box 82, Forest City, Illinois 61532; 309/597-2212

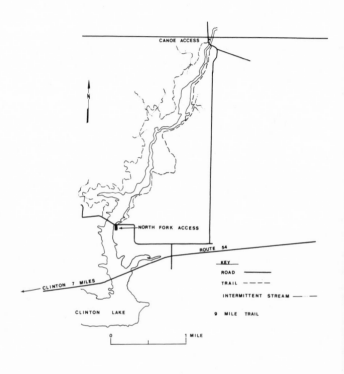

KEY

ROAD ————

TRAIL — — — —

INTERMITTENT STREAM —··—··—

9 MILE TRAIL

CANOE ACCESS

NORTH FORK ACCESS

ROUTE 54

CLINTON 7 MILES

CLINTON LAKE

N

0   1 MILE

37. Clinton Lake Recreational Area

37. Clinton Lake Recreational Area

Trail Length: 9 mile loop (14.5 kilometers)

Location: The trail, located within Clinton Lake Recreational Area, is approximately eight miles northeast of Clinton, thirty-five miles south of Bloomington, and thirty miles north of Decatur. From the east or west, Clinton Lake can be reached from Route 10.

To reach the trailhead, take Route 54 east out of Clinton for seven miles. A sign will be seen on Route 54 that says "North Fork Access Area." Turn north on this road, go over a set of railroad tracks, and follow the signs to the North Fork Access parking area.

County: De Witt

Illinois Highway Map Coordinates: G-7

U.S.G.S. Topographical Map Name and Scale: De Witt, 1:24,000

Hours Open: Clinton Lake Recreational Area is open year-round, except on Christmas Day and New Year's Day.

History and Trail Description: The controversial Clinton Lake Recreational Area was developed by the Illinois Department of Conservation (IDOC) in conjunction with the Illinois Power Company. It provides a water source for the nuclear power plant and is also designed to provide many recreation facilities for the citizens of Illinois. Presently (1984), the nuclear power plant is under construction, and many of the recreational facilities are still under proposal.

The trail described here follows the perimeter of the North Fork Canoe Area on Clinton Lake. The trail may also be started at the northern tip of the trail by the canoe access area parking lot.

The trail is newly developed and well marked with white blazes and blue ribbons on trees. Since the area is relatively new, the trail is infrequently hiked; this accounts for the trail being highly overgrown with vegetation, and at times difficult to locate.

It is highly recommended that hikers wear trousers as the vegetation can reach heights of three feet or more. Poison ivy and other plants which can cause skin irritations are found in abundance all along the trail.

Along this trail you will encounter steep hill grades, dense underbrush, dense woods, and open fields. Many footbridges exist on the trail and allow easy access over stream crossings. Many times the trail descends to lake level and then goes back into the woods on a ridge. You should pack your own water, as sources along the trail are inadequate for drinking.

Facilities: Restrooms, water, and parking facilities are available at the North Fork Access Area. A ranger station is located in the main park grounds on the lake, and additional information can be obtained there. Also available are a marina, several day-use areas with boat access, swimming, waterskiing, fishing, 135 campgrounds, and an Illinois Power Visitor's Center. All appropriate Illinois fishing rules and regulations are in effect. A trail has been proposed which, if built, will be along the southern half of the lake shore from Route 54 to the wildlife viewing platform on the northeast edge of the lake.

Permits Required: A camping permit is required.

Park Rules and Regulations: All pets must be on a leash. No swimming in streams or creeks. No groundfires permitted. Camping and cooking fires permitted in designated areas only. See Appendix A.

Mailing Address and Phone Number: Site Superintendent, Clinton Lake State Recreational Area, R.R. 1, Box 4, De Witt, Illinois 61735; 217/935-8722

38. Railsplitter State Park

Trail Length: 4 miles (6.4 kilometers)

Location: Railsplitter State Park is located two miles south of Lincoln and borders Salt Creek. The park also surrounds the Logan Correctional Center. To reach the park, exit Interstate 55 at Business 55 (exit 123) and proceed one mile to the state park sign. Turn right at the sign and go over the railroad tracks; the park is immediately to the left.

County: Logan

Illinois Highway Map Coordinates: G-6

U.S.G.S. Topographical Map Name and Scale: Broadwell, 1:24,000

Hours Open: The park is open every day of the year, except Christmas Day and New Year's Day. At certain times, due to freezing and thawing periods, the park may be closed and one must enter on foot.

History and Trail Description: The Department of Conservation initially acquired 741 acres of land from the Department of Mental Health. The following year, park development began; currently there are 751 acres of land in the park.

There are two trails in the park. The first is a short jogging trail located at the first parking facility. The other trail is a 4-mile multi-looped trail. The majority of the trail goes along Salt Creek and is known as the "Salt Creek Trail."

The trail can be reached from numerous points in the park. Maps of the park trail system can be obtained at the ranger's office, and trailboards are set up to show your location and the direction of the trail.

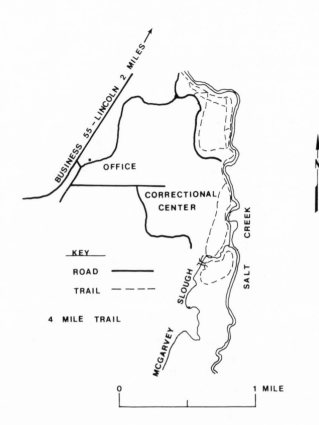

38. Railsplitter State Park

The trail can be started by the car-top boat launch. The trail then heads south, following Salt Creek and joining two other trail segments along the way. One of these trails branches west and parallels the park road, while the other trail parallels Salt Creek; this section of the trail may be inundated during the wet season. Both trails are about ten feet wide and during the winter months they are excellent ski trails.

The trail along Salt Creek soon branches west and parallels McGarvey Slough. The trail crosses a bridge, passes by a small picnic area and then makes a short loop back to the bridge.

Facilities: A ranger station located in the park offers additional information. Picnic tables, grills, restrooms, drinking water and shelters are also scattered throughout the park. A boat launch is also located in the park. Salt Creek can be fished for large- and smallmouth bass, bluegill, sunfish, crappie, catfish, bullheads, and carp. All appropriate Illinois fishing rules and regulations are in effect.

Park Rules and Regulations: No hunting allowed. See Appendix A.

Mailing Address and Phone Number: Site Superintendent, Railsplitter State Park, R.R. 3, Lincoln, Illinois 62656; 217/735-2424

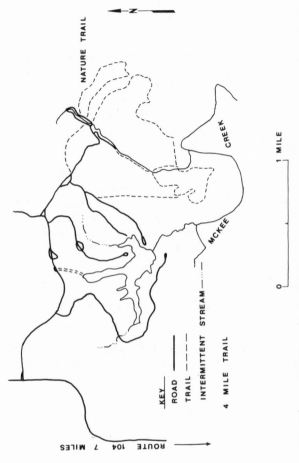

KEY

ROAD ——————
TRAIL — — — — —
INTERMITTENT STREAM ········

4 MILE TRAIL

NATURE TRAIL

MCKEE CREEK

ROUTE 104 7 MILES

N

0   1 MILE

39. Siloam Springs State Park

39. Siloam Springs State Park

Trail Length: 4 miles (6.4 kilometers)

Location: Siloam Springs State Park is located twenty-five miles east of Quincy and fifty-two miles west of Jacksonville off State Route 104. A state park sign on Route 104 points in the direction of the park. Turn north off Route 104 onto a gravel road, and the entrance to the park will be approximately seven miles down the road.

Counties: Adams, Brown

Illinois Highway Map Coordinates: H-2

U.S.G.S. Topographical Map Names and Scale: Kellerville and Fishhook, both 1:24,000

Hours Open: The park is open year-round except Christmas Day and New Year's Day. At certain times, due to freezing and thawing periods, the park is closed and access to the park is by foot only.

History and Trail Description: This area was part of the military tract of western Illinois. The land was acquired around 1852 by George Meyers, and it is thought that he claimed the land as a veteran for his service in the Black Hawk and Mexican wars. Shortly after the Civil War, the Rev. Reuben K. McCoy, a Presbyterian minister from Clayton, discovered the springs there. Quincy Burgesser, a Clayton businessman, analyzed the waters and thought that they might provide wonderful cures for all physical ailments. In 1884, Burgesser built the Siloam Forest Home Hotel, a bathing house, spring houses, and other facilities. As medical science advanced, there was a decline in the hotel business and the town. In 1935 the Siloam Springs Recreation Club purchased the site and tried to restore it to popularity. After 1940, the old hotel and bathhouses were torn down, the swimming pool was abandoned, and the springs were no longer used. Today, one can still see the sites of the hotel and springhouses while driving through the park. In 1940, the State of Illinois purchased 2,665 acres of land here. Currently there are over 3,230 acres in the park.

About 6 miles of trails are scattered throughout the park, with the main backpack trail being 4 miles. The trailhead begins at the east picnic area as soon as you go over an old steel bridge. Water bars help divert water from the trail. The trail, generally about seven feet wide, runs for about three miles on a ridge and through the woods. Backpack signposts, scattered on the trail about every quarter mile, show the distance walked. The trail crosses a stream about four times. During spring runoff, the water can be at a very high level.

At the trailhead, the trail immediately begins ascending a small hill. About two miles into the hike, an old abandoned house is seen along the trail. At 2.7 miles, you will reach the camping area. Some bathrooms and some forest tools in a tool shed are located at the camping spot. A permit must be secured from the ranger to camp at this site. Beyond the campsite, the trail connects with a wide trail that leads to the lake road. You can take this trail or turn east on the backpack trail, which leads to the trail end. The last mile of the trail goes through the woods, down a steep ridge, and across the stream a few times before connecting with an access road. At this point the road can be followed back to the trail head.

Facilities: A ranger station is located in the park to offer additional information and to issue camping permits. Shelters and playground equipment are scattered throughout the park. The park has over 160 sites available for tent, trailer and group camping. A sanitary station for trailers is nearby. Water and toilet facilities are also available. A concession stand is open during the summer months and provides boat rentals. A launching ramp and docks are available for private boats if there is enough space. The lake is stocked with large-mouthed bass, bluegill, sunfish, channel catfish, and trout. All appropriate fishing laws and regulations must be followed. Fifteen miles of equestrian trails are located in the park also.

Permits Required: A camping permit is required.

Park Rules and Regulations: No horses are allowed on the hiking trails. See Appendix A.

Mailing Address and Phone Number: Site Superintendent, Siloam Springs State Park, R.R.1, Clayton, Illinois 62324; 217/894-6205

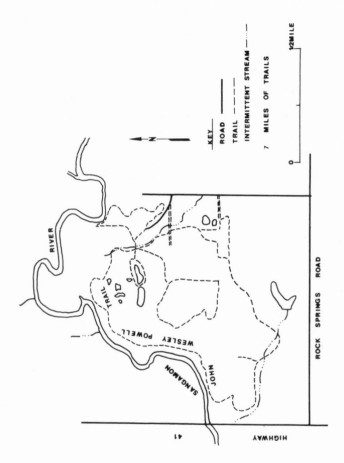

40. Rock Springs Center

40. Rock Springs Center

Trail Length: 7 miles (11.3 kilometers)

Location: Rock Springs Center is located on the southwest side of Decatur and borders the Sangamon River. The center can be reached by taking Interstate 72 to State Route 36 (Exit 30). Take Route 36 a few miles to County Highway 41. A Holiday Inn motel is situated on the corner of Route 36 and Highway 41. Proceed south on Highway 41 for about three miles and turn left at the Rock Springs Center sign. This is kown as Rock Springs Road. Go on this road for about one mile, then take a left and proceed to the park entrance.

County: Macon

Illinois Highway Map Coordinates: H-7

U.S.G.S. Topographical Map Name and Scale: Harristown, 1:24,000

Hours Open: Rock Springs Center is open year-round. The hiking trails are open Monday through Sunday from 8:00 a.m. until dusk. The Visitors' Center is open Monday through Sunday from 8:00 a.m. until 5:00 p.m.

History and Trail Description: Rock Springs Center is owned and operated by the Macon County Conservation District. It was formally opened in the mid-1970's. Prior to that time the land was held by a variety of owners, with the area being used for farming, for gravel operations, and as a dumping ground. The Center has now been set aside for the preservation of plants and animals and for education and various types of recreation compatible with the area. Currently the Center comprises 1,323 acres.

The Center's hiking trails consist of six interconnecting trails which total about 7 miles. The longest trail, about 5 miles, is called the John Wesley Powell Trail. This trail goes by the Sangamon River, a mill, a gravel pit, several ponds, and a viewing deck. At certain times of the year parts of this trail are under water.

Each trail has a trail sign for easy identification when hiking. Maps which show the locations and distances of the trails can be picked up at the Visitors' Center. The trails are all cleared and are about eight feet wide. Some areas of the trail become a single lane for a while. The trail system developed at this park can easily be walked by the whole family, although in some areas there are steep climbs. During the wet season the trails can become very muddy, so check with the Visitors' Center prior to going on the trail. The trails can also be used for cross-country skiing.

Facilities: Maps, water, toilets, and information are provided at the Visitors' Center. Only senior citizens may fish in the ponds. The Center has many programs throughout the year for the general public, including interpretive hikes and wagon tours, and demonstrations, such as ice-fishing and star gazing.

Park Rules and Regulations: Alcoholic beverages, firearms, horses, vehicles, pets and fires are not allowed on the trails. All plants and animals are protected and cannot be collected. Vehicles must use only marked roads and parking areas.

Mailing Address and Phone Number: Rock Springs Center for Environmental Discovery, 1495 Brozio Lane, Decatur, Illinois 62521; 217/423-7073

41. Robert Allerton Park

Trail Length: 15 miles (24 kilometers)

Location: Robert Allerton Park is located twenty-six miles southwest of Champaign and twenty-five miles east of Decatur. To reach the park, take Interstate 57 from the north or south to Interstate 72. Turn west on Interstate 72 and proceed to Exit 61 for Monticello. At the first road (State Route 47) turn right (west) and proceed a few miles until an Allerton Park sign is seen. Turn left (south) and follow the park signs to the entrance. Travelers coming from Decatur on Interstate 72 may turn at Exit 53 and head south to State Route 47. Turn east on this road and proceed on Route 47 to the park signs. Follow the signs to the park entrance.

County: Piatt

Illinois Highway Map Coordinates: H-7

U.S.G.S. Topographical Map Names and Scale: Cerro Gordo and Weldon East, both 1:24,000

Hours Open: The park is open daily from 10 a.m. until sunset.

History and Trail Description: Robert Allerton Park is a unique feature in the central Illinois landscape. The park consists of 1,500 acres of rolling hills, with landscaped gardens, statues, and a Georgian mansion.

Robert Allerton (1873–1964) donated the park to the University of Illinois in 1946. The gift included the 1,500 acres of woodland property which form the park, a twenty-room mansion used for conferences, 250 acres for the 4-H Memorial Camp, and 3,775 acres of land in eight farms whose income supports the park.

At the time Robert Allerton inherited the farms

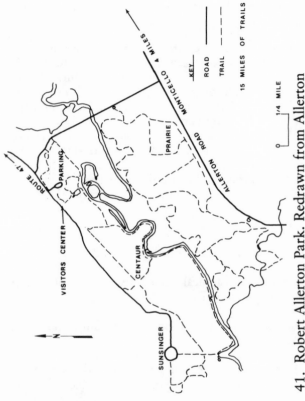

41. Robert Allerton Park. Redrawn from Allerton Park map.

from his father, the majority of the land was used for farming and grazing. The park as we see it today is the product of over seventy years of planning and development.

The Sangamon River divides Allerton Park into two sections. Houses, gardens and sculptures are set in the woodlands and meadows north of the river, while native forests and a 50-acre restored prairie can be seen by hiking or skiing the trails south of it.

The southern 1,000 acres of Allerton Park were designated as a National Natural Landmark in 1971. The floodplain forest and upland woods are excellent examples of native Illinois habitats. In this area identification of 1,032 species of flowering plants and 154 species of birds and mammals has been made.

The trail system at Allerton Park consists of hiking/skiing trails that wind their way on both sides of the Sangamon River. These trails total 15 miles, with about 7 miles of trails on the north side and 8 miles on the south of the river. The trails do not connect between the north and south; therefore, you would have to hike one side and move your vehicle to another location to start hiking the trails on the other side.

The trails are very wide, averaging about twelve feet. The trails are all dirt and very easy to follow. Trail maps are encased in metal cases and are found at most of the trail junctions and trailheads. These maps have arrows on them that identify your specific location.

The trails on the north side of the park may be started at numerous locations depending on where you park your vehicle. A good area from which to start hiking is the greenhouse, which is located close to the formal gardens. The Visitors' Center is inside the greenhouse. You can request trail maps and view a large trail map that is posted on the wall. In addition, you can purchase booklets on the park history and direct any questions to the person on duty.

Trails lead away from the gardens and head in many different directions. One set of trails takes the hiker by the Allerton House and eastward by some statues, such as "Trapper of Bear Cubs."

"Trapper of Bear Cubs," Robert Allerton Park

Another set of trails pass through the Formal Gardens and the Sunken Gardens. These gardens have a wide variety of beautiful flowers, bushes and statues. The Sunken Gardens is a large concrete-walled garden dug below ground level. From here the trail continues southwest towards the Centaur statue; another trail heads south towards the Sangamon River. Both of these trails lead through the woodlands of Allerton Park.

The trail leading down to the river heads west, paralleling the river for a long distance. As it lies within the floodplain, this trail may be inundated during wet weather. This trail connects with other trail segments which take the hiker to the Centaur and the Sunsinger statues.

In addition to these trails, you may hike the many loop trails on the north side of this park. You may also park near the Sunsinger statue and start hiking from that area.

The trails on the south side of the Sangamon River may be started at two different parking areas. The first parking area is located about two miles from Allerton House and may be found by going back out the road to the park entrance. Turn right (south) onto the road, cross the Sangamon River, and you will come to a parking area that is surrounded by a fence. The other parking area may be found by continuing down this road until you come to the T, where you join Allerton Road. Turn right and proceed until you come to the parking area on the right side.

The trails on the south side of the Sangamon River offer the most seclusion for the hiker. The area consists of woodlands and prairies. The interconnecting loop trails here wind through upland woods, through a stream valley, and above the bluffs overlooking the Sangamon River. The trail passes by the second parking area and goes over a few small bridges. Numerous birds and other wildlife may be observed while hiking the trails.

Facilities: Picnic areas, public telephones, drinking water, and restrooms are located adjacent to the main parking area near Allerton House. Restrooms and drinking water may also be found at the Visitors' Center in the greenhouse.

Park Rules and Regulations: Allerton House, other buildings in the park, and the 4-H Memorial Camp are used for conferences and camp sessions which require privacy. These facilities are not open to park visitors. Leash all dogs brought in the park. Alcoholic beverages and firearms are not allowed. Swimming is not permitted in the lakes or in Sangamon River. Do not disturb plant and animal life. Motorized vehicles are not allowed on the trails.

Mailing Address and Phone Number: Robert Allerton Park, R.R. 2, Monticello, Illinois 61856; 217/762-2721

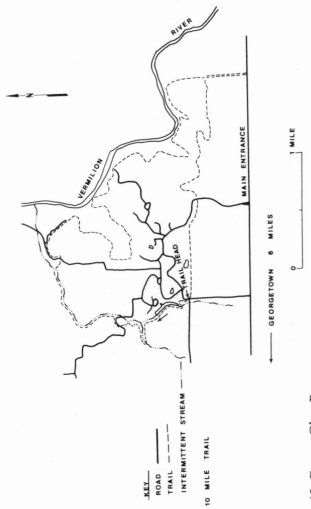

KEY

ROAD

TRAIL ------

INTERMITTENT STREAM ········

10 MILE TRAIL

N

VERMILION

RIVER

D

TRAIL HEAD

MAIN ENTRANCE

GEORGETOWN 6 MILES

0   1 MILE

42. Forest Glen Preserve

42. Forest Glen Preserve

Trail Length: 10 miles (16 kilometers)

Location: Forest Glen Preserve is located eleven miles south of Danville and six miles northeast of Georgetown. The Preserve borders the Vermilion River and the State of Indiana on the east. To reach the Preserve, take Mill Street east out of Georgetown for three miles to the Forest Glen sign. Turn left (north) onto the county road and proceed on this road for a mile. At the T junction (County Highway 27), turn right and go two miles to the preserve.

County: Vermilion

Illinois Highway Map Coordinates: H-10

U.S.G.S. Topographical Map Name and Scale: Danville S.E., 1:24,000

Hours Open: The preserve is open year-round from 8:00 a.m. to 8:00 p.m., and during the summer months from 8:00 a.m. to 10:00 p.m.

History and Trail Description: On June 16, 1966, a referendum was passed and a governing board of five trustees was appointed for the new Vermilion County Conservation District. The board quickly moved to purchase land, and in January, 1968, the first parcel of land was acquired for Forest Glen Preserve, which was opened in October of the same year. Forest Glen Preserve encompasses 1,800 acres and is considered an Illinois Nature Preserve. The Preserve has three miles of frontage along the Vermilion River, with countless species of plants and animals in the area.

The Preserve has twelve different hiking trails with the longest trail being the River Ridge Backpack Trail at

10 miles. Before hiking this trail, all hikers must register at the ranger station. The trailhead is located at the nature center parking lot.

The trail, which is marked very well with orange arrows, orange plates, or orange bands around the trees, goes clockwise around the park. The trail connects with many of the other trails in the park, and the hike may be shortened at a few locations. The trail varies in width from a single lane to a cleared path of eight feet. At times, the trail goes along the park road. The trail has many stairs, bridges, and water bars that must be crossed.

Little signposts are scattered along the first three miles of the trail, describing in general terms the plants, geology, and animals in the area. The trail goes past wooded ravines, grassy meadows, a restored tall grass prairie, several ponds, an environmental center, and an old cemetery. At about the halfway point of the hike, or at the river canoe access area, one can follow a road that leads up to an observation tower. The tower is seventy-two feet high and offers a great view of the preserve and the Vermilion River Valley.

The trail past the river canoe access area, until it meets the road again, is the most scenic and difficult section to hike. One must be in very good shape to hike this stretch of the trail. The trail goes up and down many steep ravines and crisscrosses many small streams and tributaries. The trail can be extremely wet and muddy during the rainy season, and one must be prepared for this.

If the entire trail is hiked in one day, allow a minimum of five hours to complete the trail. Tent camping is allowed at two locations along the trail. An appropriate camping permit must be secured before camping.

Facilities: Hiking, fishing, camping, and ice-fishing are some of the seasonal activities available. Picnicking is available with charcoal grills at each picnic site. A family campground offers forty-two campsites (twenty-eight with electricity), a central water supply, sanitary dumping station and restrooms. In addition, there is a tent camping area with eighteen tent sites and six group sites. Two fishing ponds are located on the grounds and have bass and channel catfish. There is an outdoor school to which 4th and 5th grade classes from schools around the county can come to study nature and conservation. Maps and other information can be obtained from the ranger station. A Visitors' Center on the grounds is open on weekends, Memorial Day through Labor Day, and has park information, exhibits, a bookstore, concessions, and restrooms.

Permits Required: A camping permit is required.

Park Rules and Regulations: No firearms, minibikes or unlicensed vehicles allowed in the park. No vehicles or horses on grass or hiking trails. No collecting of plant, animal or mineral specimens. No swimming in preserve waters. The observation tower is closed at dark, fires are allowed in designated areas only, and fishing anywhere in the Preserve is governed by Illinois rules and regulations. See Appendix C.

Mailing Address and Phone Number: Site Superintendent, Forest Glen Preserve, R.R. 1, Westville, Illinois 61833, 217/662-8028

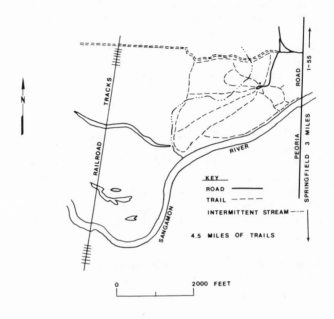

KEY

ROAD ————

TRAIL ————

INTERMITTENT STREAM ———

4.5 MILES OF TRAILS

0   2000 FEET

43. Carpenter Park

43. Carpenter Park

Trail Length: 4.5 miles (7.2 kilometers)

Location: Carpenter Park is located three miles north of Springfield. To reach the park from Interstate 55 southbound, exit off Peoria Road (exit 105) and go two miles to State Route 124. Turn right and go one block, following the signs straight ahead. If coming northbound on Interstate 55, exit at Sangamon Avenue and continue to Dirksen Parkway. Turn right at Dirksen Parkway and follow it to Peoria Road. Take a right and go on Peoria Road for one mile, cross the Sangamon River, and turn left on Route 124. Proceed ahead to the park.

County: Sangamon

Illinois Highway Map Coordinates: H-5

U.S.G.S. Topographical Map Names and Scale: Springfield West and East, both 1:24,000

Hours Open: The park is open all year (weather permitting) and hiking is allowed until sunset.

History and Trail Description: Carpenter Park is owned and operated by the Springfield Park District. The park was purchased by the Springfield Park District in 1921 and has been relatively untouched since then. In 1979, parts of the park were dedicated as a nature preserve under the Illinois Department of Conservation's Nature Preserve System.

The park displays both upland and floodplain forest, with rock outcrops along the Sangamon River. The uplands support black oak, with red oak and white oak on slopes and ravines. The floodplain supports silver maple, sycamore, scattered bur, oak, and hackberry.

The park trails comprise ten interconnecting trails

which total 4.5 miles. Most of the trails originate in the parking area. All of the trails are well marked, showing the trail name and the general direction of the trail. The trails go up and down the small hills in the park and over numerous small wooden bridges.

The Twisted Tree Trail starts from the parking lot, is about six feet wide, and narrows to a single lane which is hard to see. Twisted Tree Trail goes to the North Road Trail.

Canyon Trail, directly south of the parking lot, is a short trail that leads to the Sangamon River. This trail descends a canyon along a series of stairs, and follows a small creek to the river. During the wet season, this trail is extremely dangerous. Canyon Trail branches with the Hi-Point Trail to the east and the Wild Flower Trail at the Sangamon River.

The Wild Flower Trail connects with the Canyon Trail and parallels the river for a short distance. Since the trail is located in the floodplain, this section may be inundated during the wet season. Do not attempt to walk this trail when the water level is rising. This trail connects with the River View Trail which can be hiked to other trails in the park. All, trails in the park, except for the Canyon and Hi-Point Trails, are excellent for cross-country skiing in the winter.

Facilities: A parking lot accommodates about twenty cars. There is a picnic shelter with two fireplaces. There are restrooms but no drinking water; all water must be brought in. Do not drink any water out of creeks in the park.

Park Rules and Regulations: Motorcycles, firearms, horses, weapon devices, ground fires, and camping are all prohibited in the park. It is illegal to take any plants or trees. See Appendix C.

Mailing Address and Phone Number: Springfield Park District, 2500 South 11th Street, P.O. Box 5052, Springfield, Illinois 62705; 217/544-1751

44. Lincoln Memorial Garden

Trail Length: 5 miles (8.05 kilometers)

Location: This trail system is located on the southeast side of Lake Springfield in Springfield. To reach the Garden, southbound traffic should exit off Interstate 55 at Stevenson Drive (exit 94) and proceed eastbound on East Lake Drive for six miles. Northbound traffic on Interstate 55 can exit at the Chatham exit (exit 88) and go eastbound on East Lake Drive for about three miles. Parking is located right in front of the Gardens off of East Lake Drive.

County: Sangamon

Illinois Highway Map Coordinates: H-5

U.S.G.S. Topographical Name and Scale: New City, 1:24,000

Hours Open: The grounds are open every day of the year. Hiking is allowed from sunrise to sunset. The nature center's hours are Monday through Saturday 10:00 a.m. to 4:00 p.m. and Sunday from 1:00 p.m. until 5:00 p.m.

History and Trail Description: Lake Springfield is the water supply for the residents of Springfield and the surrounding communities, and it also provides recreational activities, such as fishing, hiking, boating and swimming.

In 1932, while Lake Springfield was being dammed and filled, Mrs. T. J. Knudson, a member of the Garden Club of Illinois, requested that the city set aside a portion of land to be developed as a living memorial to Abraham Lincoln. At the time, the surrounding area was farmland with barely a dozen trees. The Garden

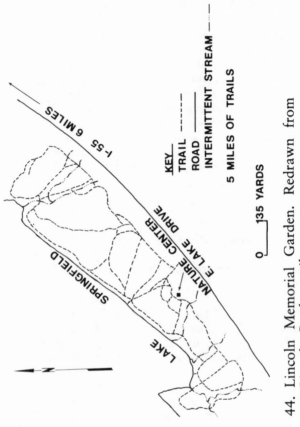

KEY
TRAIL -------
ROAD ━━━━━
INTERMITTENT STREAM ——

5 MILES OF TRAILS

0 ⌐35 YARDS

44. Lincoln Memorial Garden. Redrawn from
Lincoln Garden trail map.

Club of Illinois began planting trees in the Garden in 1932. They used shrubs, plants and trees which are native to Illinois. Today the Garden's hills are covered with maples, hickories, oaks, sweet gum, coffee tree, red bud, white dogwood, plum shad, and silver bell. The Garden is maintained by volunteers and relies on contributions. It consists of about 80 acres.

The Garden's trail system comprises eighteen interconnecting trails which total about 5 miles. All of the trails are well defined, with signposts naming each trail. The trails are all fairly easy to walk, with the longest trail (Lake Trail) being about a half mile. The trails are all well cleared, made of dirt, and are about seven feet wide. The trails go over small wooden bridges and by Lake Springfield.

The Witch Hazel Trail has a set of stairs that have to be climbed. Some of the trails are on gently rolling hills leading down to the lake. Some spots on the trails in low areas can be quite muddy in the rainy season and have water bars to help divert the water from the trail. The trail system is also an excellent area for cross-country skiing in the winter.

Facilities: A nature center is located on the grounds. The center has maps and other general information about the Garden. The center serves groups that come for field trips, and it provides office space, areas for exhibits, Sunday family programs and craft instruction. Water, soda machines, and restrooms are all located inside the nature center. A bicycle rack is located at the entrance to the park to lock your bikes.

Park Rules and Regulations: No picnicking, picking flowers, pets, bicycles, swimming, motorcycles, horses, snowmobiles, alcohol or fishing are allowed on the grounds.

Mailing Address and Phone Number: Lincoln Memorial Garden, 2301 East Lake Drive, Springfield, Illinois 62707; 217/529-1111

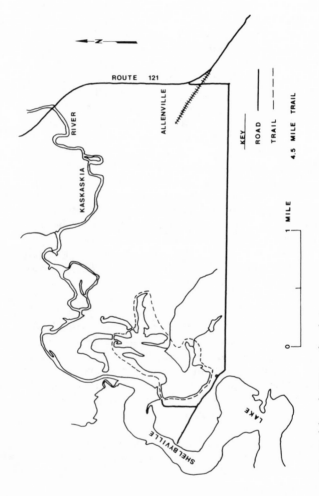

45. Fishhook Waterfowl Area

45. Fishhook Waterfowl Area

Trail Length: 4.5 miles (7.2 kilometers)

Location: Fishhook Waterfowl Area is part of the Kaskaskia Fish and Wildlife Area and is approximately ten miles southeast of Sullivan and three miles west of Allenville. To reach Fishhook Area, State Route 121 may be taken northwest out of Mattoon or east out of Sullivan. At the southern edge of Allenville, a paved road heads west. Turn west on this road, go over the railroad tracks and proceed for three miles. At about two and a half miles you will run into another road that heads north. Turn right on this gravel road and proceed to the parking area. The road is a dead end at this point.

County: Moultrie

Illinois Highway Map Coordinates: I-8

U.S.G.S. Topographical Map Name And Scale: Sullivan, 1:24,000

Hours Open: The park is open year-round.

History and Trail Description: Lake Shelbyville is an 11,000-acre impoundment between Shelbyville and Sullivan. The lands in this area are managed by the Corps of Engineers and the Department of Conservation for various recreation purposes. Lake Shelbyville is situated along the Kaskaskia and West Okaw rivers.

In the upper reaches of Lake Shelbyville are two separate wildlife units: Kaskaskia and West Okaw. The 3,700-acre Kaskaskia Unit is located along the Kaskaskia River; the 2,700-acre West Okaw Unit lies along the West Okaw River.

The trail at Fishhook starts at the parking area and boat launch. A trailboard is set up just west of the parking area. The trailboard shows the trail layout and the location of items, such as benches and bridges, that will be seen along the trail.

The trail, called the Fishook Trail, measures 4.5 miles, and is marked with wooden posts illustrated with a picture of a hiker. The trail is a mowed path about eight feet wide. At times old roads and farm roads join with the trail; therefore, hikers must keep an eye out for the trail markers to avoid getting lost. The trail goes around the water in the Fishhook Area, which is visible almost the entire length of the trail.

The trail, which goes in a counterclockwise direction, starts out by going through a small stand of woods on top of very small bluffs. From here you will see the parking lot at the entrance. Continue through this parking lot and then onto a gravel path. This path takes the hiker to an observation platform which overlooks the waterfowl area. The trail continues in a easterly direction, passing some shrub growth and farm plots on the east side of the trail.

Soon you will pass by a small pond named Lost Pond. The trail then goes west and continues into a denser forest. The hiker will go over some small wooden bridges and will follow the trail to the lake and a levee.

You will have to cross this levee and continue along the path on the other side. The trail passes close by another parking area, and from here you will have to cross another levee that goes across part of the water. This levee may be covered by water, and therefore impassable, during the wet season.

Beyond this levee the trail turns south, paralleling the Kaskaskia River. The trail continues through wooded areas and a few open fields. The trail then descends a small hill, leading to the water again. Here you will have to cross another levee. Once past this last levee, you will be at the parking area and trailhead.

Facilities: Fishook Waterfowl Area has a trailboard, a restroom, and a boat launch. Fishing is allowed anywhere in the area with all Illinois fishing rules and regulations in effect. Hunting is also permitted in the area in accordance with statewide regulations.

Permits Required: Dog training and trapping are regulated by permit.

Park Rules and Regulations: Camping is not allowed in this area. See Appendix A.

Mailing Address and Phone Number: Site Superintendent, Shelbyville Fish and Wildlife Area, R.R. 1, Box 42-A, Bethany, Illinois 61914; 217/665-3112

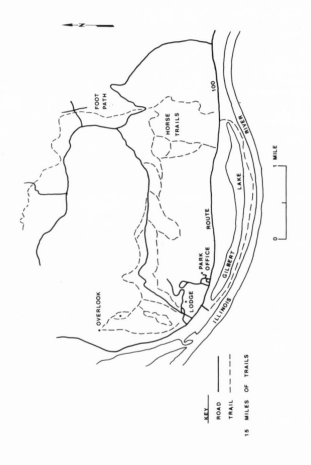

46. Pere Marquette State Park. Redrawn from park map.

46. Pere Marquette State Park

Trail Length: Various trails totaling 15 miles (24 kilometers)

Location: Pere Marquette State Park is located five miles west of Grafton on State Route 100, and twenty-five miles northwest of Alton. The park has many bluffs which overlook the Illinois River and offers many diversified forms of recreation.

County: Jersey

Illinois Highway Map Coordinates: K-3

U.S.G.S. Topographical Map Names and Scale: Grafton, Brussels and Nutwood, all 1:24,000

Hours Open: The park is open every day of the year except Christmas Day and New Year's Day. At certain times, the park may be closed due to freezing and thawing of the roads.

History and Trail Description: This park was named in memory of Father Jacques Marquette, a French Jesuit missionary priest. In 1673, Father Marquette and explorer Louis Jolliet were the first Europeans to enter what is now Illinois at the confluence of the Mississippi and Illinois rivers. A large white cross east of the park entrance along Route 100 marks where these two men landed.

In 1932, the State acquired the 2,605-acre park and adjoining 2,574-acre conservation area. They were combined into the Pere Marquette State Park by legislative action in 1967. Later acquisitions brought the park to its present total of 8,000 acres, making it the largest state park in Illinois.

The park's trail system comprises six interconnecting hiking/horseback riding trails that vary in length from a half mile to over 6 miles in length. Most of the trails begin at the Visitors' Center parking lot. At the Visitors' Center there is a signpost which shows an outline of each of the trails. The trails are all color-coded. The following is a list of some trail lengths and colors: Ridge Trail, .5 miles, green; Dogwood Nature Trail, .7 miles, blue; Goat Cliff Trail, 2 miles, orange; Hickory Trail, 6 miles, red; Horse Trail, 2 + miles, white. Most of the trails average about seven feet in width and some have benches along the trails. The trail markers consist of two holes in a tree which are colored accordingly.

The Goat Cliff Trail, Hickory Trail, and parts of the Horse Trail follow the ridges in the park. Beautiful views of the Illinois River and its backwaters can be seen from overlooks located on these trails. Goat Cliff Overlook is located on McAdam's Peak. The overlook was built in 1934 by the State of Illinois. At this point the peak is 791 feet above sea level and 372 feet above the Illinois River. A marker on this overlook describes the history of the state park and the area.

A horse trail also winds its way between Gilbert Lake and the Illinois River. Caution must be used before hiking this trail, since it may be flooded at times.

A separate hiking trail exists at the north end of the park. This trail may be started off the park road at the east end and goes northeast to the north part of the park. The trail, a single-lane path, is infrequently used, and many areas are overgrown with vegetation. The hiking path is marked with white paint blazes on the trees.

Facilities: A park office is located in the park offering maps, brochures and other general information. The park has an amphitheater which offers camp-fire programs and a boat harbor. Camping for tents and trailers offers electricity, restrooms, shower facilities and a trailer dump. There are also a lodge and cabins (reservation suggested) and picnic areas with water, playground equipment and stables for horseback riding.

Fishing is permitted on the Illinois River, contingent upon Illinois rules and regulations.

Permits Required: A camping permit is required.

Park Rules and Regulations: See Appendix A.

Mailing Address and Phone Number: Site Superintendent, Pere Marquette State Park, Box 325, Grafton, Illinois 62037; 618/786-3637

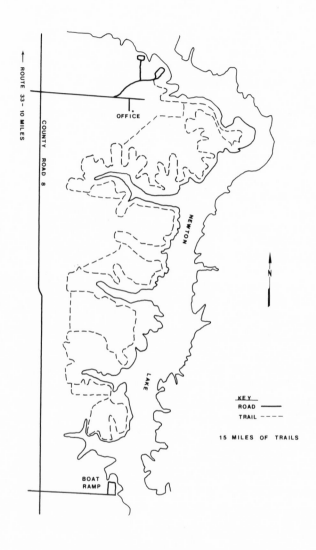

47. Newton Lake Conservation Area. Redrawn from Newton Lake map.

47. Newton Lake Conservation Area

Trail Length: 15 miles (24 kilometers)

Location: Newton Lake Conservation Area is located on the west side of Newton Lake. The park is located ten miles southwest of Newton and twenty-five miles southeast of Effingham. To reach the park, take State Route 33 out of Effingham. Fifteen miles out of Effingham there is a sign to turn south on County Road 8. Proceed on this road for ten miles, following the signs to the park entrance.

County: Jasper

Illinois Highway Map Coordinates: K-8

U.S.G.S. Topographical Map Name and Scale: Sailor Springs, 1:24,000

Hours Open: The park is open every day of the year except for Christmas Day and New Year's Day. The park closes at 10:00 p.m. daily.

History and Trail Description: Newton Lake was impounded by the Central Illinois Public Service Company (CIPS) to provide water for its Newton electric power generating plant. In 1979, the Illinois Department of Conservation (IDOC) signed a twenty-five year lease with CIPS which designates the 1,755-acre Newton Lake and 540 acres of shoreland as a day-use conservation area. By agreement, recreational activities in the area consist of bank and boat fishing, picnicking, hiking, and horseback riding. CIPS financed the initial recreational development of the area.

The trail system consists of a 15-mile hiking/horseback riding trail. The trail starts at a horse trail parking lot at the north access area. A trailboard there shows the trail layout along with an arrow pointing to the direction of the trailhead. The trail is well marked with metal poles that have arrows indicating the direction of the trail and orange ribbons hanging from trees.

The trail parallels the lake and its coves for more than ten miles. The trail also winds around grasslands and along fields. Animals, such as whitetail deer, Canada geese, mallards, blue heron, and pintails, may be observed when hiking. The trail is about six feet wide and is mowed to keep it clear. Generally on flat land, the trail does go up and down in some areas. At a few points, the trail crosses intermittent streams, which can be fairly high during the wet season. Benches are located on the trail at about 3 and 7 miles, where the trail intersects the lake. In addition, at mile 7 there is a wooden platform on the lake that can be used as a fishing pier. At about 4.5 miles the hiker will come across a junk pile scattered around the trail.

The hiker has the option of returning on different loops so that the hike can be reduced in length if desired; the six return loops are all clearly marked. The most scenic and forested areas on the trail are located on the second half of the trail. The return loops generally pass through open grasslands with little shade available.

Facilities: A site office is located in the park to provide information. Currently, there are no concessions or rental services available at the site. Water is available at the site office and toilets are located by the parking area. There are no camping facilities at Newton Lake; primitive camping may be found at Sam Parr State Park which is sixteen miles from the lake, and there is a private campground about four miles south of the dam.

Park Rules and Regulations: Swimming, camping, ice-fishing and hunting are prohibited. See Appendix A.

Mailing Address and Phone Number: Site Superintendent, Newton Lake Conservation Area, R.R. 4, Newton, Illinois 62448; 618/783-3478

PART IV

Hiking Trails in Southern Illinois

SOUTHERN ILLINOIS

48. Beall Woods State Park
49. Washington County Conservation Area
50. Pyramid State Park
51. Kinkaid Lake Trail
52. Giant City State Park
53. Cedar Lake Trail
54. Garden of the Gods
55. Ferne Clyffe State Park
56. Bell Smith Springs Recreation Area
57. River-to-River Trail
58. Beaver Trail
59. Heron Pond Little Black Slough Nature Preserve

Figure 4. Hiking trails in southern Illinois

48. Beall Woods State Park

Trail Length: 8 miles of interconnecting trails (12.9 kilometers)

Location: Beall Woods State Park is located three miles east of Keensburg and six miles south of Mt. Carmel. The southeastern edge of the park borders the Wabash River. To reach the park, take State Route 1 south out of Mt. Carmel or north out of Carmi. In Keensburg a sign points to the direction of the park. Turn east and proceed down a gravel road for three miles, following the signs to the park entrance.

Illinois Highway Map Coordinates: L-10

County: Wabash

U.S.G.S. Topographical Map Name and Scale: Keensburg, 1:24,000

Hours Open: The park is open year-round except on Christmas Day and New Year's Day. At certain times, due to freezing and thawing periods, the park is closed and access to the park is by foot only.

History and Trail Description: The state park derives its name from the Beall family that owned the land from 1861 to 1962. Beall Woods is the only sizable, near-virgin deciduous forest left in Illinois. The stand has several distinct forest sites, ranging from well-drained, rolling uplands, to low areas subject to frequent flooding and standing water. The area has over sixty-four species of trees and over one hundred different birds. Many large sycamores grow in the bottomland area, with some sycamores, shumard's oak, bur oak, and big shellbark hickory trees measuring over three feet in diameter. On one of the trails you can view the largest Shumard

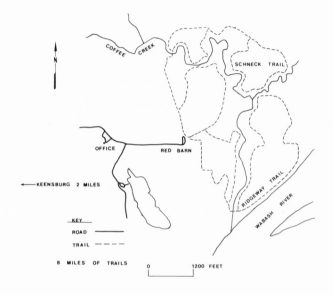

COFFEE CREEK

SCHNECK TRAIL

OFFICE

RED BARN

←— KEENSBURG 2 MILES

RIDGEWAY TRAIL

WABASH RIVER

KEY

ROAD ———

TRAIL – – – –

8 MILES OF TRAILS

0   1200 FEET

48. Beall Woods State Park. Redrawn from park map.

Red Oak tree in the United States. The tree is over 150 years old and measures 16.5 feet in circumference.

The state initially purchased the property for $287,000 from Mr. James Bower in 1965. Mr. Bower had threatened to clear the land of trees and farm the area. A group of conservationists then persuaded the state to buy the land and preserve it in its natural state. The Bower family did get to keep its mineral rights; some of their oil wells may be observed from the Ridgeway Trail. A coal mine extends underneath Beall Woods and the Wabash River. The coal company is mining only forty percent of the coal under the park, leaving the remaining coal columns to support the forest to lessen the chance of land subsidance.

The current acreage in the park is 635; 329 acres of this property lie within the Illinois Nature Preserves and is registered as a National Natural Landmark. The United States Register of National Landmarks lists the landmark as the "Forest of the Wabash."

The trail system in Beall Woods consists of five interconnecting trails that measure 8 miles. Each trail has a particular name and is marked with a distinctive symbol. All trails can be started at the Red Barn Nature Center. The Schneck trail has been closed by the park because a sizable population of pileated woodpeckers thrives there, and the state wants to protect the woodpecker from human encroachment.

A trailboard behind the Red Barn Nature Center shows the trail layout. Each trail is well marked with a wooden post which has the trail name and the trail symbol carved on it.

All the trails are about eight feet in width and well traveled. The trails are located in the nature preserve; therefore, no pets, food, or drinks are allowed on the trail. All the trails are to be hiked in the direction indicated on the map.

The White Oak Trail has an oak leaf for its symbol, the Tulip Tree Trail, a tulip, the Sweet Gum Trail, a sweetgum leaf, and the Ridgeway Trail, a cardinal.

All of the trails are fairly short and easy to follow. The Tulip Trail measures 1.5 miles and follows the edge of a small rock cliff with Coffee Creek in the valley. From the Tulip Trail, you may join the Sweetgum Trail by crossing Coffee Creek at Rocky Ford and climbing some stairs. During the wet season, crossing at Rocky Ford may be dangerous due to high water. The Sweet Gum Trail parallels Coffee Creek for a short distance and has some nice views of rock outcrops. This trail intersects with the Schneck Trail, currently closed, and then circles back to Rocky Ford. From here the trail can be hiked back to the Red Barn, where more trails may be reached.

The White Oak Trail begins as a loop off of the Tulip Tree Trail. This trail offers the greatest variety of vegetation and forest conditions. Many large trees may be seen in the valley floor from this trail. The Ridgeway Trail then connects with the White Oak Trail. Some stairs must be climbed and then a small bridge must be crossed on this trail. You will hike by the largest Shumard Red Oak tree in the United States off of the Ridgeway Trail. The trail then loops back to the junction of the White Oak Trail.

Facilities: A site superintendent's office is located on the grounds to offer additional information. Picnic areas, water, park stoves, and restrooms are provided near the Red Barn and the park lake. A boat launch is located on the lake and fishing is allowed contingent upon Illinois fishing rules and regulations. The Red Barn Nature Center has materials for the public, old pictures of the site, and displays of plants and animals that may be seen at the park.

Park Rules and Regulations: No pets, food or drinks allowed on any of the trails. No camping allowed at the park. See appendixes A and C.

Mailing Address and Phone Number: Site Superintendent, Beall Woods State Park, R.R. 2, Mt. Carmel, Illinois; 618/298-2442

49. Washington County Conservation Area

Trail Length: 7 mile loop (11.3 kilometers)

Location: Washington County Conservation Area is located four miles south of Nashville. To reach the park, north—and southbound traffic may take State Route 127. Four miles south of Nashville a sign on Route 127 points to the park. Turn east on a gravel road and proceed for one mile to the park entrance.

County: Washington

Illinois Highway Map Coordinates: L-6

U.S.G.S. Topographical Map Name and Scale: Beaucoup, 1:24,000

Hours Open: The park is open all year except on Christmas Day and New Year's Day. At certain times, due to freezing and thawing periods, the park is closed and access to the park is by foot only.

History and Trail Description: In 1959 the State of Illinois acquired 160 acres that is now known as Washington County Conservation Area. One year later Washington County Lake was built; it covers 248 acres, with a maximum depth of twenty-five feet and a shoreline of 13.3 miles. The area varies in its abundance of cover, with fallow fields, stands of hardwood timber, pine stands, and small cultivated fields. Current acreage in the park is now over 1,417 acres.

The park trail, a 7-mile loop known as the Wacca Lake Trail, can be started west of the concession stand. A parking lot and boat launch area are located at the concession stand. A wooden sign south of the boat launch reads, "Wacca Lake Trail." The trail is marked with white wooden rectangles nailed onto trees and fences. These trail markers are very scarce during the

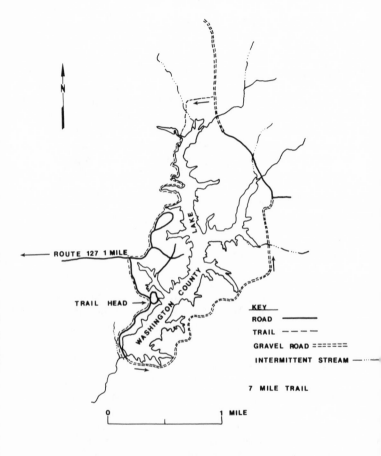

49. Washington County Conservation Area

first few miles of the trail since the trail follows the park road.

The trail goes counterclockwise around the lake following the park road for the first five miles. Shortly after starting the trail, you will walk by the dam and see the entire lake. After three and a half miles you will go past a gate and continue on a dirt road. At the northern tip of the lake the trail leaves the road and starts into the woods. At this point you will see trail markers.

The trail through the woods is a single lane and is used infrequently. The trail goes up and down small hills through the woods and crosses a few creeks. One of the creeks has a wooden pole placed across it with a steel cable for a handrail. You should be very cautious when using this pole: the cable swings very easily and could leave you in the creek.

The trail parallels the lake and offers some beautiful views. The trail eventually meanders to the Shady Rest Camping Area. At this point, the trail comes out of the forest and follows the road in the camping area back to the park entrance. From here, you can go back to the starting point, following the park road.

Facilities: A park office on the grounds offers additional information. The park has several picnic sites that have tables, grills, drinking water, restrooms and, playground equipment. A concession stand is located on the lake and offers food, drinks, and fishing tackle; it also rents boats. Hunting is permitted only in restricted areas. Tent and trailer camping is available in the park, along with electricity, a trailer disposal area, and a shower building. Fishing is allowed in the lake with all Illinois fishing laws and regulations in effect.

Permits Required: A camping permit is required.

Park Rules and Regulations: No fishing off of the docks. See Appendix A.

Mailing Address and Phone Number: Site Superintendent, Washington County Conservation Area, R.R. 3, Nashville, Illinois 62263; 618/327–3137

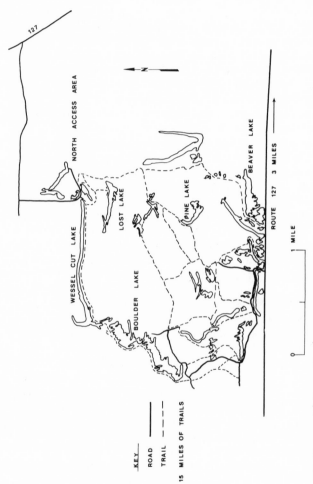

KEY

ROAD

TRAIL

15 MILES OF TRAILS

50. Pyramid State Park

50. Pyramid State Park

Trail Length: 15 miles (24.2 kilometers)

Location: Pyramid State Park is located six miles southwest of Pinckneyville. To reach the main park entrance, north and south traffic may take State Route 127. A sign for the park is located three miles south of Pinckneyville. Turn west on this road and go approximately three miles to the park entrance.

Trails may also be reached from the north access area. To reach the north access area, go two miles north of the park road on Route 127 to a gravel road. Turn west on this road, go over a set of railroad tracks, pass by a coal company building and proceed for one and a half miles to the park entrance. There is a sign as soon as you cross the railroad tracks which says "Pyramid State Park, North Area."

County: Perry

Illinois Highway Map Coordinates: M-6

U.S.G.S. Topographical Map Name and Scale: Pinckneyville, 1:24,000

Hours Open: The park is open all year except on Christmas Day and New Year's Day. At certain times, due to freezing and thawing periods, the park is closed and access to the park is by foot only. The park closes at 10:00 p.m. except to campers.

History and Trail Description: Pyramid State Park gets its name from one of the major coal companies in Perry County that was strip-mining land in this area. The park was formerly used as Southern Illinois University's Research Area. In 1965, the State of Illinois acquired 1,600 acres of land and have since increased the acreage to over 2,528 acres.

The park features rough topography with multiple ridges and cuts that resulted from mining operations between 1930 and 1950. Numerous lakes and ponds were created by the strip-mining opeation; these vary in size from .01 to 24 acres, and include over 135 acres of water. The park is now heavily wooded with cottonwood, box elder, sycamore, small oak, and hickory trees.

The trail system in the park consists of an 8-mile backpack trail and 7 miles of additional trails. The park board states that the backpack trail measures 10 miles; our measurement differs. The main trailheads for the backpack trail may be started at the east end or the west end of the park, or from short connecting trails in the center of the park. At the west end the trail may be found at the first camping area as you enter the park. The eastern part of the trail may be found by going back out of the park and going east for two blocks and parking in the area of Little Beaver Lake.

Horseback riders may also ride on parts of the backpack trail. Some of the sections of the trails are off limits to horses and are marked accordingly.

The trail at both ends is well marked with a wooden trailboard bearing the trail name and length. The trail is about eight feet wide and generally follows mine spoil ridge tops. It offers some beautiful views of the numerous small ponds and lakes in the park. The trails in the center of the park are all well marked with wooden posts bearing the name and direction of the trail.

If you start hiking the trail from the east end, you will come across another trail that, within three miles, intersects with the east end trail. This trail, which goes west and passes by Pine Lake, is a loop trail centered in the park. From here one can hike around numerous small lakes and pick up other connecting trails to go to other areas in the park.

Shortly after the trail intersection, the trail passes Beehive Lake, which is at the north park access. A side trail off the main trail leads past Beehive Lake and to the road in the north access area.

Lost Lake is to the south, and a connecting trail

takes you to this lake. Soon you will see Wesslen Cut Lake from the north side of the trail. The trail parallels this lake for about one and a half miles.

The trail then goes between Boulder Lake and Wesslen Cut Lake, paralleling the west side of Boulder Lake. Close to the south end of Boulder Lake, the trail crosses the park road and goes by Pine Grove Picnic Area. A shelter, picnic tables and restrooms are available here. Beyond Pine Grove Picnic Area, the trail passes by an open field and goes to the campground on the west side of the park.

There is no designated camping along the backpack trail, but there are numerous hike-in campsites available in the center of the park.

Facilities: A park office located in the park has additional information. Many picnic areas, which have tables, restrooms and stoves, are scattered through the park. Over 100 tent and trailer campsites are in the park. Water is available at the park office. There are also boat launches on the larger lakes. Fishing is allowed on any of the lakes in the park contingent upon all Illinois fishing rules and regulations. Horse trail parking is located west of the park office.

Restrooms, picnic tables, grills, a boat launch and camping facilities are available at the north access area.

Permits Required: A camping permit is required.

Park Rules and Regulations: No vehicles on the trails. Horse camping area is restricted to horse campers only. No horses are allowed at the north end of the park. Horses must stay on the trails and are not permitted on or along roads, except where the trail crosses the park road. Camping is permitted only in designated areas. Ten is the maximum horsepower on the lakes. Swimming, diving and bathing in the lakes are prohibited. No fires are permitted on the ground. See Appendix A.

Mailing Address and Phone Number: Site Superintendent, Pyramid State Park, R. R. 1, 115-A, Pinckneyville, Illinois 62274; 618/357-2574

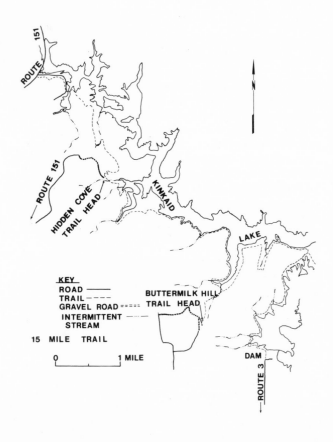

51. Kinkaid Lake Trail

51. Kinkaid Lake Trail

Trail Length: 15 miles (24 kilometers)

Location: Kinkaid Lake is located west of Murphysboro. The trail may be started either at the southern end next to the dam or at Johnson Creek Recreation Area off State Route 151. To reach the dam area, take State Route 149 west out of Murphysboro for six miles. There is a turnoff to the north just beyond Kinkaid Creek. Follow this gravel road to the parking area by the dam and spillway. To reach Johnson Creek Recreation Area, continue on Route 149 to the junction of Route 3. Turn north on Route 3 and proceed to State Route 151. Turn north on Route 151 and proceed for four miles to the site entrance.

County: Jackson

Illinois Highway Map Coordinates: N-6

U.S.G.S. Topographical Map Names and Scale: Oraville and Raddle, both 1:24,000

Shawnee Sportsman Maps: T.8S., R.4W., T.8S., R.3W., and T.9S., R.3W.

Hours Open: Hiking is permitted from sunrise to 10:00 p.m. Johnson Creek Campground is open year-round. Picnicking is permitted from sunrise to 10:00 p.m. The beach is open between 10:00 a.m. and 7:00 p.m.

History and Trail Description: Johnson Creek Recreation is the newest campground facility opened by the U.S. Forest Service in the Shawnee National Forest. The site was opened in 1981 and offers many recreation opportunities for the public. Kinkaid Lake has a surface area of approximately 3,000 acres and a shoreline of 81 miles. The lake's main purposes are to supply water and to provide recreation. Prior to the lake being impounded, the land was primarily cropland, grasslands, and woodlands.

The main hiking trail parallels Lake Kinkaid from Johnson Creek Recreation Area all the way to the dam.

This trail, the Kinkaid Lake Trail, is marked with white diamonds painted on trees at a height of about six feet. The trail is basically a footpath, but at times it joins old roads.

If you hike the entire trail in one direction, you will have to shuttle a vehicle to the other end; or, you camp along the trail and return on the same route the following day. To reduce the length of the trail, the U.S. Forest Service set up two areas along the trail where you may leave a vehicle or arrange to be picked up. The two other trailheads are called the Hidden Cove Trailhead and the Buttermilk Hill Trailhead. To get to the Hidden Cove Trailhead parking areas, take Route 151 south out of Johnson Creek Recreation Area. Go for two miles until a hiker sign is seen. Turn east and follow the signs to the parking area. To reach the Buttermilk Hill Trail parking area, take Route 151 south to Route 3. Turn east on Route 3 and proceed for three miles until another hiker sign is seen. Turn north on a gravel road and proceed for one and a half miles to the parking area. The trail distance from Johnson Creek Recreation Area to Hidden Cove Trailhead is 3.2 miles; from Johnson Creek Recreation Area to Buttermilk Hill Trailhead is 9.2 miles.

The trailhead at Johnson Creek Recreation Area may be started at the beach area or the tent camping area. Both locations have parking areas. From the hike-in campground parking area the trail crosses a small wooden bridge over Johnson Creek. The trail goes by the eastern edge of the hike-in camping area and then into the woods.

The trail from Johnson Creek Recreation Area to Hidden Cove Trailhead goes through upland woodlands and past some open fields. The trail passes many old roads and jeep trails in this area. Caution must be used when hiking this area because it is very easy to lose the trail and start hiking an unmarked section. There is a trailboard with a map at the Hidden Cove Trailhead.

From here the trail goes to Lake Kinkaid and parallels the lake all the way to the dam. The trail goes up and down many hills and over many small creeks. Many rock formations, as well as some beautiful views of the lake, may be seen. The trail at many points goes to the lake shore and offers the hiker a nice spot to dip his hat to cool off. In addition, the hiker may wish to bring along a fishing pole. Fishing is available in the many small coves and streams.

Five and a half miles from the Hidden Cove Trailhead, you will see a wooden sign pointing to the direction of Buttermilk Hill Trailhead and Buttermilk Hill Beach. The trail can be hiked to Buttermilk Hill Beach, passing by many beautiful coves and offering some good views of the lake. Prior to reaching the beach, the trail parallels the bluffs above the lake. The trail spur becomes part of a road and goes downhill to the beach area. Beyond the beach, the trail continues along the shores of the lake a few miles to the dam and spillway. From the dam, the trail continues down the hill and finally to the parking lot below the spillway.

Facilities: Johnson Creek Recreation Area has numerous picnic facilities, a boat launching area, a beach, restrooms and water. There are forty-three single camping units, eleven double units, nine triple units, and twelve hike-in camping units. Fishing is allowed on Lake Kinkaid, contingent upon Illinois fishing rules and regulations.

Buttermilk Hill Beach has picnic tables, restrooms, and garbage cans. Lifeguard services are not available. No pets, food, camping or beverages are allowed by the beach area.

Permits Required: A camping permit is required.

Park Rules and Regulations: Primitive camping is permitted anywhere on the hiking trail. All pets must be kept on a leash. See Appendix B.

Mailing Address and Phone Number: District Ranger, U.S. Forest Service, 2221 Walnut, P.O. Box AA, Murphysboro, Illinois 62966; 618/687-1731

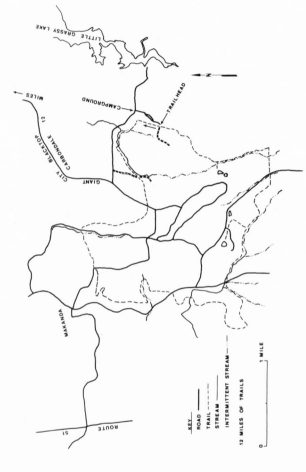

52. Giant City State Park

52. Giant City State Park

Trail Length: 12 mile loop trail (19 kilometers)

Location: Giant City State Park is located twelve miles south of Carbondale. To reach the park, take State Route 51 south out of Carbondale to Makanda. Turn east and proceed through Makanda to the park entrance. An alternative route, and a more direct one, is Giant City Blacktop Road. If you are coming from the east on Route 13, turn left (south) on Giant City Blacktop Road. Proceed for twelve miles to the park. This route goes to the entrance to the campground and to the trailhead for the hiking trail.

Counties: Jackson and Union

Illinois Highway Map Coordinates: N-6

U.S.G.S. Topographical Map Name and Scale: Makanda, 1:24,000

Hours Open: The park is open year-round except on Christmas Day and New Year's Day. The horseback campground is open May 1 through November 1. The lodge is open from March 15 to November 1 of each year.

History and Trail Description: In 1927, the State of Illinois acquired 1,162 acres of land that is now Giant City State Park. The park is part of the Shawnee National Forest and lies within the Shawnee Hills, which vary in elevation from 500 to 1,060 feet.

The name "Giant City" has been given to the park because of the groups of huge blocks of sandstone located throughout the park. Fern Rocks Nature Preserve is located at the northeastern edge of the park; all nature preserve rules must be observed. The park currently has over 3,696 acres.

Giant City State Park lies outside the glaciated area

in Illinois. At one time the area was a lowland plain that slowly emerged from the sea. As the region gradually rose, a stream which had flowed over it cut the valleys deeper. Only isolated ridges and knobs are now left. Wherever the rocks are hard and resistant, they stand as steep walls along the valley; wherever they are soft, they have worn down to gentle slopes.

Some indicators of ancient man are also found in the park. A feature called "Stone Fort" is located at the top of an eighty-foot sandstone cliff. This fort is a great wall of loose stone that partially encloses several acres. It has been suggested that these structures might have been used as a defensive fortification, as corrals for wild or domesticated animals, as game traps, or for ceremonial purposes.

The main hiking trail in the park is a 12-mile trail known as the Red Cedar Hiking Trail. The park also has numerous nature trails, a trail built for the blind, and an extensive horse trail winding its way through the park.

The Red Cedar Trail starts and ends at the camping area located off Giant City Blacktop Road, although the trail may be started at various locations in the park. The trailhead begins by the tent camping area, where there is a parking area.

At the start of the trail a large trailboard shows the trail layout and points to the direction of the trail. The trail is marked with white bands painted on the trees. An orange spot is painted in the middle of this white band. One white band on the tree means that the trail continues ahead while two bands means that the trail changes directions. The trail is also marked with fifteen numerical markers on trees. These markers correspond to special features on the trail. These features are described in the Red Cedar Hiking Pamphlet which may be obtained from the site superintendent.

The trail begins and ends at the campground and goes in a counterclockwise direction. Starting out as a six-foot wide trail, it becomes a single-lane footpath for most of the hike. From the campground to marker number 2, the trail goes through the woods, over Indian

Creek, past a closed park road, and finally to Giant City Road. The trail crosses this road and parallels an open field for a short distance until reaching the woodlands again. There is an old cemetery along the trail with a few old grave markers still visible, some dating back to 1871.

Beyond the cemetery, you cross a small stream, pass through the woods, and, before reaching the park road, go around a gate. Within the next few miles you will pass under some power lines, go by numerous rock out-crops, hike a ridge top, go past waterfalls, and finally arrive at the backcountry camping area. Restrooms are available at this camping area, but there is no water. From the Red Cedar Camping Area the trail passes through open pasture, past numerous small creeks, and through woods and beautiful valleys. Two small ponds just off the trail are stocked with fish. From there the trail goes past another waterfall, over a park road, along wildlife food plots, over Indian Creek, and then finally back to the starting point.

The trail goes up and down small hills in the park and at one point goes above fifty-foot cliffs. Some areas of the trail may become difficult to hike because of the slope. The trail also passes by a few small waterfalls that are extremely beautiful during the wet season. Great caution must be used when crossing over wet rocks and rock outcrops and when hiking by the cliffs. In addition, some of the streams that must be crossed might be quite high at different times of the year and may be very dif-ficult to cross. Water should be carried along the entire hike, and it is advisable to wear long pants since the trail goes through and by shrubs, thorns, sharp rocks, and poison ivy.

The trail also crosses the road a few times during the hike, and it is possible to hike any of the roads back to the starting point if the hiker does not want to com-plete the trail.

Facilities: A park office is located in the park where you may request additional park information. Numerous picnic areas, which have shelters, picnic tables, water and restrooms, are scattered throughout the park. A Class A campground complete with electricity, sanitary station, and showers is available for tent and trailer camping. A horse camping area, group camping area and another tent camping area are available in the park also. Fishing is allowed in the numerous streams, ponds and at the Little Grassy Lake access area. All Illinois fishing rules and regulations apply. A lodge and cabins are also located in the park. Hunting is allowed in certain areas of the park.

Permits Required: All camping in the park requires a permit, including the backcountry camping site located along Red Cedar Hiking Trail.

Park Rules and Regulations: All plants, animals and cultural features are protected by law. See appendixes A, C, and D.

Mailing Address and Phone Number: Site Superintendent, Giant City State Park, R.R. 1, Makanda, Illinois 62958; 618/457-4836

53. Cedar Lake Trail

Trail Length: 15 miles (24 kilometers)

Location: Cedar Lake is located eleven miles south of Murphysboro off of State Route 127. To reach the trailhead, take Route 127 nine miles south of Murphysboro. turn left (east) onto Dutch Ridge Road and follow the trail sign two miles to the trailhead. The trail may also be accessed south of Dutch Ridge Road by turning east onto Pomona Road or on the gravel road marked "300 N."

County: Jackson

Illinois Highway Map Coordinates: N-6

U.S.G.S. Topographical Map Name and Scale: Pomona, 1:24,000

Shawnee Sportsman's Maps: T.10S., R.1 & 2W.

Hours Open: Cedar Lake Trail may be hiked year-round (weather permitting).

History and Trail Description: Cedar Lake Reservoir was jointly sponsored by the City of Carbondale and the U.S. Forest Service. The primary purpose of the Cedar Lake Reservoir is to provide a water supply for Carbondale with secondary recreational opportunities. Construction of Cedar Lake was completed in December 1973 and reached normal lake level during the winter of 1975. The entire shoreline is in public ownership, with the City of Carbondale owning and managing the northern half and the U.S. Forest Service owning and managing the southern half.

Cedar Lake Hiking Trail parallels the western leg of Cedar Lake, becomes a loop around Little Cedar

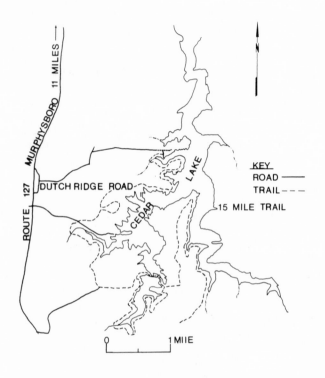

53. Cedar Lake Trail

Lake, and then follows the ridge top between the west and east legs of Cedar Lake making its way to a gravel road.

To reach the trailhead, follow Dutch Ridge Road for two miles to a dead-end parking area. At this parking area a trailboard is located, along with white paint blazes on wooden posts. The entire trail is marked with these white diamonds painted on trees. The trail is basically a single-lane trail for most of the length but at times runs into an old road and becomes part of it for a short distance.

The trail heads south from the parking area, following the ridge top, and then goes down to Cedar Lake, where it parallels the lake heading south.

The first three miles of the trail are probably the most beautiful. Many unique bluffs, rock formations, and cliffs are seen along this section. The trail goes up and down small winding hills and crosses a few small creeks which flow into the lake.

The trail then crosses Pomona Road, where metal hiker markers are posted. From here the trail goes through an open field for a short distance, down to a creek bed, and back into the woods. The trail continues to parallel the lake for a short distance and crosses numerous small creeks. You will soon ascend a hill and go past small rock overhangs, telephone wires, and an open field. From here continue south to the third road or access point.

At this third access point, on top of the hill, there is a small turnaround area for the cars. You will be able to look west and see a beautiful view of the valley. The trail continues south of this little parking area and goes east atop the ridge, following it for a short distance. The trail is very wide at this point, since it is an old road bed. The trail goes by a gate and then continues downhill towards Cedar Lake.

Once the hiker has made it down to Cedar Lake, he will have the option of hiking around Little Cedar Lake or going over the spillway and following the trail in the area between the two branches of Cedar Lake.

If you follow the trail around Little Cedar Lake,

Hiker passing over the rock spillway between Cedar Lake and
Little Cedar Lake

you will follow the shores of this lake for almost the
entire length of the trail. You will get good views of the
lake from most parts of the trail. Little Cedar Lake is
also referred to as Presley Lake and is managed by the
U.S. Forest Service. The spillway for Little Cedar Lake
is made of naturally outcropped stone, uncovered when
Cedar Creek was filled in with soil. You will cross this
stone spillway when passing between Little Cedar Lake
and Cedar Lake.

The trail continues on the east side of Little Cedar
Lake and then connects with a branch of the trail which
heads off in a westerly direction.

If you take this branch of the trail, you will soon
be climbing a small hill along a wide, abandoned road.
The trail goes north following the top of the ridge and
offers views of Cedar Lake both to the west and to the
east. The trail continues north and down to the area
where the east and west parts of the lake meet. From
here the trail will continue south, paralleling the shores
of Cedar Lake.

The trail follows the shores of the lake for a good
distance, going by many small coves, creeks, and islands
visible in the lake. The many small creeks offer some

good fishing spots. The trail then follows a stream valley and ascends a hill while moving toward an open field. The trail at this point becomes a mowed path with marked wooden posts scattered along the trail all the way to the road and to the end of the trail. By looking south from the end of the trail, you will see the Cedar Lake valley.

Retracing your footsteps, you can follow the trail back to your original starting point.

Facilities: No facilities exist along the trail and the hiker must carry his own water.

Park Rules and Regulations: 10 horse power motor limitation on the lake. No houseboats or pontoon boats allowed. No skiing. No overnight mooring permitted on the lake. Fishing by pole and line only. No hunting on City of Carbondale land. All motor vehicles must stay on designated roadways. No cross-country travel allowed. Primitive camping is permitted anywhere along the trail. See Appendix B.

Mailing Address and Phone Number: District Ranger, Shawnee National Forest, 2221 Walnut, P.O. Box AA, Murphysboro, Illinois 62966; 618/687-1731

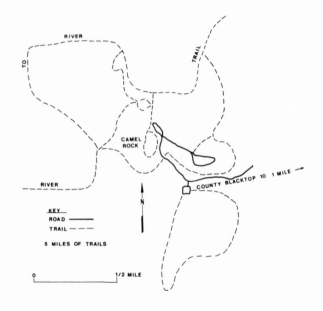

54. Garden of the Gods. Redrawn from Forest
Service Map.

54. Garden of the Gods

Trail Length: 5 miles (8.1 kilometers)

Location: Garden of the Gods Recreation Area is located six miles northeast of Herod and fifteen miles south of Harrisburg. To reach this area, take State Route 34 south out of Herod to Karber's Ridge Blacktop. Turn left (east) on Karber's Ridge Blacktop. Go about three miles to County Blacktop 10, take a left, and follow the signs to the entrance. As an alternative to this route, take State Route 1 to Karber's Ridge Blacktop, turn right (west) and proceed to County Blacktop 10. Take a right and follow the signs north to the site.

County: Saline

Illinois Highway Map Coordinates: N-8

U.S.G.S. Topographical Map Names and Scale: Karber's Ridge and Herod, both 1:24,000

Shawnee Sportsman's Map: T.10S., R.7E. and T.11S., R.7E.

Hours Open: The site is open year round.

Trail Description: The trail system at Garden of the Gods consists of interconnecting trails that wind their way around the bluffs and rock formations. The hiking trails also connect with the River-to-River Trail at three different locations.

The main parking area is the easiest location from which to start hiking the trails. A large shelter here describes how the rocks and bluffs were formed over two hundred million years ago. A short paved trail, about one-eighth of a mile long, leads away from the shelter and takes you past several interesting rock formations, such as Camel Rock and Devil's Smoke Stack. The trail then loops back to the parking area.

At the northern tip of the parking lot and just north of the paved trail, you will run into the main hiking trail system. A wooden post has a copy of the trail map on it. A small gate also marks this location. The trail heads north from this point.

All of the trails in the Garden of the Gods area are marked with white paint blazed on the trees. The River-to-River Trail is blazed with blue paint.

Soon you will come to a trail junction. If you turn west you will reach another trail junction. A wooden sign identifies both Mushroom Rock and Noah's Ark for one trail, and another sign points to the direction of Shelter Rock. You may proceed along either trail. Both trails have beautiful rock formations.

If you take the Noah's Ark trail, you will walk by two interesting rock formations. The trail continues north and will soon intersect the River-to-River Trail. At this point you may go west or east.

The trail for Shelter Rock takes you past additional rock formations and finally to the River-to-River Trail. A sign will also be seen which reads "Lower Trail." This

Noah's Ark rock formation, Garden of the Gods

trail leads you to the valley below the rock formations. From here, the trail crosses the park road and you will encounter another set of bluffs.

The trail follows the base of these bluffs for a short distance, offering beautiful views of the rock formations. The Garden of the Gods camping area is directly above these bluffs.

The trail then circles these bluffs and comes to a trail junction. The trail to the right takes you back to the River-to-River Trail, while the branch to the left leads up the bluffs back to the picnic/camping area. A short walk along the road will take you back to the main parking area.

Facilities: Garden of the Gods has picnic facilities, with picnic tables, grills, restrooms, and water available. The campground has ten tent or trailer units, restrooms and water.

Permits Required: A camping permit is required and may be obtained from the ranger or from a pay station at the entrance to the campground.

Park Rules and Regulations: See Appendix B.

Mailing Address and Phone Number: District Ranger, Shawnee National Forest, Elizabethtown, Illinois 62931; 618/287-2201

KEY

ROAD ——————

TRAIL — — — —

STREAM ——————

INTERMITTENT STREAM —·——·——

6 MILES OF TRAILS

GOREVILLE

W. CRAWFORD AVE.

ROUTE

37

CAMPING AREAS

0   1 MILE

N

55. Ferne Clyffe State Park

55. Ferne Clyffe State Park

Trail Length: 6 miles (9.6 kilometers)

Location: Ferne Clyffe State Park is located one mile south of Goreville and twelve miles south of Marion. The park can be reached by taking State Route 37 south out of Marion. Northbound travelers on Interstate 57 can exit on State Route 146 and proceed east eleven miles to Route 37. Turn north on Route 37 and proceed for eight miles to the park entrance. Southbound Interstate 57 motorists can exit on State Route 148 and proceed three miles east to Route 37. Proceed south on Route 37 seven miles to the park entrance.

County: Johnson

Illinois Highway Map Coordinates: N-7

U.S.G.S. Topographical Map Names and Scale: Goreville and Lick Creek, both 1:24,000

Hours Open: The park is open year-round except on Christmas Day and New Year's Day. At certain times, due to freezing and thawing periods, the park is closed and access to the park is by foot only.

History and Trail Description: In the summer of 1778 George Rogers Clark and his Kentucky "Long Knives" passed through and camped close to the park en route from Fort Massac to Kaskaskia in their conquest of the Illinois country. On the site of Clark's camp is a marker erected by the Daughters of the American Revolution.

This section of the state was formerly the winter hunting grounds of the Indians. The last Indians to use it were the Cherokee, who travelled across southern Illinois in 1838–1839 and were allowed to hunt north and south of their route. The farthest north they hunted was Ferne Clyffe State Park.

The State of Illinois initially acquired about 119 acres of land here in 1949. Prior to this, Miss Emma Rebman owned most of the land for many years and had in fact operated the area as a park. Miss Rebman took pleasure in naming various points in the park, including Job's Coffin, Alligator Cave, Hawk's Cave, and Round Bluff. In 1960 a sixteen-acre fishing lake was built near the northeastern foot of Round Bluff. The maximum depth of the lake is twenty-one feet and the shoreline is about one mile. The park now has over 1,073 acres.

Ferne Clyffe State Park is a scenic area of valleys, dells, canyons, and brooks. As you enter the park, you will soon come to a place along the road where an excellent view of the valley can be had. Ferne Clyffe has a central valley with a number of gorges and canyons. In the winter, these gorges offer beautiful views of frozen waterfalls. There are several so-called caves in the park; these are not truly caves but great ledges of rock that make an arched roof.

The trail system in the park consists of eight separate trails that total over 14 miles. These trails are scattered throughout the park and offer the hiker beautiful views of the park canyons, waterfalls, wildflowers, shelter bluffs, and unique rock formations. The main trail described here is the Happy Hollow Trail, which at six miles is the longest trail in the park. This is the only trail in the park on which horseback riders are allowed.

There are four separate trailheads for Happy Hollow Trail. You can reach the first trailhead by parking at Bluff View Picnic Area. From here go west across the park road and down the hill. You will see a wooden sign at this point showing the Happy Hollow Trail layout. The other three trailheads may be reached by going to W. Crawford Avenue in Goreville, the tent camping area, and the horseback camping area.

Hiking from the Bluff View Picnic Area, just past the trailboard, you will cross a small stream and come to a trail junction where there is a wooden trail sign. This sign points to the directions of the wildlife food plots and backpacking area, horse, tent and group camping, and to the direction of Goreville.

Going toward Goreville, you will gradually climb through a sparsely wooded area. You will pass some rock outcrops and continue uphill to the top of the bluffs. At this point you will be walking northeast, paralleling the bluffs, and will start seeing some homes on the west side of the trail. When you come to a road in Goreville, you are at the end of the trail and you will see a metal hiker marker. From here you can retrace your footsteps back to the trailboard.

Going in the other direction, toward the wildlife food plots and backpack camping area, you will hike on a wide dirt road which passes newly planted wildlife food plots. The backpack camping area is located one-half mile away. There are five backpacking campsites here, along with restrooms. From the camping area continue along the trail for a short distance until you reach the bluffs. At this point, the trail heads into the forest. The trail follows the top of the bluff for a distance and then turns into a footpath. The trail then descends the bluffs, reaching the valley floor close to the creek. The trail parallels the creek for a short distance. A trail marker, a three-foot wooden pole with a horseshoe on it, can be seen. The trail then crosses perennial creeks a few times and heads north, paralleling a creek.

The trail follows this creek all the way back to the original trail junction. At certain times of the year, the trail along the creek may be extremely muddy and at certain times flooded. Prior to reaching the original trail junction you will see a wooden sign that points to the backpacking area. Shortly beyond this sign are two trails that head east back to the tent camping area and horseback camping area.

Facilities: The park has a site superintendent's office where one may request additional information. Several picnic areas are located throughout the park and have picnic tables, park stoves, restrooms, playground equipment, and water. There are camp sites for tents, trailers, horseback riders; also, there is a backpack camping area. Electricity, a disposal station, and a shower building are available. Fishing is allowed in the lake with all Illinois fishing rules and regulations applying.

Permits Required: All campers must secure a camping permit.

Park Rules and Regulations: Boats are not permitted in the lake. See Appendix A.

Mailing Address and Phone Number: Site Superintendent, Ferne Clyffe State Park, P.O. Box 120, Goreville, Illinois 62939; 618/995-2411

56. Bell Smith Springs Recreation Area

Trail Length: 10 miles (16.1 kilometers)

Location: Bell Smith Springs Recreation Area is located nineteen miles southwest of Harrisburg and seven miles northwest of Eddyville. To reach the site, southbound traffic from State Route 145 can turn right (west) onto Burden Falls Road, which is also Forest Road 402. Proceed to a T junction with Forest Road 447. Turn left (south) and proceed to Forest Road 848. Turn right on Forest Road 848 and proceed on a gravel road either to Hunting Branch Picnic Area or to the parking area past Red Bud Campground.

Northbound traffic on Route 145 can turn left onto Eddyville Road in Eddyville and proceed until it joins Forest Road 848. Proceed as described above.

County: Pope

Illinois Highway Map Coordinates: N-8

U.S.G.S. Topographical Map Name and Scale: Stonefort, 1:24,000

Shawnee Sportsman's Map: T.11S., R.5E

Hours Open: The site is open year-round

History and Trail Description: Bell Smith Springs Recreation Area is another recreation site built by the Civilian Conservation Corps in the late 1930s and early 1940s. The area consists primarily of deeply dissected stream valleys cut into sandstone, steep bluffs, sheer cliffs, and small waterfalls. Over 1,260 acres are part of this site.

The trail system in Bell Smith Springs Recreation Area consists of various interconnecting loop trails that

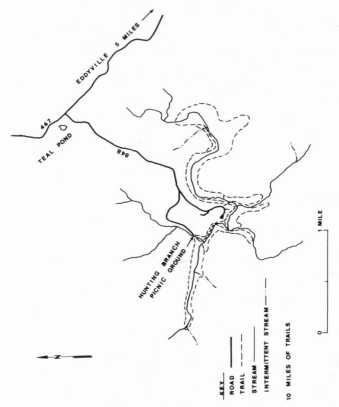

N

KEY

ROAD ——————
TRAIL — — — — —
STREAM ——————
INTERMITTENT STREAM ——————

10 MILES OF TRAILS

0   1 MILE

EDDYVILLE 5 MILES

447

TEAL POND

848

HUNTING BRANCH
PICNIC GROUND

56. Bell Smith Springs Recreation Area

wind through stream valleys and above the bluffs in the park. All of the trails are marked with color-coded diamonds painted on the trees and rocks. You can start hiking the trail system from the Hunting Branch Picnic Grounds or from the parking lot by Red Bud Campground. We recommend starting the hike at the parking lot south of Red Bud Campground because a detailed trail layout is available in one of the information boards.

If you start hiking the trail from Hunting Branch Picnic Grounds, you will start heading west and hike around Mill Branch Creek. The trail going around Mill Branch Creek is marked with orange and white diamonds painted on the rocks and trees along the trail. The trail meanders along the contours of the hill above the creek valley. As you hike this trail, beautiful views of the rock stream valley below appear. The creek bed consists of rock which has been eroded by the creek, thereby leaving numerous small waterfalls along the length of the creek. The trail then comes down toward the feeder creek, which it crosses. From here the trail ascends the hill and you will be above the creek bed again. The trail continues east toward the center of the park; the hiker will soon see white diamonds painted along the trails. The diamonds signify that the trails lie within the center of the recreation area.

You can continue to hike the trails above the bluffs or walk down one of the trails to the stream valley below. On the bluffs, beautiful views of the valley below and of the many pools of water are always visible. You will soon come to a natural arch that must be crossed. Where the trail crosses it, the arch is about forty feet high and about nine feet wide. The trail goes right over the arch, allowing a view of the opening of the arch and the ground below. For a better view of the arch, the hiker can take one of the trails down into the valley. Just before the arch, there are some metal bars wedged into the side of the cliffs which extend to the valley below. We do not recommend climbing down these metal bars. The trails that lead to the natural arch have white dia-

Natural arch, Bell Smith Springs Recreation Area

mond blazes painted on the trees with a black circle painted in the middle of the diamond.

Beyond the arch, the trail is blazed in blue starting near the Fox Gap area. This trail, referred to as the "Sentry Bluff Trail," follows the top of the bluffs and offers beautiful views its entire length. The trail goes past Boulder Falls and Sentry Bluff, and then it descends a rock ledge to the stream bed. This rock ledge is extremely slippery when wet, so you must proceed with caution. The trail then goes back to the top of the bluffs on the other side and toward the center of the park. At the center of the park you can descend some stairs to the stream valley below. The stairs were carved out of the rock cliff. From the stream bed you can follow a myriad of trails that branch out in all directions. It is possible to take the lower trail along the north side of Mill Creek to the spring that gave the area its name.

The trails at Bell Smith Springs may be hiked in any direction and you may vary the distances by taking different trails.

Facilities: The Hunting Branch Picnic Grounds has seven picnic units. The Red Bud Campground has twenty-two tent or trailer units, and restrooms and water are available. In addition, nine tent or trailer units are available at Teal Pond Campground located on Forest Service roads 447 and 848.

Permits Required: A camping permit is required here.

Park Rules and Regulations: See Appendix B.

Mailing Address and Phone Number: District Ranger, Shawnee National Forest, Vienna, Illinois 62995; 618/658-2111

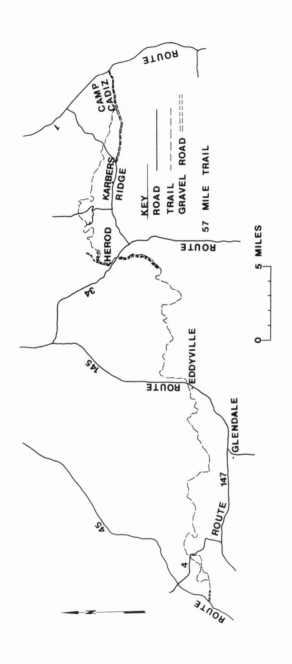

57. River-to-River Trail

57. River-to-River Trail

Trail Length: 57 miles (92 kilometers)

Location: The River-to-River Trail is located in the southeastern portion of the Shawnee National Forest. The trail may be started at either end, at Camp Cadiz or off State Route 45 north of Vienna. To reach Camp Cadiz, take State Route 13 east out of Harrisburg or west out of Shawneetown to Route 1. Turn south on Route 1 for about twelve miles, go past Karber's Ridge Blacktop about three and a half miles to County Road 4 (a gravel road). Turn right (west) on this road and drive about three miles. Camp Cadiz is on the north side. Overnight parking at Camp Cadiz is located on the east side of the campground close to the horse corrals. Camp Cadiz may also be reached by taking State Route 34 south out of Harrisburg for fifteen miles to Karber's Ridge Blacktop. Turn left (east) and go through the town of Karber's Ridge. One mile past the town of Karber's Ridge is County Road 4. A sign for Camp Cadiz will also be seen here. Turn right on County Road 4 and proceed for five miles to Camp Cadiz.

To reach the west access of the trail, take State Route 45 north out of Vienna, Illinois for five miles. A Forest Service sign along Route 45 (at the site of the radio tower) has the words "Trigg Section" written on it. Turn east on a gravel road and follow this road for one and a half miles until you see blue blazes on the trees (there are also orange letters on trees indicating the start of the River-to-River Trail [eastern section] and the Max Creek Trail going north). Vehicles can be parked off the side of the road at any point here.

Counties: Hardin, Gallatin, Saline, Pope, and Johnson

Illinois Highway Map Coordinates: N-9, N-8 and N-7

U.S.G.S. Topographical Map Names and Scale: Saline Mines, Karbers Ridge, Creal Springs, Herod, Eddyville, Waltersburg, Glendale and Bloomfield, all 1:24,000

Shawnee Sportsman's Maps: T.11S., R.9, 8E., T.10S, R.7, 8E., T.11S., R.6, 7E., T.12S., R.3, 4, 5, 6E.

Hours Open: The trail may be hiked year-round.

Trail Description: The River-to-River Trail is a 57-mile trail which may be started in Camp Cadiz and hiked west to Route 45 north of Vienna, or it may be started in Vienna and hiked east.

The trail utilizes existing hiking trails, dirt and gravel roads, and one section of state highway. The trail is marked with blue blazes in the form of the letter "i" that are visible on trees and wooden posts along the trail. The west part of the trail is marked with orange blazes and blazes that say "RR." The trail is well traveled, and parts of the trail are currently being re-blazed or re-routed due to logging operations.

The trail is a multi-purpose trail, used by hikers as well as horseback riders. In fact, the trail goes right through two large horse campgrounds.

The trail crosses some major roads during the course of the hike, and, if the hiker chooses to do so, he could plan a shorter trip.

Camping is permitted anywhere along the trail portion that lies within the Shawnee National Forest; parts of the trail go by private property, so know your location on the trail. We recommend that you carry the Shawnee Sportsman's Maps whenever you hike this trail.

In our opinion, the River-to-River Trail is one of the most challenging and difficult trails in Illinois. The hiker will encounter a variety of terrain and vegetation, pass wildlife watering ponds, wildlife food plots and openings, cross numerous streams, go by sixty-foot cliffs, and follow many existing old farm and jeep roads.

From the east trailhead, the trail heads west away from Camp Cadiz through an open field and then goes downhill. Between Camp Cadiz and Karber's Ridge Blacktop, you will cross a small creek, climb a hill, and then come to an old road. The trail follows this road for a few miles, going past a few wildlife food plots and water holes. The trail then comes to a gravel road and follows it north, going over Karber's Ridge Blacktop; it then heads west along another old dirt road.

You will travel up and down many hills in this area and will have some good views from the ridge tops. Within two miles the trail will go by an old cemetery located on the south side of the trail. The headstones are so old that no writing is visible on them. Past the cemetery are two old, abandoned houses and a trail junction. Continue hiking west past these houses until you see some trail markers. This area may be very confusing; therefore, the hiker must keep an eye out for the blue blazes. The trail then connects with other trails in the High Knob Picnic Area.

A horse ranch is located on a road beyond High Knob Picnic Area. Follow the road north for a short distance; the trail then goes into the woods, paralleling the road. You will cross the road again, and then the trail will become part of an old dirt road once more. This part of the trail is rough in some areas because it is severely eroded. Continue on this road for about one and a half miles, going up a hill; at the top of a ridge, the trail will branch off into the woods again.

The trail will head west now. This part of the trail is very pretty, with pine trees and other conifers all along the trail. You will cross a new logging road. Some of the trees were cut down, so you must look closely for the trail here. Next you will come to a paved road that leads to the Garden of the Gods Recreation Area. A sign at this point says "River-to-River Trail."

Cross this road and continue off into the woods again. At this point, you have entered the Garden of the Gods Recreation Area. After climbing a large hill, you will reach another trail which goes south. This trail leads to the Garden of the Gods area and is marked with white diamonds blazed on the trees. If you choose to do so, you may hike to the Garden of the Gods area and hike some of the trails there (see Garden of the Gods Trail Map).

The River-to-River Trail makes a half-loop around the Garden of the Gods area and then continues as a wide path going west. It follows the ridge tops of the hills, goes up and down stream valleys, and then comes to a gate and a gravel road. This is Forest Service Road 114. Take this road west for about one mile until it joins another gravel road. Turn south on this gravel road and follow it for about one mile to the town of Herod at Route 34.

The hiker then follows Route 34 south for about a half mile to Blackmen Cemetery Road. Turn south on this gravel road and go about four miles until it becomes a dirt road. Walking along these gravel roads for this long distance is the most unpleasant part of the trail.

The trail passes by Hogg Cemetery and then heads west. You must cross a perennial stream and continue west and then north. The trail is extremely confusing to find south of Hogg Cemetery and you will have to watch closely for the trail markers. There are also other trails which connect with the River-to-River Trail. These trails come from One Horse Gap Area and wind their way throughout the area.

Once past the One Horse Gap Area, you will hike along a ridge top, passing many wildlife food plots and ponds. The trail then turns north to a small cemetery. The trail follows a gravel road west and continues straight where the main road heads south. Becoming part of an old road again, the trail goes over the East Fork of Little Lusk Creek, and proceeds uphill. The trail then starts heading south, as you are on a ridge top.

The trail heads into the woods again for a short time and then connects with another dirt road. Follow this road for a few miles, heading downhill towards Lusk Creek. During periods of high water this creek may be impassable.

Lusk Creek offers the hiker a good spot to rest and enjoy the beautiful scenery in the area. From here the trail goes uphill to another trail on top of the ridge. The trail then heads west where it comes to a road. As you cross the road the trail starts heading south, paralleling the road for about one mile.

The trail crosses the road again. At this point, follow this gravel road for about one and a half miles to Route 145 in Eddyville. Cross Route 145 and follow Pope County Road in Eddyville to Eddyville Road. One block south of the Eddyville Post Office is a signpost indicating the horse trail. Follow that road (it becomes a gravel road) west until it turns south, passing through woods again.

The section west of Eddyville all the way to Little Bay Creek (parallel with the Illinois Central Railroad) is extremely difficult to follow as there are several primitive roads, hunters' trails, and other unmarked trail intersections. By following the numbering system for wildlife openings and waterholes as listed on the Shawnee National Forest Sportsman's Maps, the true River-to-River Trail is more easily determined.

Continuing westward, the trail meanders through dense forest land, up and down ridges, and across perennial streams. Crossing the Cedar Creek East Branch may be hazardous; however, a new bridge along the road at this same crossing may provide a safer alternative. West of Cedar Creek the trail is broken at several locations and the blazes are not always easily visible.

As the trail meanders north, you follow the split that goes north and continues northwest; this is the Cedar Creek Trail. Eventually, the trail goes due south for a half mile where it meets with Tunnel Hill Road (Route 4) and turns west to McCormick's Cedar Lake Campground.

Also, at the trail junction for Cedar Creek Trail you may continue west along the established River-to-River Trail. The River-to-River Trail continues southward along Tunnel Hill Road, curves east, and then enters the woods once again. As you go west, you will eventually join the Cedar Creek Trail junction coming out of Cedar Lake Campground. At this point you may hike on either trail; both trails take you back to trailhead at the Trigg Section. You have the option of following the Max Creek Trail which meanders up and down the valley of

Max Creek while crossing the creek six times, or you can follow the original River-to-River Trail, which passes through several open areas, moves on top of ridges, and passes through many areas altered by logging operations. Either section of the loop back to the Trigg Section trailhead is approximately two miles long.

Facilities: Camping is allowed anywhere along the River-to-River Trail so long as it is within the Shawnee Forest. Camping is also allowed at Garden of the Gods, at Camp Cadiz, and at McCormick's Cedar Lake Campground. Camp Cadiz has eleven campsites, horse campsites, a water pump, toilets, and group campsites.

Trail Rules and Regulations: See Appendix B.

Mailing Address and Phone Numbers: District Ranger, Shawnee National Forest, Elizabethtown, Illinois 62931, 618/287-2201, and District Ranger, Shawnee National Forest, Vienna, Illinois 62995; 618/658-2111

58. Beaver Trail

Trail Length: 7.5 miles (12 kilometers)

Location: The Beaver Trail trailhead is located at Camp Cadiz camping area in the Shawnee National Forest. The River-to-River Trail also starts at the same campground. To reach Camp Cadiz, southbound traffic may take State Route 1 twelve miles south of State Route 13. Go past Karber's Ridge Blacktop about three and a half miles to County Gravel Road 4. Turn right (west) and go for about three miles to Camp Cadiz. As an alternative to this route, take Route 34 south out of Harrisburg for about fifteen miles to Karber's Ridge Blacktop. Turn left (east) on Karber's Ridge Blacktop and proceed for six miles. One mile past the town of Karber's Ridge you will reach County Gravel Road 4. Turn east and follow the road for about five miles to Camp Cadiz. Camp Cadiz is located on the north side of the road and is identified with a sign.

County: Hardin

Illinois Highway Map Coordinates: N-9

U.S.G.S. Topographical Map Name and Scale: Saline Mines, 1:24,000

Shawnee Sportsman's Map: T.11S., R.9E.

Hours Open: Camp Cadiz is open year-round.

History and Trail Description: Beaver Trail is a 7.5-mile trail which has its trailhead at Camp Cadiz. The trail may also be started at the trail end at Rim Rock National Trail. The trail is marked with white painted diamonds blazed on trees along the trail.

Parking is available at Camp Cadiz on the east side

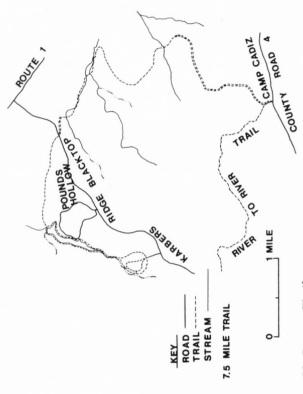

KEY
ROAD ———
TRAIL - - - - -
STREAM ———

7.5 MILE TRAIL

0   1 MILE

58. Beaver Trail

of the camping area, close to the horse area. From here, go northwest to a gravel road. This gravel road is the start of the Beaver Trail.

Follow this gravel road for about one and a half miles. The trail branches off into the forest. The trail then proceeds to go up and down the stream valleys and crosses Beaver Creek, the trail's namesake.

You will reach an old road that runs through the forest. This road proceeds first in a northeasterly direction and then in a northwesterly direction. You will intersect many other old roads while following this section of the trail, and you must be careful to keep an eye out for the white paint blazes on the trees.

You will then come across Karber's Ridge Blacktop. From here, the trail heads back into the forest and becomes a single-lane path to its end.

Between Karber's Ridge Blacktop and Pounds Hollow Lake, the trail goes up and down difficult hills, over creeks, and by rock outcrops. This section of the trail probably offers the hiker the most pleasant scenery along the trail. The trail goes downhill to the lake by the earthen dam.

The trail crosses this dam and follows the northern shore of Pounds Hollow Lake. The trail parallels the entire lake shore and offers the hiker some good views of the lake. At the end of the lake the trail goes up the stream valley, paralleling the lake's feeder creek. Crossing this creek, the trail heads south toward Rim Rock. The trail goes completely around Rim Rock and then back toward Pounds Hollow Lake.

On top of Rim Rock is a National Recreation Trail, a short nature trail paved its entire length. Views of the lake can be seen from the top of Rim Rock, and you can take the stairs down to the base of the rock. While hiking down these stairs, you will pass between some large rock formations.

Facilities: Camp Cadiz has about ten tent campsites, with additional sites for horseback riders. Restrooms, water, grills, and a horse area are all located at Camp Cadiz. Pounds Hollow Recreation Area has seventy-six campsites, picnic areas, shelters, water, restrooms and a beach house. Rim Rock Recreation Area is a day-use area with no camping allowed there.

Permits Required: A camping permit is required at both Camp Cadiz and Pounds Hollow.

Park Rules and Regulations: See Appendix B.

Mailing Address and Phone Number: District Ranger, Shawnee National Forest, Elizabethtown, Illinois 62931; 618/287-2201

59. Heron Pond–Little Black Slough Nature Preserve

Trail Length: 6.5 miles (10.5 kilometers)

Location: Heron Pond–Little Black Slough Nature Preserve comprises two of three separate units within state holdings, which include Heron Pond–Wildcat Bluff, Goose Pond, and Little Black Slough. The main hiking trail is located at Goose Pond and Little Black Slough area. To reach this site, northbound or southbound traffic may take either Interstate 55 or Interstate 57 and exit onto State Route 146. Three and a half miles west of Vienna or about two miles east of Route 37, there is a sign on Route 146 for Wildcat Bluff. Turn south on this gravel road and proceed five miles to a dead-end road. There is a turnaround parking area at the dead end and a wooden sign which reads "State of Illinois Nature Preserve–Little Black Slough Trail." Immediately to the south of the parking area is a fifty-foot drop to the valley below. This bluff is known as Wildcat Bluff.

To reach Heron Pond by car, take State Route 45, five miles south out of Vienna. A sign on Route 45 points to the direction of Heron Pond. Turn right (west) and proceed for nearly two miles to another sign for Heron Pond. Turn right (north) onto a gravel road and proceed to the Heron Pond parking area.

County: Johnson

Illinois Highway Map Coordinates: 0-7

U.S.G.S. Topographical Map Names and Scale: Karnak and Vienna, 1:24,000

Hours Open: The sites are open every day of the year.

History and Trail Description: Heron Pond–Little Black Slough was acquired by the Illinois Department of Con-

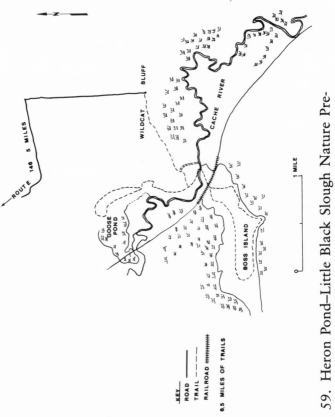

59. Heron Pond–Little Black Slough Nature Preserve

servation to preserve one of the finest remaining cypress swamps in the state. The nature preserve is part of a diverse landscape and harbors hundreds of different plant species. In addition, a variety of environments—such as floodplain forest, moist and dry slope forest, barren sandstone ledges, dry limestone glades, and prairie—may be found here.

The Little Black Slough Trail measures 6.5 miles. This trail also connects with the Goose Pond Spur Trail. Two trails may be accessed from the parking area at Heron Pond: the Heron Pond Trail, a 1.5-mile trail, and the Cypress Trail, a half-mile trail. The trails described here are the Little Black Slough and Goose Pond Trails.

From the parking area at Wildcat Bluff, you must go around a gate and then proceed west along a wide abandoned road. This trail follows the bluff for a short distance; from the bluffs you will see many beautiful views of the valley below. Within a mile you will reach a Y in the trail. Stay to the left, and you will soon reach a wooden post which has a picture of a backpacker painted on it. Also, on the left side of the trail is a rock with a metal marker etched with the following words: "Little Black Slough, Illinois Department of Conservation acquired this land in 1975 with the help of Illinois Chapter of the Nature Conservancy and Westvaco Corporation." Shortly after this sign you will reach another Y in the trail. Proceed to the right and follow the trail down towards the valley. A sign on the valley floor points to Goose Pond. This short loop trail, an extension of the Little Black Slough Trail, goes around a bald cypress pond know as Goose Pond.

Proceeding along the Little Black Slough Trail, you will reach the Cache River. At this point you must cross the river, going over some rocks. During the wet season, the river may be impassable; therefore, the trail cannot be followed past this point. Shortly after crossing the river, you will see an old, abandoned house and shed. This house is a reminder of earlier settlements in this area. From here, the trail crosses a set of railroad tracks and heads towards Boss Island. This section of the trail becomes a loop. You will pass by sections of pine and sycamores trees. The trail along this branch is marked with yellow rectangles on the trees.

After completing the loop, retrace your steps to the trailhead. It is possible to hike to the Heron Pond area via the railroad tracks. By following the tracks southeast for about one mile, you will reach the Heron Pond site.

Facilities: There are no facilities here, although the Heron Pond parking area has restrooms and a trailboard set up.

Park Rules and Regulations: This area is protected under the Illinois Nature Preserves. Camping, horses, pets, vehicles and firearms are prohibited. Plants, animals and other natural features of this area are protected by law. See Appendix C.

Mailing Address and Phone Number: Site Superintendent, Ferne Clyffe State Park, P.O. Box 120, Goreville, Il 62939; 618/995-2411

Appendixes

Bibliography

APPENDIX A

Rules and Regulations Pertaining to Public Use of State Parks, Memorials, Conservation Areas, State Forests and All Other Properties Owned, Managed or Leased by the Department of Conservation—Article XX

The following rules and regulations apply to all areas and facilities owned, leased or supervised by the Illinois Department of Conservation.

It Shall Be Unlawful:

Section 1. Aircraft

a. For any seaplane, pontoon plane, or float-plane to land on or otherwise use any water area under the management of the Department, except in cases of emergency.

b. For any aircraft to land on Department property, except in those areas designated as authorized airstrips or landing areas for aircraft, except in an emergency situation.

Section 2. Alcoholic Beverages and Drugs—Possession, Consumption, Influence

a. For any person to possess or consume alcoholic beverages with the exception of beer and wine. Possession and consumption of beer or wine shall be limited to those persons of the age of 19 years or over. However, this does not prohibit the consumption of alcohol by persons legally of age at places where alcohol is legally offered for sale on State property under the jurisdiction of Department of Conservation.

b. For any person to possess or consume or to be under the influence of intoxicating beverages, including beer or wine, in an area which is posted with signs indicating that such possession or consumption is unlawful.

c. For any person to possess or use any drug defined as unlawful in the Cannabis Control Act, Section 704 (Ill. Rev. Stat., Chap. 56, 1/2 Sec. 704) and the Controlled Substances Act, Section 1402 (Ill. Rev. Stat., Chap. 56, 1/2 Sec. 1402) except those drugs which are prescribed and authorized by a licensed physician.

Section 3. Animals—Pets,—Dogs, Cats—Noisy, Vicious, Dangerous Animals—Horses—Livestock—Animal Waste

a. For any persons to allow or otherwise permit an unleashed dog, cat, or other domesticated animal in any area, except that field trials may be conducted and hunting dogs may be used on any area so posted as open to hunting or where permission is specifically granted by the Department of Conservation to utilize such hunting dogs. All leashed animals shall at all times be under the specific physical control of a responsible person. Persons responsible for dogs or other animals must have proof their animal has a current rabies inoculation or a valid license.

b. For any person to keep a noisy, or vicious, dangerous dog or animal or one which is disturbing to other persons, on Department of Conservation controlled properties and remain therein after being asked by the Site Manager or assigned employees to leave.

c. For any person to ride or lead any horse in any area except on designated bridle paths or equestrian areas, except that horses may be permitted in any area at field trials and special events authorized by the Department of Conservation. Horse patrols of the Division of Law Enforcement or Site employees of the Department in the performance of their duties are not excluded from any area under the control of the Department.

d. For any person to allow livestock to roam or graze on any state controlled lands except when authorized by proper lease, license or written agreement approved by Illinois Department of Conservation.

e. For any person responsible for an animal not to dispose of his animal's waste in proper containers or as may be provided by the Department of Conservation.

Section 4. Boats and Other Watercraft

a. For any person to operate any sailboat, rowboat, houseboat, pontoon boat, or boat propelled by machinery or other watercraft in any pond, lake, river, canal, or other body of water where posting clearly indicates that certain specific boating usage is prohibited. However, Department of Conservation employees operating watercraft in carrying out official duties and personnel of cooperating agents or agencies operating watercraft as authorized by the Department of Conservation may be exempt from boating regulations in this Section or in specific sites' rules as determined by Department of Conservation supervisory managers in order to provide management actions for enhancing or saving the resource base or the safety and welfare of the using public.

b. For any person to use an outboard motor on any body of water under the jurisdiction of the Department that has less than 60 acres. However, this does not exclude the use of electric trolling motors on these bodies of water.

c. For any person to use an outboard motor of a size larger than 10 hp on any body of water under the jurisdiction of the Department that has more than 60 acres of water area except departmentally supervised waters of over 500 acres and portions of canals may have specific regulations approving locations for larger sized motors with exact use allowed posted.

d. For any person to allow his boat or other watercraft to remain on any of the public recreational and fishing areas under the jurisdiction of the Department beyond the date of December 1st of each year.

Section 5. Capacity of Areas—Usage Limitation

a. For any person to violate the rules and regulations pertaining to posted usage capacity of campgrounds, picnic grounds, or other areas where limited facilities make it necessary to control use by persons and/or motor vehicles. Site Managers and Law Enforcement Officers of the Department of Conservation are authorized to close such facilities to additional persons until such time as the number of users falls below the capacity posted within the area.

Section 6. Camping—Campfires

a. For any person to use a tent or trailer, or any other type of camping device except in designated camping areas, and persons camping in such designated areas shall obtain a camping permit as soon as possible from authorized site personnel.

b. For any person to build any area except in campstoves provided by the Department of Conservation or in charcoal or other types of metal grills which are furnished by the visitor and approved by the site manager or ranger or at a specific campfire site designated by the Department of Conservation.

Section 7. Destruction of Property—Flora—Fauna—Man-made and Inanimate Natural Objects

a. For any person to injure or remove any animal, plant, or part thereof or attempt to disturb any agricultural crop, except as otherwise provided by permit, law regulation, or by program activity under the dirct supervision of an authorized employee.

b. For any person to remove, take, mutilate, deface or destroy any property, equipment, improvement, sign or building.

Section 8. Disorderly Conduct

a. For any person to act in such disorderly or unreasonable manner as to alarm or disturb another and to provoke a breach of the peace. Provided by Criminal Code of 1961, Section 26-1, (a) (1) (Ill. Stat., Chap. 38, Sec. 26-1, (a) (1)).

b. For any person to enter into any area for lewd or unlawful purpose deliberately to look into or through any window, doorway or other opening of any, dwelling, tent, trailer, or camping device. Provided by Criminal Code of 1961, Section 26-1 (a) (6), (Ill. Rev. Stat., Chap. 38, Sec. 26-1, (a) (6)).

Section 9. Group Activity

a. For persons to use Department of Conservation facilities in groups of more than 25 persons unless written permission is obtained from the Department of Conservation in advance.

b. For groups of 15 or more minor persons under the age of 18 to gather in any area unless at least one responsible adult accompanies each such group of 15 individuals.

Section 10. Littering

a. For any person using Department of Conservation facilities to discard, abandon, place, or deposit on Department of Conservation properties, except in containers provided, all wire, can, bottle, glass, paper trash, rubbish, garbage, cardboard, wood boxes or other insoluble animal, vegetable, metal, or mineral materials.

b. For any person to bring into Department of Conservation property any of the items listed in item 10a above, with the express purpose of disposing, abandoning, or leaving any of these types of materials on Department of Conservation property whether they are left or placed in proper containers or not.

Section 11. Prohibited Fishing Areas—Cleaning of Fish—Fishing Content

a. For any person to take fish from the waters of any area contrary to the rules and regulations of the Department, and further any fish or parts of fish remaining from cleaning must be placed in a proper refuse container that is provided by the Department of Conservation or removed from the area upon leaving.

Section 12. Restricted Area—Metal Detection Devices

a. For any person to enter or remain in any area when such area has, in whole or in part, been closed to use by visitors. Site Managers and Law Enforcement Officers of the Department of Conservation, as well as other peace officers, are authorized to prohibit the use of such closed areas and it shall be unlawful for any person to disobey the rules and regulations posted relative to such closed areas.

b. For any person to enter or remain on any portion of a dedicated nature preserve where posted rules and regulations prohibit such entry to protect the natural fauna or flora within such area.

c. For any person to operate a metal or mineral detection device except portable hand carried devices may be used by anyone in Department of Conservation properties that are not classified or zoned as State Historical, Archaeological, or Nature Preserve Sites. In addition, persons must obtain a permit from the Department through the site superintendent in advance indicating the location where these devices may be used. Furthermore, only a small penknife, ice pick or screwdriver may be used by permittee in area designated to recover find. After completing detection activity, permittee must return the work area to its original state. No shovels, picks or entrenching devices of any size may be used.

Section 13. Resisting/Obstructing a Peace Officer

For any person to resist or obstruct the performance of a peace officer acting within his official capacity. Provided by Criminal Code of 1961, Section 7-7 (Ill. Rev. Stat. Chap. 38, Sec. 7-7).

Section 14. Soliciting/Advertising/Selling

For any person to place signs or distribute advertising of any type in any area or make an attempt to make sales of any kind or solicit sales of any kind without first obtaining a permit in writing from the Department of Conservation.

Section 15. Swimming/Wading

For any person to swim, wade or bodily enter into the water at any location unless designated by posting and when lifeguards are on duty; the only exception would be as may be allowed by authorized waterfowl hunters, water skiers, wading anglers, or scuba divers.

Section 16. Vehicles—Operation on Roadway—Speed—Parking—Illegal Transportation

a. For any person to operate any motors vehicle other than on roadways specifically posted as trafficways by the Department of Conservation, or to operate a snowmobile or other tracked vehicle commonly known and defined as an all terrain vehicle in any area unless specific permission is granted by the Department, through the Site Manager to operate such vehicles on posted trails; or for any person to ride any motor driven bicycle, minibike or motorcycle except if licensed and on roadways designed for vehicular use.

b. To exceed a speed of 20 mph unless it is otherwise posted by sign on any paved, concrete, asphalt or other all-weather roadway, or to exceed 10 mph unless otherwise posted by sign on any unpaved, gravel or dirt roadway or in any parking area. No vehicle may be driven upon any roadway or in any parking area at a speed which is greater than is reasonable and proper with regard to traffic conditions, or in a manner that endangers the safety of any person or property. The fact that the speed of a vehicle does not exceed the applicable maximum speed limit does not relieve the driver of the duty to decrease speed when approaching and going around a curve, when approaching a hill crest, when traveling upon any narrow or winding roadway, or when any special hazard exists with respect to pedestrians or other traffic or by reason of weather or roadway conditions.

c. For any person to park a motor vehicle in any prohibited area which is posted with signs, or to park a vehicle in any area for the purpose of repair, except those immediate repairs necessary to remove the vehicle from the area immediately.

d. For any person to transport, carry, possess, or have any alcoholic liquor within the passenger area of any motor vehicle except in the original package and with the seal unbroken.

Section 17. Weapons and Firearms—Display and Use

For any person, except authorized peace officers, to display or use on state controlled lands, except as authorized legally by the Department on hunting, field trial, target, or special event areas, any gun including shotgun, rifle, pistol, revolver, air or BB gun, sling shot, bow and arrow, switchblade knife with spring loaded blade, throwing knife, towahawk, or throwing axe.

Source: IDOC Article XX pamphlet

APPENDIX B

Regulations Governing the Occupancy and Use of Developed Recreation Sites on National Forests

The Secretary of Agriculture's regulations (36 CFR 261) provide in part for regulating the occupancy and use of developed recreation sites. A violation of these regulations is subject to a penalty of not more than $500 or 6 months imprisonment, or both.

These regulations have been made by the Secretary of Agriculture to increase the overall enjoyment of recreation in the National Forests. They are common-sense rules meant to control actions that cause damage to natural resources and facilities, as well as actions that cause unreasonable disturbance for National Forest visitors. Observance of these rules will make your visit and the visits of others more pleasant and enjoyable.

Definitions

The following definitions which appear in 36 CFR 261.2 apply to all regulations quoted in this publication.

"Campfire" means a fire, not within any building, mobile home, or living accommodation mounted on a motor vehicle, which is used for cooking, personal warmth, lighting, ceremonial, or aesthetic purposes. "Fire" includes campfire.

"Camping" means the temporary use of National Forest System lands for the purpose of overnight occupancy without a permanently fixed structure.

"Camping equipment" means personal property used in or suitable for camping, and including any vehicle used for transport and all personal property in possession of a person camping.

"Developed recreation site" means an area which has been improved or developed for recreation.

"Forest development road" means a road wholly or partly within or adjacent to and serving a part of the National Forest System and which has been included in the Forest Development Road System Plan.

"Forest development trail" means a trail wholly or partly within or adjacent to and serving a part of the National Forest System and which has been included in the Forest Development Trail System Plan.

"Forest officer" means an employee of the Forest Service.

"Person" means natural person, corporation, company, partnership, trust, firm, or association of persons.

"Permission" means oral authorization by a forest officer.

"Permit" means authorization in writing by a forest officer.

"State law" means the law of any State in whose exterior boundaries an act or omission occurs regardless of whether State law is otherwise applicable.

"Stove fire" means a campfire built inside an enclosed stove or grill, a portable brazier, or a pressurized liquid or gas stove, including a space-heating device.

Prohibited Acts

The following represents a partial listing of acts prohibited on recreation sites in the National Forests. All of the regulations are published in Title 36 of the Code of Federal Regulations and copies of the same on file at all Forest Supervisor and District Ranger Offices.

Sanitation

Failing to dispose of all garbage, including any paper, can, bottle, sewage, waste water or material, or rubbish either by removal from the site or area, or by depositing it into receptacles or at places provided for such purposes. (261.11d)

Cleaning or washing any personal property, fish, animal, or food at a hydrant or at a water faucet not provided for that purpose. (261.14c)

Placing in or near a stream, lake, or other water any substance which does or may pollute a stream, lake, or other water. (261.11c)

Depositing in any toilet, toilet vault, or plumbing fixture, any bottle, can, cloth, rag, metal, wood, stone, flammable liquid, or other substance which could damage or interfere with the operation or maintenance of the fixture. (261.11a)

Depositing any body waste except into receptacles provided for that purpose. (261.14q)

Dumping or leaving in a refuse container, dump, or similar facility, refuse, debris, or litter brought as such from private property or from land occupied under permit. (261.11e)

Possessing or leaving refuse, debris, or litter in an exposed or unsanitary condition. (261.11b)

Operation of Vehicles

Operating or parking a motor vehicle or trailer except in places developed for this purpose. (261.14m)

Operating a bicycle, motorbike, or motorcycle on a trail unless designated for this use. (261.14n)

Operating a motorbike, motorcycle, or other motor vehicle for any purpose other than entering or leaving the site. (261.14o)

Placing a vehicle or other object in such a manner that it is an impediment or hazard to the safety or convenience of any person. (261.10f)

Failing to stop a vehicle when directed to do so by a forest officer. (261.12c)

Blocking, restricting, or otherwise interfering with the use of a road, trail, or gate. (261.12e)

Building Fires

Building, attending, maintaining, or using a fire outside of a fire ring provided by the Forest Service for such purpose, or outside of a stove, grill or fireplace. (261.14b)

Leaving a fire without completely extinguishing it. (261.5d)

Camping

Occupying between 10 p.m. and 6 a.m. a place designated for day use only. (261.14e)

Failing to remove all camping equipment or personal property when vacating the area or site. (261.14f)

Placing, maintaining, or using camping equipment except in a place specifically designated or provided for such equipment. (261.14g)

Without permission, failing to have at least one person occupy a camping area during the first night after camping equipment has been set up. (261.14h)

Leaving camping equipment unattended for more than 24 hours without permission. (261.14i)

Destruction of Property

Cutting, killing, destroying, girdling, chipping, chopping, boxing, injuring, or otherwise damaging or removing, any timber, tree or other forest product, except as authorized by permit, timber sale contract, Federal law or regulation. (261.6a)

Mutilating, defacing, removing, disturbing, injuring or destroying any natural feature or any property of the United States. (261.9a)

Public Behavior

Engaging in fighting, or in threatening or abusive behavior. (261.4a)

Inciting or participating in a riot. (261.4b)

Making unreasonable noise. (261.4c)

Pets and Animals

Bringing in or possessing an animal, other than a seeing eye dog, unless it is crated, caged, or upon a leash not longer than six feet, or otherwise under physical restrictive control. (261.14j)

Bringing in or possessing in a swimming area an animal, other than a seeing eye dog. (261.14k)

Bringing in or possessing a saddle, pack, or draft animal, except as authorized by a sign. (261.14l)

Business Activities

Selling or offering for sale any merchandise, conducting any kind of business enterprise, or performing any kind of business enterprise, or performing any kind work unless authorized by Federal law, regulation or permit. (261.10c)

Distributing any handbill, circular, paper or notice without a permit. (261.14p)

Posting, placing, or erecting any paper, notice, advertising material, sign, or similar matter without a permit. (261.10g)

Audio Devices

Operating or using in or near a campsite, developed recreation site, or over an adjacent body of water without a permit, any device which produces noise, such as a radio, television, musical instrument, motor or engine in such a manner and at such a time so as to unreasonably disturb any person. (261.10h)

Operating or using a public address system, whether fixed, portable, or vehicle mounted, in or over an adjacent body of water without a permit. (261.10i)

Fireworks and Firearms

Discharging or igniting a firecracker, rocket or other firework, or explosive. (261.14d)

Discharging a firearm or any other implement capable of taking human life, causing injury, or damaging property: (1) in or within 150 yards of a residence, building, campsite, developed recreation site or occupied area, or (2) across or on a Forest Development road or a body of water adjacent thereto whereby any person or property is exposed to injury or damage as result of such discharge. (261.10d)

Interfering with Forest Officer

Threatening, resisting, intimidating, or interfering with any forest officer engaged in or on account of the performance of his official duties in the protection, improvement, or administration of the National Forest System. (261.3)

Other Prohibited Acts

Constructing, placing, or maintaining any kind of road, trail, structure, fence, enclosure, communication equipment, or other improvement without a permit. (261.10a)

Occupying any portion of the site for other than recreation purposes. (261.14a)

Conducting, demonstrating, or participating in a public meeting assembly, or special event, except as authorized by permit. (261.10j)

Abandoned Personal Property

Abandoning a vehicle, animal or personal property. (261.10e)

Additional rules may be established at individual developed sites where determined necessary by the Regional Forester or Forest Supervisor.

Such rules will be established by an order that is posted in such locations and manner as to reasonably bring the prohibition to the attention of the public.

Source: U.S. Department of Agriculture Forest Service/PA-1199.

APPENDIX C

Regulation of Public Use of Illinois Dedicated Nature
Preserves—Article 64

It is Unlawful:

1. For any person to enter any dedicated nature preserve or portion thereof if such area has been closed to visitors by notice posted by the Department of Conservation or a duly authorized agent thereof.

2. For any person to possess or consume or be under the influence of intoxicating beverages, including beer, or dangerous or narcotic drugs in any dedicated nature preserve.

3. For any person to camp or place a tent or trailer or any type of camping device in a dedicated nature preserve.

4. For any person to cut, break, injure, destroy, take or remove any tree, shrub, timber, flower, plant, or other natural object including rocks, soil, or water from a dedicated nature preserve; except that small quantities of such materials may be collected and removed for scientific or educational purposes by written permit from the owner, the Department of Conservation and the Illinois Nature Preserves Commission, and except for management under direct supervision of a designated agent.

5. For any person to kill, cause to be killed, harass, pursue, or take any animal, whether mammal, bird, fish, reptile amphibian, or invertebrate on its nest or habitat in a dedicated nature preserve; except that small quantities of such materials may be collected and removed for scientific or educational purposes by written permit from the owner, the Department of Conservation and the Illinois Nature Preserves Commission, and except for management purposes under the direct supervision

of a designated agent with the approval of the Illinois Nature Preserves Commission and the Department of Conservation.

6. For any person to conduct scientific research in a dedicated nature preserve without a written permit from the owner, the Department of Conservation and the Illinois Nature Preserves Commission.

7. For any person to possess a firearm, airgun, slingshot, bow and arrow, or any other weapon within the boundaries of any designated nature preserve, except authorized peace officers and as authorized for management and control measures for wildlife population control under the supervision of a designated agent with the approval of the Illinois Nature Preserves Commission and the Department of Conservation.

8. For any person to take, mutilate, deface, move, or destroy any structure, improvement, work, or sign, or any stone, soil, or other natural object or material in any dedicated nature preserve, except for management under the direct supervision of a designated agent.

9. For any person to operate a motor vehicle in any dedicated nature preserve other than on designated roadways or parking areas or to park a motor vehicle except in designated parking areas, except for maintenance and management vehicles operated by designated agents.

10. For any person to operate a motor vehicle in a reckless manner, or to exceed posted speed limits on roadways within any dedicated nature preserve.

11. For any person to build or light any fire or willfully or carelessly permit any fire which has ignited or been caused to ignite or which is under his charge and care to spread or extend to or burn any part of a dedicated nature preserve, except for prescribed burning for vegetation management under the direct supervision of a designated agent.

12. For any person to discard rubbish of any kind in any dedicated nature preserve except in designated containers provided by the Department of Conservation or a duly authorized agent thereof.

13. For any person to bring or allow to enter into

a dedicated preserve any dog, cat, horse, or other animal or pet, except that horses may be brought into areas where bridle trails are designated and posted.

14. For any person to engage in disorderly conduct within any dedicated nature preserve.

15. For any person to engage in any sporting or athletic activity, including swimming, within the boundaries of any dedicated nature preserve.

16. For admittance to be granted to groups of 25 or more persons to any nature preserve unless written permission from the Department of Conservation or other owner has been secured in advance. Groups of 25 or more will be granted permission to visit preserves if the groups do not exceed the capacity of the facility. The Site Superintendent of the affected facility shall grant permits, in advance, to groups wanting to use the facility.

17. For any group of minors to enter any dedicated nature preserve without adequate supervision. At least one responsible adult shall accompany each group of not more than 15 minors.

18. For any person to plant or disperse any native or non-native plant species or their parts into any dedicated Illinois Nature Preserve without the written approval of the Illinois Department of Conservation and the Illinois Nature Preserves Commission.

19. For any person to release or disperse any native or non-native animal species into any dedicated Illinois Nature Preserve without the written approval of the Illinois Department of Conservation and the Illinois Nature Preserves Commission.

Criteria that will be used to evaluate requests under parts 18 and 19 include:

a. Is there evidence that the species formerly occurred on the preserve or that the habitat was suitable and was probably occupied by the species.

b. Are the habitat and other ecological conditions presently suitable and adequate to support the species.

c. What is the source of origin and genotype of the proposed introductions and is it the same as that was originally occurring on the preserve.

   d. Will the introduction threaten the population for
which it is being taken.
   e. Will the introduction threaten any species or
communities presently considered desirable on the preserve.

   *Source: "A Directory of Illinois Nature Preserves;
Illinois Department of Conservation and Illinois Nature
Preserves Commission, 1982."*

APPENDIX D

The National Trails System Act and the National Recreation Trails in Illinois

The National Trails System Act (Public Law 90–543, as amended) was passed in 1968 and established a nationwide network of trails consisting of four categories: National Scenic Trails, National Historic Trails, National Recreation Trails (NRT) and connecting trails. National Recreation Trails provide a variety of outdoor recreation uses in or reasonably accessible to urban areas. National Scenic Trails are extended trails so located to provide for maximum outdoor recreation potential and for the conservation and enjoyment of the nationally significant scenic, historic, natural or cultural qualities of the areas through which such trails pass. National Historic Trails are extended trails which follow as closely as possible and practicable the original trails or routes of travel of national historical significance. Connecting or side trails also make up the National Trails System. Connecting trails provide additional points of public access to national recreation, national scenic, or national historic trails or which will provide connections between such trails.

Presently eight National Scenic Trails, five National Historic Trails, and 715 National Recreation Trails have been designated for inclusion under this Act.

The bulk of the system consist of NRTs which generally are in or near urban areas and provide for a wide variety of trail experiences. In Illinois there are thirteen trails designated as NRTs, totalling 90.1 miles. In addition, the eastern end of the Mormon Pioneer National Historic Trail is located in Nauvoo, Illinois, and the beginning point for the Lewis and Clark National Historic Trail is at Wood River, Illinois.

The most recent amendment to the National Trails System Act directs the Secretary of the Interior to study two additional trail routes for possible inclusion in the National Trails System. These include the Illinois Trail, which generally follows the Illinois River and the Illinois and Michigan Canal, and the Trail of Tears, which passes through the southern end of the state.

Following is a list of the National Recreation Trails that are located in Illinois as of May 1, 1983.

1. The Illinois Prairie Path
2. Rim Rock Trail
3. Inspiration Point Trail
4. Greenbelt Bikeway
5. Virgil L. Gilman Nature Trail
6. Starved Rock State Park Trail System
7. Red Cedar Hiking Trail
8. Camp Camfield Nature Trail
9. Roby Recreation Trail
10. Eberley Park Fit-Trail
11. Lake Forest Bike Trail
12. Shag Bark Nature Preserve Trail
13. Great Western Nature Trail

For additional information on this program contact: National Park Service, Midwest Regional Office, 1709 Jackson Street, Omaha, Nebraska 68102

Source: Modified from National Park Service, "Directory of Sources of Trails Information."

APPENDIX E

Where to Order Maps for Illinois

The U.S.G.S. publishes a series of standard topographical (topo) maps for Illinois. The unit of survey is a quadrangle bounded by parallels of latitude and meridians of longitude. If you live east of the Mississippi River, U.S.G.S. topo maps may be ordered from:

> Eastern Branch Distribution
> U.S. Geological Survey
> 1200 South Eads Street
> Arlington, Virginia 22202

If you live west of the Mississippi River, U.S.G.S. topo maps may be ordered from:

> Western Distribution Branch
> U.S. Geological Survey
> Box 25286, Federal Center
> Denver, Colorado 80225

Topo maps for Illinois may also be ordered from the Illinois State Geological Survey at:

> Illinois State Geological Survey
> Natural Resources Building
> 615 East Peabody Drive
> Champaign, Illinois 61820

Topo maps may also be purchased at selected sporting or camping goods stores throughout the state.

The Illinois Department of Transportation (IDOT) prepares and publishes various special-purpose state, county, township and city maps that are available for sale to the general public. A description of the maps available for Illinois and their prices may be obtained from IDOT at the following address:

> Map Sales
> Illinois Department of Transportation
> 217 Administration Building
> 2300 Dirksen Parkway
> Springfield, Illinois 62764

The Shawnee Sportsman's Maps are printed in cooperation with the Illinois Department of Conservation and U.S. Department of Interior, Fish and Wildlife Service. These Sportsman's Maps may be obtained by contacting one of the following Forest Service offices:

Forest Supervisor
Shawnee National Forest
Route 45 South
Harrisburg, Illinois
62946

District Ranger
Shawnee National Forest
Elizabethtown, Illinois
62931

District Ranger
Shawnee National Forest
Jonesboro, Illinois
62952

District Ranger
Shawnee National Forest
Murphysboro, Illinois
62966

District Ranger
Shawnee National Forest
Vienna, Illinois 62995

APPENDIX F

Illinois Map Reference Libraries

Many libraries maintain reference files of the published maps of the United States Geological Survey (U.S.G.S.). In Illinois, U.S.G.S. topo maps are deposited and may be viewed in the libraries listed below:

Aurora: Aurora Public Library

Carbondale: Morris Library, Southern Illinois University

Charleston: Library, Eastern Illinois University

Chicago: Chicago Public Library

Library, Loyola University of Chicago

Library, University of Chicago

Library, University of Illinois at Chicago

The John Crerar Library, Illinois Institute of Technology in Chicago

De Kalb: Northern Illinois University Library

Edwardsville: Library, Southern Illinois University

Elgin: Gail Borden Public Library

Evanston: Northwestern University Library

Galesburg: Knox College Library

Kankakee: Library, Olivet Nazarene College

Macomb: Map Library, Western Illinois University

Monmouth: Library, Monmouth College

Normal: Illinois State University Library

Peoria: Peoria Public Library

Rock Island: Augustana College Library
Springfield: Illinois State Library
Urbana: University of Illinois Library

Source: "U.S.G.S. Illinois Map Index, 1979"

APPENDIX G

Telephone Numbers for Weather Forecasts for Selected Areas in Illinois

The following phone numbers may be used by hikers to find out the weather conditions and forecasts for certain areas in Illinois.

Chicagoland forecast—312/976-1212

Moline–Quad Cities and surrounding area—309/762-1726

Peoria area forecast—309/697-8620

Rockford area forecast—815/963-8518

St. Louis and area forecast—314/928-1198

Springfield area forecast—217/492-4949

APPENDIX H

Other Hiking Trails in Illinois

The following list of hiking trails and distances was compiled by the authors by writing to the park or organization or by telephone. The appendix is divided into three sections: northern, central, and southern Illinois. Each trail has either the park or trail name, trail owner/administrator, and the trail length. These trails include Boy Scout and Girl Scout trails, state parks, forests, conservation areas and nature preserves, forest preserves, county and city parks, not-for-profit parks, and conservation districts. (Note: Short trails were not measured, but were listed or described as less than 4 miles in length.)

Northern Illinois

Chicago Lake Front Path, Chicago Park District, 20-mile trail

Oxpojke Trail, Bishop Hill Heritage Ass., 11-mile trail

Boone County Bicentennial Heritage Trail, Boone County Bicentennial Commission, 30-mile trail

Sac–Fox Trail, Boy Scouts, 15-mile trail

Black Hawk Trail, Boy Scouts, 20-mile trail

Kishawaukee–Barb Wire, Boy Scouts, 10-mile trail

Chief Chicagou Trail, Boy Scouts, 14-mile trail

Mitigwaki Trail, Boy Scouts, 13-mile trail

Veteran Acres, Crystal Lake Park District, short trail

Sannauk, De Kalb Park District (DPD), short trail

Chief Shabbona, DPD, short trail

Russell, DPD, short trail

P.A. Nehring, DPD, short trail

Afton, DPD, short trail

Randall Oaks, DPD, short trail

Crabtree Nature Center, Forest Preserve District of Cook County (FPDCC), 3-mile trail

River Trail Nature Center, FPDCC, 2.5 mile trail

Little Red School House Nature Center, FPDCC, 3-mile trail

Sand Ridge Nature Center, FPDCC, 3.5-mile trail

Arie Crown Forest Preserve, FPDCC, 3.2-mile trail

Fullersburg Forest Preserve, Forest Preserve District of Du Page County (FPDDC), 1.5-mile trail

West Du Page Woods, FPDDC, 2-mile trail

Nelson Lake, forest Preserve District of Kane County (FPDKC), short trail

Burnidge Forest Preserve, FPDKC, short trail

Tyler Creek Forest Preserve, FPDKC, short trail

Campton Forest Preserve, FPDKC, short trail

Lone Grove Forest Preserve, FPDKC, short trail

Oakhurst Forest Preserve, FPDKC, short trail

Trail of the Old Oakes, Forest Preserve District of Will County (FPDWC), short trail

Heritage Trail, FPDWC, short trail

Goodenon Grove Forest Preserve, FPDWC, short trail

Plum Creek Nature Center, FPDWC, short trail

Nettle Creek Nature Trail, Illinois Department of Conservation (IDOC), short trail

Illinois Beach State Park, IDOC, 2-mile trail

Johnson Sauk Trail State Park, IDOC, 4-mile trail

Apple River State Park, IDOC, 5 trails, 1-mile each

Lowden State Park, IDOC, 2 trails, 1.5-mile each

Castle Rock State Park, IDOC, 3.5-mile trail

Silver Spring State Park, IDOC, 3.5-mile trail

Goose Lake State park, IDOC, 1.5-mile trail

Chain of Lakes State Park, IDOC, 2 trails, 4 miles of trails

Black Hawk State Park, IDOC, short trail

Volo Bog State Park, IDOC, short trail

Franklin Creek State Preserve Area, IDOC, 3 trails, 1-mile each

Illini State Park, IDOC, 2.5-mile trail

Old School Forest Preserve, Lake County Forest Preserve District (LCFPD), 5.5-mile trail

Greenbelt Forest Preserve, LCFPD, 4-mile trail

Spring Bluff Preserve, LCFPD, 2.5-mile trail

Old School Preserve, LCFPD, 3-mile trail

Van Patten Woods, LCFPD, 3-mile trail

Harrison–Benwell, McHenry County Conservation District (MCCD), 2-mile trail

Burrow's Woods, MCCD, 3-mile trail

Marengo Ridge, MCCD, 3.5-mile trail

Queen Anne Prairie, MCCD, short trail

Deep Cut Marsh, MCCD, short

Rush Creek Conservation Area, MCCD, 3-mile trail

Northwoods Park, Morton Park District, 3 miles of trails

Nature Center Area, Park District of Highland Park, 3 miles of trails

Loud Thunder Forest Preserve, Rock Island County Forest Preserve District, 2-mile trail

Aldeon Nature trail, Rockford Park District, 1.5-mile trail

Hammel Woods, Will County Forest Preserve District (WCFPD), 3 miles of trails

Messenger Woods, WCFPD, 1-mile trail

Runyon Preserve, WCFPD, short trail

Thorn Creek Woods, WCFPD, 2-miles of trails

Hononegah, Winnebago County Forest Preserve District (WCFPD-2), 1-mile trail

Kieselburg, WCFPD-2, 1-mile trail

Espenscheid, WCFPD-2, short trail

Blackhawk Springs, WCFPD-2, 7.5 miles of trails

Kishwaukee River, WCFPD-2, 1.5-mile trail

Kilbuck Bluffs, WCFPD-2, 1.5-mile trail

Fuller Memorial, WCFPD-2, 3 miles of trails

Severson Dells, WCFPD-2, 3 miles of trails

Seward Bluffs, WCFPD-2, 3 miles of trails

Four Lakes, WCFPD-2, 1-mile trail

Pecatonica River, WCFPD-2, 3 miles of trails

Colored Sands, WCFPD-2, 3 miles of trails

Central Illinois

Rapatuck Trail, Boy Scouts, 16-mile trail

Carl Sandburg Trail, Boy Scouts, 16-mile trail

Lincoln Circuit Trail, Boy Scouts, 16-mile trail

Court House trail, Boy Scouts, 11-mile trail

Cedar Creek Trail, Boy Scouts, 10-mile trail

Lincoln Trail Hike, Boy Scouts, 16-mile trail

Lake Bloomington, Bloomington Park District, 3-mile trail

Lake of the Woods County Park, Champaign County Park District, short trail

Scovill Gardens, Decatur Park District (DPD), short trail

Wildwood Park, DPD, short trail

Baker Woods, DPD, short trail

Big Creek Riding Center, DPD, short trail

Fairview Park, DPD, short trail

Friends Creek Regional Park, DPD, 2.5 miles of trails

Garman Park, DPD, short trail

Hidden Springs State Forest, IDOC, 5 miles of hiking trails, 17 miles of fire lanes

Peoria and Galena Trail and Coachhead, Girl Scouts, 10-mile trail

Spring Lake Conservation Area, IDOC, 1.8-mile trail

Crawford County Conservation Area, IDOC, 1-mile trail

Turkey Bluffs Fish and Wildlife area, IDOC, 5 miles of trails

Piney Creek Nature Preserve, IDOC, 2 miles of trails

Big River State Forest, IDOC, various lengths of horsetrails

Nauvoo Historical Site, IDOC, 1.5-mile trail

Beaver Dam State Park, IDOC, 7 miles of trails

Sangchris Lake State Park, IDOC, 2.5-mile trail

Spittler Woods State Park, IDOC, 3 short trails

Ramsey Lake State Park, IDOC, 2-mile trail

Lincoln Trail State Park, IDOC, short trail

Fox Ridge State Park, IDOC, 7 miles of short trails

Kickapoo State Park, IDOC, 1-mile trail

Moraine View State Park, IDOC, 3 miles of trails

Delabar State Park, IDOC, 2 miles of trails

Walnut Point State Park, IDOC, 2.5-mile trail

Sam Parr State Park, IDOC, 2-mile trail

Weldon Springs State Park, IDOC, 4.5 miles of trails

Wolf Creek State Park, IDOC, 6 miles of trails

Henderson County Conservation Area, IDOC, 2 miles of trails

Marshall County Conservation Area, IDOC, 3.5 miles of trails

Kankakee River State Park, IDOC, 3-mile trail

Iroquis County Conservation Area, IDOC, 2-mile trail

Weinberg–King State Park, IDOC, 1.5-mile trail

Kinsbury Nature Trail, Kingsburg Park District, 2.5-mile trail

Spring Lake Park, Macomb Park District, 3.5-mile trail

Fort Daniel Conservation Area, Macon County Conservation District (MCCD), 1.5-mile trail

Griswold Conservation Area, MCCD, short trail

Forest Park, Peoria Park District (PPD), short trail

Detweiller Park, PPD, short trail

Robinson Park, PPD, short trail

Natural Lands Area, Putnam County Conservation District (PCCD), 1.5-mile trail

Fox Run Conservation Area, PCCD, 1.5-mile trail

Miller–Anderson Woods, PCCD, 1-mile trail

Sangamon State University Nature Trail, Sangamon State University, short trail

Wildlife Sanctuary Park, City of Springfield, 1.5-mile trail

Gurgens Park, Springfield Park District (SPD), short trail

Lincoln Park, SPD, short trail

Timberbrooke Park, SPD, short trail

Walnut Valley Park, SPD, short trail

Washington Park, SPD, short trail

Spoon River Trail, Spoon River Drive Ass., 55-mile trail

Greenbelt Bikeway, Urbana Park District, 2.5-mile trail

Kennekuk Cove County Park, Vermillion Conservation District, 6 short trails

Southern Illinois

Gordon F. Moore Community Park, Alton Park and Recreation Commission, short trail

Eagle Trail, Boy Scouts, 10-mile trail

Lewis and Clark Trail, Boy Scouts, 13-mile trail

Grafton–Marquette Trail, Boy Scouts, 10-mile trail

Sam Dale Lake Conservation Area, IDOC, 3.5-mile trail

Lusk Creek Canyon Nature Preserve, IDOC, short trail

Saline County Conservation Area, IDOC, 5 miles of trails

Cave-in-Rock State Park, IDOC, 1-mile trail

Fort Massac State Park, IDOC, 4.5 miles of trails

Fort De Charles Historic Site, IDOC, 3 miles of trails

Dixon Springs State Park, IDOC, 2 miles of trails

Eldon Hazlet State Park, IDOC, 3 miles of trails

Lake Glendale, U.S. Forest Service, 3-mile trail

Pounds Hollow Recreation Area, U.S. Forest Service, 3-mile trail

Stephen Forbes State Park, IDOC, 1-mile trail

Red Hills State Park, IDOC, 2.5-mile trail

Lake Murphysboro State Park, IDOC, 3.5-mile trail

Wayne Fitzgerrell State Park, IDOC, 1.5-mile trail

Hamilton County Conservation Area, IDOC, 1-mile trail

Trail of Tears State Forest, IDOC, 40 miles of fire trails

Randolph County Conservation Area, IDOC, 7 miles of trails

SIU-C Campus Lake Trail, Southern Illinois University at Carbondale, short trail

SIU-E Nature Trail, Southern Illinois University at Edwardsville, short trail

Wood River Massacre Historical Trail, Trails Incorporated, 10-mile trail

APPENDIX I

Illinois and National Hiking Organizations

Many of the trails listed in this book are located at parks (both public and private), forest preserve districts, Shawnee National Forest and other not-for-profit lands. Some of these parks have rangers or park interpreters who offer guided nature trail walks. Other times, various hiking groups or organizations offer hiking outings. Many times the hiker might be interested in joining a local or national hiking club or organization to participate in hiking outings or to help in developing a new trail. This appendix was written for the hiker who wishes to find hiking organizations in Illinois and nationally which offer hiking outings, or support other trail activities.

The following list shows the organizations which are involved in sponsoring hiking outings, or which support trail-related activities.

A. Illinois Hiking Organizations

Sierra Club, Great Lakes Chapter, 53 West Jackson Boulevard, Chicago, Illinois 60604. The Sierra Chapter in Illinois has its headquarters in Chicago and is called the Great Lakes Chapter. The Great Lakes Chapter has thirteen thousand members statewide and offers many hiking outings by the various regional groups. The chapter has thirteen regional groups in Illinois. The following list shows the names of the local groups and the towns where they have their meetings. For additional information on each of these groups contact the chapter office in Chicago.

Regional Group	Town
Blackhawk	Rockford
Chicago	Chicago
Des Plaines	Mount Prospect
Du Page	Glen Ellyn
Eagle Bluff	Moline
Heart of Illinois	Peoria
Kaskaskia	Belleville
North Suburban Group	Lake County
Piasa Palisades	Alton
Prairie	Champaign
Sangamon	Springfield
Sauk–Calumet	Park Forest
Shawnee	Carbondale

American Youth Hostels, Inc., 3712 North Clark Street, Chicago, Illinois 60613. The American Youth Hostels is a non-profit volunteer organization which sponsors many recreational activities, including hiking trips.

The Prairie Club, 6 East Monroe, Room 1507, Chicago, Illinois 60603. The Prairie Club is a not-for-profit organization set up to promote outdoor recreation in the form of walks, outings, camping and canoeing. In addition, the Club also pursues the preservation of suitable areas in which outdoor recreation may be increased, such as the establishment and maintenance of camps.

Illinois Department of Conservation, Bureau of Lands and Historic Sites, 405 East Washington Street, Springfield, Illinois 62706. Each spring the Department offers spring volk walks at their state parks. These walks are family oriented and provide all age groups an inexpensive way to enjoy some of the state parks in Illinois. For more information on the state parks which are participating in this program, contact the Department.

In addition, many local colleges and universities in Illinois have recreation clubs or groups that sponsor organized hiking outings. These colleges and universities may be contacted directly to receive information on their outings.

A source of hiking outings for families with children is through their local scout troops. Both the Boy and Girl Scout troops in Illinois sponsor many hiking outings in the state, as well as on many of the trails which are listed in this book.

B. National Hiking Organizations

Sierra Club Headquarters, 530 Bush Street, San Francisco, California 94108

American Hiking Society, 1701 18th Street, N.W., Washington, D.C. 20009

C. Illinois and National Organizations That Either Support, Protect or Expand Trail Activities

The following groups or organizations are involved in many areas of trail support or activities. These include:

Illinois Department of Conservation, c/o Trail Specialist, 405 East Washington Street, Springfield, Illinois 62706

Illinois Prairie Path, P.O. Box 1086, 616 Delles Road, Wheaton, Illinois 60187

Northeastern Illinois Trail Association, 2860 Orange Brace Road, Riverwoods, Illinois 60015

Illinois Parks and Recreation Association, 250 East Wood Street, Palatine, Illinois 60067

National Trails Council, 13 West Maple Street, Alexandria, Virginia 22301

National Campers and Hikers Association, Inc., 7172 Transit Road, Buffalo, New York 14221

National Park Service, Midwest Regional Office, 1709 Jackson Street, Omaha, Nebraska 68102

Friends of the Illinois and Michigan Canal National Heritage Corridor, P.O. Box 867, Ottawa, Illinois 61350

The organizations listed in section A and B also support trail activities, in addition to offering hiking outings.

Selected Bibliography

This reading list is not meant to be exhaustive; rather, it contains works related to the subject and the trail areas which the hiker might find useful.

Bohlen, H. D. *An Annotated Checklist of the Birds of Illinois*. Volume 9. Springfield: Illinois State Museum, 1978.

Bretz, J. H., and S. E. Harris. *Caves of Illinois*. Report of Investigation 215. Urbana: Illinois State Geological Survey, 1961.

Calder, Jean. *Walking. A Guide to Beautiful Walks and Trails in America*. New York: William Morrow and Company, 1977.

Carra, Andrew J. *The Complete Guide to Hiking and Backpacking*. New York: Winchester Press, 1977.

Changnon, Stanley A. *Illinois Weather and Climate Information. Where to Find It*. Circular 123. Urbana: Illinois State Water Survey, 1975.

Changnon, Stanley A., and David Changnon. *Record Winter Storms in Illinois, 1977–1978*. Urbana: Illinois State Water Survey, 1978.

Changnon, Stanley A., and Floyd A. Huff. *Review of Illinois Summer Precipitation Conditions*. Urbana: Illinois State Water Survey, 1980.

Condit, Carlton. *Fossils of Illinois*. Springfield: Illinois State Museum, 1954.

Cote, William E., et. al. *Guide to the Use of Illinois Topographic Maps*. Urbana: Illinois State Geological Survey, 1972, revised 1978.

Dubberdt, Walter F. *Weather for Outdoorsmen*. New York: Charles Scribner's Sons, 1981.

Dunlop, Richard. *Rand McNally Backpacking and Outdoor Guide*. Chicago: Rand McNally, 1981.

Evers, Robert A., and Lawrence M. Page. *Some Unusual*

Natural Areas in Illinois. Urbana: Illinois Natural History Survey, 1977.

Fritz, Arnold W. *Lake Shelbyville Fishing Guide.* Springfield: Illinois Department of Conservation, 1971.

George, Jean C. *The American Walk Book. Major Historic and Natural Walking Trails from New England to the Pacific Coast.* New York: Dutton Publishers, 1978.

Harris, Stanley E., Jr., William C. Horrell, and Daniel Irwin. *Exploring the Land and Rocks of Southern Illinois, A Geological Guide.* Carbondale: Southern Illinois University Press, 1977.

Hoffmeister, Donald F., and Carl O. Mohr. *Fieldbook of Illinois Mammals.* New York: Dover Publications, Inc., 1972.

Howe, Walter A. *Documentary History of the Illinois and Michigan Canal, Legislation, Litigation, and Titles.* Springfield: Illinois Department of Public Works and Buildings, 1956.

Illinois Department of Commerce and Community Affairs. *The Weekend Book. A Guide to Small Adventures in Illinois.* Springfield: Illinois Department of Commerce and Community Affairs, 1981.

Illinois Department of Conservation. *Recreation Areas Guide.* Springfield: Illinois Department of Conservation, 1980.

———. *Outdoor Recreation in Illinois: The 1983 Policy Plan.* Springfield: Illinois Department of Conservation, 1983.

———. *Elements of Forestry with Special Reference to Illinois.* Springfield: Illinois Department of Conservation, 1973.

Illinois Nature Preserves Commission. *Illinois Nature Preserves System, 1981–82 Report.* Springfield: Illinois Nature Preserves Commission, September 1983.

Illinois State Geological Survey. *Guide to Rocks and Minerals of Illinois.* Urbana: Illinois State Geological Survey, Sixth Printing, 1976.

Irwin, Roderick R., and John C. Downey. *Annotated Checklist of Butterflies of Illinois.* Biological Notes 81. Urbana: Illinois Natural History Survey, 1973.

Jones, Douglas M., et. al. *Causes for Precipitation Increase in the Hills of Southern Illinois.* Report of Investigation 75. Urbana: Illinois State Water Survey, 1974.

Jones, G. Almut, and David T. Bell. *Guide to Common Woody Plants of Robert Allerton Park.* Champaign: Stipes Publishing Company, 1976.

Kjellstrom, Bjorn. *Be An Expert with Map and Compass, the Orienteering Handbook.* New York: Charles Scribner's Sons, 1975.

Learn, C. R., and Mike O'Neal. *Backpacker's Digest.* Northfield: DBI Books, Incorporated, Northfield, Illinois, 1976.

May, George W. *Down Illinois Rivers.* Ann Arbor: Edmund Brothers Inc., 1981.

Meves, Eric. *Guide to Backpacking in the U.S. Where to Go and How to Get There.* New York: Collier Books, 1979.

Mohlenbrock, Robert H. *Spring Woodland Wildflowers of Illinois.* Springfield: Illinois Department of Conservation, 1980.

————. *Giant City State Park, An Illustrated Handbook.* Springfield: Illinois Department of Conservation, 1981.

Nixon, Charles M., et. al. *Distribution of the Gray Squirrel in Illinois.* Biological Notes 105. Urbana: Illinois Natural History Survey, 1978.

Parmalee, Paul W. *Reptiles of Illinois.* Springfield: Illinois State Museum, 1955.

————. *Amphibians of Illinois.* Springfield: Illinois State Museum, 1954.

Proudman, Robert D., and Reuben Rajala. *AMC Field Guide to Trail Building and Maintenance.* 2nd edition. Appalachian Mountain Club, 1981.

Rockford Map Publishers. *Illinois State Atlas.* Rockford Map Publishers, 1980.

Roos, Herbert H. *A Synopsis of the Mosquitoes of Illinois.* Biological Notes 52. Urbana: Illinois Natural History Survey, 1965.

Roseboom, Donald P., Ralph L. Evans, and Thomas E. Hill. *Effect of Agriculture on Cedar Lake Water Quality.* Urbana: Illinois State Water Survey, 1979.

Runkel, Sylvan T., and Bill F. Alvin. *Wildflowers of Illinois' Woodlands*. Wallace Homestead Book Company, 1979.

Schiffman, Ted, and Susan Lariviere. *Amphoto Guide to Backpacking Photography*. New York: American Photographic Book Publishing, 1981.

Shcreiber, Lee. *Backpacking: A Complete Guide to Why, How and Where for Hikers and Backpackers*. New York: Briarcliff Manor, Stein and Day, 1978.

Smith, P. W. *The Fishes of Illinois*. Urbana: University of Illinois Press, 1978.

Tacoma Mountain Rescue Unit. *Outdoor Living: Problems, Solutions, Guidelines*. Tacoma, Washington: Mountain Rescue Unit.

Thomas, Lowell J. *First Aid for Backpackers and Campers: A Practical Guide to Outdoor Emergencies*. New York: Rinehart and Winston, 1978.

Voigt, John W., and Robert H. Mohlenbrock. *Prairie Plants of Illinois*. Springfield, Illinois.

Voss, John, and Virginia S. Eifert. *Illinois Wild Flowers*. Springfield: Illinois State Museum, 1951.

William, H. B. *Geology Along the Illinois Waterway— A Basis for Environmental Planning*. Urbana: Illinois State Geological Survey, Circular 478, 1973.

Wilson, John W., and A. Stanley Changnon. *Illinois Tornadoes*. Circular 103. Urbana: Illinois State Water Survey, 1971.

Winterringer, Glen S. *Poison Ivy and Poison Sumac*. Springfield: Illinois State Museum, 1963.

Winterringer, Glen S., and Alvin C. Opinot. *Aquatic Plants of Illinois*. Springfield: Illinois State Museum, 1966.

Wright, A. G. *Common Illinois Insects and Why They are Interesting*. Springfield: Illinois State Museum, 1955.

Walter Zyznieuski is an environmental planner for the Illinois Department of Energy and Natural Resources (ENR). He has authored a number of informational booklets and environmental reports for ENR and holds a B.S. in geography and environmental planning from Southern Illinois University, Carbondale.

George Zyznieuski is a service technician for Solar Energy Products, Inc., in Skokie, Illinois. He has a B.S. in industrial technology from Illinois State University and has done graduate work in alternative energy and energy conservation.